RUSSIAN AMERICA

RUSSIAN AMERICA

The Great Alaskan Venture
1741-1867

HECTOR CHEVIGNY

Binford & Mort Publishing
Portland, Oregon

In memory of a friend and teacher

CLARENCE ANDREWS

Foreword

As a nation we are of the opinion that the history of the settlement of this continent is a complete exemplification of the dictum that the course of empire is always westward. We hold that events of importance to our growth moved solely in one direction, from the Atlantic seaboard to the Pacific. There is, however, one cross-grained element: the Russian occupation of Alaska, our one state originally settled from Asia.

Its name was not Alaska until we bought it in 1867. Until then it was Russian America. Russia had possessed it for 126 years. Her claim to it by right of discovery from Siberia went back to 1741. As evidence of her long tenure, many a native still clings to the Russian Orthodox faith. The presence of Russians in their huge American colony was, moreover, felt throughout the Pacific. They established a trade that extended from New England to the Orient. New Archangel, their capital, was the first seaport in western America, North or South, and it remained the only one for the many years Spain kept her colonial ports closed to foreigners. New Archangel was a town of a thousand people before San Francisco had a hundred. It came to have a cathedral, a seminary, a college, and such other distinctions as two institutes for scientific research. It also had a shipyard, for years the only one north of Hawaii. From that yard in 1841 was launched the first steam vessel built in the Pacific.

Until the arrival of the Russians, the Pacific was so neglected an ocean that even hard-to-miss Hawaii lay undiscovered by Europeans. The governments of Europe having an interest in America sprang to attention quickly enough on learning that Russia, that power whose movements had always been peculiarly disturbing, was in what her people called the Eastern Ocean. England, France, and Spain all sent inquiring expeditions. Mexico, ordered to do so forthwith by Spain, hastily extended herself up the coast, creating present-day California. England reached for the Pacific Northwest, eventually bringing on the spectacular surge of the United States to the Far West, the end result of which was the incorporation of California into the Union along with the new territories named Oregon and Washington.

The Russians quickly caused the Pacific to become a busy sea. What had drawn them into it was their discovery of its vast wealth in fur seal and sea otter, an animal that could then be caught by the thousands. This soon brought the British in their trading ships, followed by the Yankees, some of whom went into virtual partnership with the Russians. In those days furs were like gold, silver, or precious stones—wealth itself. Far more of the United States was won by the hunt for furs than by the quest for gold. No fur had ever been found to equal the value of the sea otter. For it the Chinese proved ready to pay high in tea and silk. The foundations had been laid for the long and profitable trade between China and the United States.

To sum up, the Russians were the catalysts of our history in the Pacific, accounting even for the fact that today we and not the British have Hawaii. And there is the direct result that we have Alaska, which was for sale only to the United States, with whom the Russian government, whose action caused unforgotten bitterness at home, wished to seal forever a friendliness that had prevailed for over sixty years.

Its colony in America was the final phase of a great adventure on which the Russian nation embarked in the sixteenth century. I have been fascinated by the subject for thirty years, since 1934, when I came on the materials that led to my first two books in the field. And now I have attempted to tell the whole of the story in broad outline from its remote beginnings. New information on many points has been turned up in recent years. Fresh light has been shed on the character of the colony, its ethos as it developed over the years, the good or evil done the natives, the forces that brought it into being in the first place, and those that put an end to it. Like all frontiers, Russia's brought out her best and her worst. A number of her best were spectacular figures indeed. My scope has, of course, imposed limitations. Many more explorations were made, Russian and foreign, than I even mention. And other things of the sort have been left out which bulk large in the regional histories of Alaska.

Various technical simplifications have been made. Russian dates are given as they appear in the texts. Translatable names of Russian ships are in English. Modern place names are used wherever possible. Some old place names had to be used because the new ones mean something else; Leningrad hardly connotes Saint Petersburg, capital of the tsars. Place names are spelled mainly in accordance with the American-Oxford Atlas.

The word "mile," unless specified as nautical, means the English statute mile, to which I have reduced practically all indications of distance given in the sources. The Russian verst equals two-thirds of a mile.

Some may appreciate a word on the spelling of Russian names, which is far more a matter of rule than it was when many an old book was written. Sovereigns' names are in familiar English (e.g., Alexander). Other names are usually spelled in accordance with the Library of Congress system of transliteration, which follows the Russian letter by letter (e.g., Aleksandr). I have excepted from this system those names which, although they belonged to Russians, came from some other European language. Those names are given their original spellings (e.g., Hagemeister, from the German).

After my thirty years of probing in this field I am beholden to so many scholars for their advice and information that an adequate listing would be too large to honor anyone on it. I therefore ask forgiveness for singling out only the five who have most closely advised me of late. They are: Dr. Helen A. Shenitz, longtime librarian of the Alaska Historical Library, Juneau; Dr. Richard A. Pierce, Professor of Russian History, Queens University, Kingston, Ontario; Dr. Robert Magidoff, Director, Slavic Program, New York University; Dr. Morgan Sherwood, Assistant Professor of American History, University of Cincinnati; His Grace the Most Reverend Vladimir Nagosky, Bishop of the Eastern Orthodox Church in Japan, who as a priest long served the natives of Alaska. I owe a special debt to Dr. Shenitz and Dr. Pierce for doing me the great service of going over the first draft of my manuscript. To all these kind friends I am enormously grateful.

HECTOR CHEVIGNY

Contents

SIBERIA

GULF OF ANADYR

BERING

SEA

St. Michael

KUSKOKWIM RIVER

NUSHAGAK RIVER

St. Paul I.
PRIBILOF. ISLANDS
St. George I.

BRISTOL BAY

ALASKA PENINSULA

ALEUTIAN ISLANDS

UNALASKA

ATTU

AGATTU

THE NORTH PACIFIC AREA TODAY

RUSSIAN AMERICA

YUKON RIVER

Cook Inlet

KENAI PENINSULA

Prince William Sound

Nuchek I.

Montague I.

Resurrection Bay

• Mt. St. Elias

Bay of Yakutat • Yakutat

Sitka (New Archangel)

Kodiak I.

Kodiak

KODIAK I.

Three Saints Bay

PACIFIC OCEAN

ALEUTIAN ISLANDS

50   0   50   100   150   200 MILES

I

The Beginnings

For speed, vigor, and daring, nothing in the history of the white race surpasses the feat of the Russian frontiersmen who, beginning in 1579, conquered Siberia. They numbered no more than a few thousand. They had no charts, no foreknowledge of what lay ahead, no instruments to guide them other than their own senses. Yet within sixty years they had that huge expanse in hand to its Pacific shore. They reached also for Manchuria and Mongolia. Possessed apparently by a passion for distance, they went on expanding the Russian empire for 250 years. Although unschooled in ocean navigation, after learning in 1741 how far America lay from Asia, they set out for it, doing so in vessels in which today only madmen would venture on those northern waters.

The land to which they came, a second Scandinavia in size, character, and variety of climates, the land now called Alaska, was soon down on the maps as Russian America. The Russians, although at no one time did their numbers ever reach even a thousand in the whole of the vast country, much of which was guarded by murderous savages, nevertheless possessed themselves of it by establishing some forty posts scattered as far as the Yukon. Nor did that satisfy their craving for distance. They reached for Hawaii and sought to extend themselves all down the American seaboard to Spanish California, where indeed they had a post that stood for twenty-nine years.

History was in a measure made to repeat itself in reverse

3

when the Russians effected their conquests in Asia. In a sense they settled an old score, the fact that 350 years before they had been conquered by the Mongols of Asia, who for generations had held them in costly subjection, and had left them destitute and otherwise deeply affected.

Indeed a distinct age came to a close for the Russians when, in 1237, the Mongols struck. Despotism was unknown. "Tsar" was a word that meant the emperors of Greek-held Constantinople, whence Russia had derived her Orthodox Christianity. Among the country's several divisions were two republics with written constitutions, one the great city-state of Novgorod. And in all sections the ruling princes were to a degree subject to the will of citizens' assemblies.

From the time they emerged as a nation the Russians had been an aggressively independent people, disposed to govern themselves. Even gangs of workmen elected their own bosses. The lowest had their rights. Serfdom had yet to appear. There was no flogging, no torture, no putting to death even for murder. The very first code of laws had done away with all forms of corporal punishment in favor of fines. The Kievan Age, the period is called, after the fact that the cultural center was the beautiful old city of Kiev, which had four hundred churches. Moscow was nothing as yet, a small town under petty princes in the thinly populated northeast.

The nation prospered. A river people adept at navigating the Volga and their many other waterways, the Russians briskly traded among themselves and abroad. Merchants were the dominant element in the lusty, hearty society. And the richest and most aggressive of all were the merchants of Novgorod, Europe's great mart for Russia's sable and the other furs that were her chief stock-in-trade.

In those days a large fur trade called for ever-expanding frontiers. The hunters, ignorant of conservation, were forever on the move in search of places where the animals had not been killed off. The hunting expeditions were financed chiefly by the Novgorodian merchants, who paid also for new communities in the wilds, thereby adding to the domain of their republic, whose citizens' assembly regarded princes as hired hands. But the day of real power for Russian princes had, unknown to them, long been in the making in the depths of Asia.

Barbarian onslaughts were not new to the Russians; their cities were well fortified; but nothing had been seen to equal the mounted horde of savages that appeared, moving with great speed over the frozen ground, in December of 1237. At its head rode Batu Khan, grandson of Genghis Khan, late ruler of the Mongol nation and the world's foremost genius at the art of murder. Batu's striking force was made up of 50,000 disciplined Mongols and Tatars armed with helmets, breastplates, the Tatar crossbow, and a cutlass heavy as a meat-ax. Behind them came the reserves and the laborers, 70,000 more men, bringing up extra horses and supplies on the backs of camels. By failing to lay aside their differences in time, the princes of Russia contributed to the catastrophe that followed.

Riazan was the first city to take the blow. It fell in five days, so clever were the Mongols at the art of siege. Terror was another of their weapons. "No eye was left open to weep for the dead," says the chronicle of the event. People were roasted alive, flayed alive, impaled. Every corpse was minus an ear; as the American Indians took scalps, the Mongols cut off ears. When the killing was over and the city had been sacked, it was put to the torch.

The united army that belatedly took the field against the invaders was cut down. When the conquest was over, death had been met by at least a quarter of the population, which had numbered some four million. Kiev was in ashes, as were most of the towns and villages that had stood in the path of the Mongols. Novgorod survived and would continue to do so but, like all the places left standing, at the cost of heavy exactions.

Batu Khan's intention had been to devastate all Europe, which awaited him in terror, but he got no farther than Hungary, where he received changed orders from Mongolia. After returning to Russia, he proceeded to make it his home, establishing his capital, which he called Sarai, on the lower Volga. Here he pitched his great tent of cloth-of-gold and, seated on a throne of gold, he received the Russian nobles who came at his command or to beg his favor, requiring them to prostrate themselves and to remain in that most un-Russian posture until it pleased him to let them stand. The Tsar Khan, as he came to be called, had his portrait periodically taken about the country in order that similar homage might be done him in all its parts.

Not two generations before the appearance of Batu in Europe, the Mongols had been a people utterly without distinction, small in number, no more than a million, and mostly nomads, tent-dwellers forever on the move in search of new pasturage for the horses, the two-humped camels, and the other animals they bred. What notions of civilization they had had come to them from the Chinese, who had long had them under subjection of a sort, annually sending soldiers among them to collect tribute in the form of furs and domestic animals.

Not that they were tractable, these Asian counterparts of the early American Plains Indians. War was their passion. They were constantly embattled, among themselves and against their neighbors, notably the Manchus and the several peoples of Turkic stock called Tatars. When they could, they plundered the caravans carrying trade goods between Peking and the Moslem cities of Turkestan. They were forever in hope of annihilating the guards at the gates of China's Great Wall and of sacking the cities beyond. But thought of real conquest was not in them until the rise of the man who took the name Genghis Khan, inventor of many a war device unknown until his time.

Genghis welded his tiny, hitherto un-united nation into the most efficient war machine on earth, pressing even such old enemies as the Tatars into his service. At his death in 1227 he left his people in possession of North China, Manchuria, all of Mongolia, a good part of Siberia, and much of Turkestan. Well schooled in his methods, his heirs took the rest of China, Korea, and many a land to the west, including Russia, which was thus made a partner with China at the opposite end of the mighty Mongol empire.

Having no culture to impose, the Mongols were content to let their subject peoples keep their old ways. The wish was for profit. Foreign administrators, chiefly Chinese, were employed to manage the huge domain. The tribute imposed was an annual tenth of everyone's income, payable in gold or goods. This vast flow of wealth went largely to Karakorum in Mongolia, seat of the Grand Khans, as Genghis's heirs came to style themselves. Here, by the labors of artisans from all over the world, many of them slaves, a spectacular palace was erected, the roof of which was upheld by twenty-four columns of gold. But though the court of the Grand Khans was to receive ambassadors from even the Pope, never was its life to be touched to any depth by civilization.

Fine furs were much prized at Karakorum. No small part of its wealth came from Siberia, whose natives were made to pay an annual tenth of their peltry. Tribute in furs was called *yasak*, after Yasa, the name for Genghis's code of laws. The collecting of yasak was farmed out to willing chiefs, who empowered others, with the result that Karakorum received sable from as far as the Arctic. The natives took to extracting yasak on their own behalf, the stronger tribes from the weaker, the custom spreading to all parts of Siberia. This ready-made taxation system was one day to be of great interest to the Russians.

For the long while the Russians were under the Mongol yoke, well over two hundred years, they too were a source of furs to their masters. Sarai, the Mongol capital on the Volga, a town which to its end remained a place of tents and mud-brick structures, was given its share of Chinese and other foreign administrators. They organized a system of bureaus, one for every activity, from the care of the roads to the extracting of tribute. A census was periodically taken; the income of every man was ascertained; the population was policed against escape movements. Russians had to have passports to go about their own country.

The old foreign trade was practically gone, replaced by a new one conducted at Sarai, where traders from as far as Venice bought slaves and goods taken in tribute. So many were enslaved that Russia lost most of her artisans. Russian slaves and military conscripts did duty all over the Mongol empire, including China.

At the outset of the occupation some of Russia's bravest men had counseled acceptance of the situation and even collaboration, seeing in this course the only way to rebuild and keep the nation intact. Neighboring countries were eager only to seize the opportunity to reach for Russian soil. Although the Tatars who had come with the Mongols, and who kept coming by the thousands, brought with them the Mohammedanism so dreaded in Western Europe, no help ever came from that quarter. The Russians stood alone throughout their historic ordeal.

Caught between the Moslem Tatars, who settled mostly along the eastern boundary, and the Catholic countries encroaching from the south and west, the Russians came to feel beleaguered religiously as well as territorially. Their sense of isolation deepened as Constantinople, their spiritual capital, fell to Moslem Turks. The old friendliness toward foreigners was gone. Only he who was Orthodox could be fully trusted. By the same token, the man, whatever his race, who adopted Orthodoxy qualified as a Russian. The mark of the new nationalism was a deep and passionate love for the soil of Russia, every foot of which must some day be won back.

The country was poor, drained of its wealth, practically without industries. The economy had been set back to a primitive age. Furs were the money of the people, serving even to pay wages. Gangs of hungry robbers roamed about and infested the rivers, pillaging what little commerce was left. Nor did the situation improve as Mongol power waned. A new despotism had been taking over.

No longer was Moscow an insignificant town. It had grown mightily over the years, as people fled to its vicinity and as its princes, pupils in Mongol rapacity, used the chaotic situation to widen their domain at the expense of their neighbors. By 1480 Moscow's power was such that it stopped paying tribute to the Mongols. Something else it stopped was the existence of the state of Novgorod. And with the incorporation of the old republic into Muscovy went the last hope of restoring the past. Never again would merchants be dominant. The princes had triumphed.

Moscow retained many a feature of Mongol rule, notably the bureaus, which were housed in the Kremlin. Tribute was still collected. Also as before, the population was policed against escape movements. Everyone still had to have a passport when going even from town to town. Serfdom appeared, as a reward for nobles serving the new order. The Muscovite nobles were a brawling, turbulent lot, like the Tatars, whose dress and weapons they affected. Asia had left a deep imprint. Kindly treated was the criminal whose only punishment was slit nostrils, branded cheeks, and fingers chopped away.

Moscow's soldiers, whose duties included keeping the people in the villages and on the lands, at work for their lords, in many cases themselves joined the thousands who managed to flee to the distant south, out of easy reach of Moscow. Here the refugees, who came to be called Cossacks, established embattled communities for the preservation of their independence, warrior republics governed in the old way, strictly by majority vote. So strongly was the principle held that even in the midst of a battle a leader might be deposed and a new one elected.

The Cossacks baited and harried Moscow, often going far from their bases to raid and plunder. Yet they also served Moscow, enlisting as units in its foreign wars and always guarding the border. In this they reflected the attitude of the entire nation. Moscow was to be served when it was a case of holding or restoring the soil of Russia.

The explosive energies of the Cossacks and others like them found full expression after 1547, when a youth of seventeen who was to go down in history as Ivan the Terrible received the crown of Moscow, inaugurating a reign that was to last thirty-seven years. He was the first formally to call himself Tsar. More than anyone, he solidified the power of Moscow, yet in his own curious way he was a great man. Gifted with vast energy, he was determined to bring Russia out of her poverty by restoring her old foreign trade. It was a project of formidable dimensions.

The country had lost all friendly contact with the outside world. The Tatars kept closed the trade routes to the east. As for the routes to the south and west, neighboring nations deemed it expedient to keep the Russians poor. There was no seaport; the Baltic was closed off from Muscovy. Yet Ivan had his will. With the enthusiastic aid of the Cossacks, he broke the power of the Tatars along the eastern boundary. He cleared a path to German markets and established Archangel as a port on the White Sea, the sea lane to which was opened by the English, Ivan's first commercial allies. The trade was small, practically all in furs, the one commodity Russia could produce in quantities, but it was a lucrative trade. Europe, with all its new wealth from overseas, was never a better market for sable.

A word that harked back to old Novgorod was *promyshlennik—promyshlenniki* in the plural—signifying free-lance exploiters of natural resources, notably furs. There would have been little peltry had Moscow not allowed all their old freedom of movement to the fur-hunting promyshlenniki. Men with a sure instinct for rivers and forests, they went where they pleased, traveling in bands, electing their own leaders, sharing their tools, and, at season's end, the profits, among themselves and with the traders who financed their expeditions. Now, what with the great new demand for skins, they were busy indeed, so busy that by Tsar Ivan's twentieth year on the throne they had the available fur grounds practically hunted out. On the domestic market sable reached such a price that a single pelt could buy a fifty-acre farm. Russia's new trade seemed destined to be short-lived.

The sole hope for a solution lay in opening Siberia—a name that area had yet to acquire. And Moscow had taken steps to that end, commissioning a private merchant family for the purpose. But this action had roused the powerful Moslem trading city of Bukhara in faraway Turkestan. Bukhara, whose merchants were dependent on furs for the conduct of their trade with the Chinese, viewed itself as heir of a portion of the old Mongol empire and therefore solely entitled to the yasak garnered from the natives of western Siberia.

Bukhara rushed in Moslem missionaries, troops, and even cannon, no doubt from the Chinese. Strength was concentrated at Sibir, the fort guarding the only good route into the country from Russia. Thus the Russians had first of all the problem of reducing Sibir, a task that appeared to require a large army, with so little hope of success in that vast wilderness that even Tsar Ivan feared to take the risk.

The man who bid for the honor of solving the problem was one Ermak Timofeivich, leader of a large band of fellow Cossacks engaged in piracy on the Volga. Tsar Ivan, who wanted them all very much for hanging by hooks thrust through the ribs—his punishment for molesting commerce on the rivers—sent soldiers to capture them, but they escaped. The next thing anyone knew, Ermak was on his way to attack Sibir, his army consisting of 850 men, most of them his old followers, with arms and supplies furnished by the merchant family commissioned to exploit Siberia. This was in the fall of 1579.

Ivan was furious when he heard, fuming that only harm could come of such an expedition, but the Bukharians proved no match for Cossacks. Ermak took Sibir within two years, and with it its store of yasak—sable, ermine, bear, and other peltry to the value of 100,000 rubles, a fabulous sum in those days. Bells rang all over Moscow when the news came. Ermak shrewdly sent all the yasak as a personal gift to Ivan, who responded by pardoning all concerned for their crimes, sending Ermak the insignia of a national hero, and promising reinforcements. The name Cossack was always to be enshrined in Siberia. One testimonial was to be the creation of a specially privileged regiment, the Siberian Cossacks, whose duties would include carrying the mails. But Ermak Timofeivich lived to see none of these honors. He died fighting to hold the country, and so did most of his men. Only 125 survived. By the time they returned home, to wild acclaim and laden with furs enough to keep them the rest of their lives, the fur rush to Siberia was on.

The promyshlenniki deserted their old forests. Hurriedly they were followed over the Urals by merchants and traders bringing goods. Footloose men of all sorts joined the rush, including many a wanted criminal hopeful of earning a pardon by emulating Ermak. The government poured in builders and supplies for the construction of forts. This work was pressed with great vigor by Boris Godunov, who succeeded Ivan in 1584. Western Siberia was in hand within twenty years, held by a line of forts stretching from the Arctic to the highlands bordering the south.

The forts—future towns, most of them—were centers for the capture of the country's ready-made taxation system, based on the claim of an overlord to yasak, which occasionally had to be enforced. The garrisons were made up of regular army troops and Cossacks of the Siberian regiment, who served as scouts for new fort sites and had the honor of collecting the yasak. Moscow insisted on a strict accounting. Every fort had its bookkeepers to keep track of amounts paid or payable by the tribes within its area.

The line of forts went on advancing at the rate of some sixty miles a year across that trackless expanse of marsh, rivers, forests, and tundra, on the way encountering natives of many sorts and all degrees of submissiveness. The Russian leadership, which never centered in any one man, was a queer, often antagonistic mixture of governmental and private initiative. The antennae of the movement were the bands of promyshlenniki, self-governing and self-employed, financed by traders who were often with them. Sometimes they worked as official pathfinders. More often they were on their own, searching out the haunts of the sable, doing so usually hundreds of miles ahead of the advancing forts. They were followed by the Cossacks in search of new fort sites, since they knew that where the promyshlenniki led good fur grounds were sure to be, and therefore habitations of natives having yasak to pay.

And there was an illegal element—bands of men who had good reason to stay well ahead of the advancing government. They were the outlaws, the wanted men who had found their way into the new country, deserters from the forts and the like. Their numbers increased by the year, augmented in particular by runaways from the forced-labor camps after Moscow instituted the practice of exiling its unwanted to Siberia. The record often refers to them as promyshlenniki, for they too were factors in the advance. The yearners for pardons among them were quick to offer the government new and rich places they discovered.

The ever-expanding occupation constantly called for new men. The Church, which had arrived quickly on the scene, contributed by turning natives into Russians through baptism, giving them Slavic names. The native who turned Orthodox no longer had to pay yasak and could bid to join the garrison forces or the promyshlenniki. The Russians were, moreover, given to mating quickly with the women of lands they penetrated. Always the children were baptized. From them came many of the promyshlenniki of the future, a new breed of frontiersmen even more daring than their fathers, fearful least of all of distance, restless, curious beyond measure, having always to see what lay ahead if only for the sake of seeing it.

Siberia still seemed endless when the men of the advance reached the Lena River, on which they founded Yakutsk in 1632. Then, farther on, for the first time to the east, they saw mountains, all along the horizon, the peaks of the Stanovoi range, seven hundred miles from the Lena over very rough ground. What those mountains concealed may well have been ascertained by wandering promyshlenniki or outlaws before 1639, but that is the year of record for the discovery. The commander of Yakutsk ordered Cossack leader Dimitrii Kopylov to take twenty-four men, form a packhorse expedition, scout a pass over the Stanovois, and see what lay beyond.

Having surmounted the barrier, Kopylov followed a river that was to be named Okhota ("The Hunt") and was brought to a great bay overhung with fog and shored by tons of bleaching driftwood. The fort one day to be placed here would be named Okhotsk, and the bay the Sea of Okhotsk. The Russians had reached the Pacific. Kopylov's sight of it in 1639 was just sixty years after Ermak's crossing of the Urals in 1579. Siberia had been traversed within a lifetime. The distance come, as the zigzag travel then went, up one river and down another, was at least 5800 miles.

Their restless energy only heightened by the years, they now devoted themselves to expansion in the south and in the north, where spectacular feats of Arctic exploration were performed. As for their doings in the south, it is only a detail in the story that by subduing the fierce Buriats they established such future towns as Irkutsk. The south, although it did not produce the best furs, had a special attraction for them. In that direction lay China and the country of the Mongols, who were unremembered by no Russian.

Movements toward China and Mongolia had been in the making a long while, since the early 1600s, when forts, notably Tomsk, were first placed along the highlands bordering southwestern Siberia. The men who established those forts did so in acute awareness that beyond those highlands lived their old masters, for whom they had mingled feelings of apprehension, curiosity, and longing to put them in tribute-paying subjection. It was known that the Mongols had long since returned to nomadic life and that most of them were now peaceable, but the fact also was that they were still a highly independent people and had acquired a measure of sophistication. What restrained the bold spirits at the forts was Moscow, which forbade penetration of Mongolia, the bureau in charge contending that the likely reward would be more trouble than profit.

China, which was known to lie somewhere beyond the country of the Mongols, was thought of as a land rich and beautiful beyond compare, with a people wise and clever above all others.

Nor was this legend, which had surely come down to the Russians from the Mongols, without a certain proof. From no other country came so many unique and lovely things for luxurious living: silk, satin, cottons of exquisite weave, perfumes, condiments, exotic candies—all of which was to say nothing of the medicinals, obtainable from no other source. These commodities were sold to Europe by the Bukharian merchants of Turkestan, who profited mightily, having no competitors in the caravan trade with China; only they knew the route, which they kept a tight secret.

Moscow yearned for a share of the trade, but the oldest records gave no clue to the road. Then, around 1615, the Kremlin realized that the Mongols would of course know all about routes across their country. Perhaps they might be persuaded to talk and even give a safe-conduct for an exploratory mission to Peking. An inquiring expedition was ordered sent to the Mongols from Siberia.

This expedition, bearing gifts, set out up the Yenisei River in 1616, at its head two Cossacks who went with the brash determination of also asking for tribute and submission to the Tsar. The man they planned to see was the Altyn Khan, a lineal descendant of Genghis and ruler of a substantial part of northwest Mongolia.

Regarding routes to China, the Altyn Khan was exactly the man to see. He traded often with the Chinese, selling them camels, cattle, and horses. He was an astute businessman with a fine instinct for politics, but the full truth about that was not to be apparent to the Russians until some years thence. They found him encamped on the grassy highland steppe, surrounded by his herds and the tents of his people. After carefully appraising the gifts his visitors brought, he made them welcome, showing as much curiosity about them as they felt about him. He was well aware of the growing strength of his new neighbors to the north.

The Cossack who was spokesman led up to the subject of submission by putting it in the light of an alliance. The Khan listened with great interest until he understood the price. But he was not offended, only amused. The information desired by Moscow was granted.

Two years later, in 1618, with the Khan's directions and safe-conduct in hand, Russia's first mission to China set out from Tomsk, the embassy consisting of another pair of Cossacks. And when, some two years after that, they were back at Tomsk, it was with nothing substantial to show for their long journey. China was indeed a wondrous country, they said; they had been politely received, they were shown many a marvel in Peking, including birds that talked, but the officials were uninterested in trade.

The Chinese told all Europeans that they neither needed nor desired trade. The barbarian world had nothing to offer, so complete was Chinese culture. Goods brought by ignorant foreigners, in the manifest belief that China must be in want, might sometimes be bought but only out of politeness. No binding agreement to buy could ever be made. Apparently any great need for furs was denied, despite the old and regular barter in that commodity with the Bukharians and other Asians, people whom the years had taught not to infringe on the privileges granted them.

Aside from all that, as Moscow could see by the report of the mission, Peking was an unconscionable distance away—five thousand miles of roundabout travel, a thousand of the miles over the Gobi Desert, a journey of four months for the hardiest and a year for the soft. Moscow shelved the thought of China and renewed the order to stay out of Mongolia. And there the matter rested until 1632, sixteen years after the mission to the Altyn Khan, who now astonished the commander of Tomsk by sending a message saying he was ready to discuss submission to the Tsar.

All these years the Khan had remembered the suggestion of an alliance with the Russians as reward for submission. And now he expected trouble with the Kalmyks, a branch of his people, partly in Russia, who were developing ambitions to reunite the Mongol nation and to reconquer China if not also Russia. The Khan wanted his independence, and Moscow, which also had a nervous eye on the Kalmyks, sent him another mission, with the result that, 405 years after his forebears conquered Russia, he acknowledged himself one of Russia's tribute-paying vassals. With him as ally, the Russians were soon happily deep in Mongolia, seeking alliances with other khans, playing politics against the Kalmyks, and working to put themselves in control of this borderland of China.

And Moscow was given trade with China. The Altyn Khan, no man to pass up a business opportunity, put his camels to work freighting goods between Tomsk and Peking, himself acting as middleman. He was to keep up the trade for twenty years, and to bring the Russians great quantities of tea and fix it as an essential in their diet. For them that was to change commerce with China from a luxury to a necessity.

Another borderland of China, this time Manchuria, began undergoing penetration by the Russians when, in the early 1640s, a party of them came over the mountains from Yakutsk. They found a mighty river, the Amur, an Asian Missouri in length and navigability, three thousand miles long, flowing in a great arc from west to east and joining the Pacific at the southern extremity of the Sea of Okhotsk. Such a waterway was vital to the future of eastern Siberia, inasmuch as the Yakutsk region was hemmed in from the sea by the Stanovoi Mountains. But that advantage was not seen by the Russians at the time. They had as yet no notion of venturing on the Pacific. What they did see was the value of the Amur Valley as a bread basket for the cold and rugged Yakutsk region.

The Amur natives, a gentle people, had grain fields, orchards, cattle. Fish could be caught most of the year; sable abounded. And the country lay unprotected. When asked by the Russians for tribute, the natives protested that they paid it to China, but no Chinese soldiers were about. Nor were Manchu forces in evidence. The Manchu lords and their retinues were in China, making use of a turbulent situation to install themselves as rulers over the Chinese for the next two and a half centuries.

The ensuing invasion of the Amur wrote no pretty page in the history of the Russians. Moscow's Bureau for Siberia, which held all power over the country, could do little about controlling a region so remote and complex. No better haven had been found for outlaws, to whom the great river offered thousands of hiding places. The lawlessness was abetted by the very commander of Yakutsk, who to his own profit farmed out the collecting of tribute—in this case grain and beef as well as furs—to an unscrupulous promyshlennik contractor whose method was to slaughter the unsubmissive natives, seize their property, and burn their villages—with, he was wont to say, "God's help."

What with the doings on the Amur, the activities of the Russians in Mongolia, where the Kalmyks continued to threaten war, and the strivings of the Manchus to control China, the Far East took on the aspect of a caldron coming to a boil. The Manchus, who heard all about the atrocities on the Amur, were grimly aware that the Russians appeared to be China bound, but for a long while they were too preoccupied to do more about the situation than send a few counter-agents into Mongolia and a small force into the Amur—a force which quickly met defeat. At length, in 1658, for the purpose of clearing out the Amur, the Manchus organized an army which, according to one Chinese historian, numbered ten thousand.

For the first time since their arrival in Asia, Russians met thorough defeat. After that the few not driven out of the Amur Valley stayed well out of sight, the Manchus having installed a resident guard. The loss of the Amur was heard of with no regret at Moscow's Bureau for Siberia, which indeed promised Peking cooperation in keeping the peace. The bureau was under the necessity of establishing direct trade with China, the Altyn Khan having died and his trade with him.

Over the years that followed, years of peace on the Amur, Moscow sent Peking a number of trade missions accompanied by ambitious caravans laden with furs and goods of the highest quality. The Manchus bought, but, like the Chinese of old, would not agree to buy in the future. The frustrated Russians were given to understand that every caravan would be a gamble. The situation began approaching a resolution when, in 1668, the Amur was reinvaded. The Yakutsk region just across the mountains had come to be one large prison farm, so many were the forced-labor exiles at the various forts. The tension was heightened by disaffection among the garrison Cossacks. Events were tripped off by a mutiny at one of the forts, which was stripped of even its cannon by the Cossacks and exiles, who then set out for the Amur under the leadership of a popular war prisoner, an able Polish officer named Nikefor Chernigovskii. Peking's guard proved powerless to stop them. Having rebuilt the old Russian fort of Albazin, they proclaimed a Cossack republic with Chernigovskii as elected head. The news brought all the footloose men on the run and set off three more mutinies. In vain Moscow's Bureau for Siberia promised death to all who joined Chernigovskii. Within a year he had some ten thousand men.

Nor, as time passed, did Peking seem able to do more than send letters of protest. Ten years went by, during which the Amur occupation continued to grow, and Chernigovskii, like Ermak before him, offered Moscow his conquest in hope of pardons for all concerned. The Bureau for Siberia refused, provoking its critics, who pointed out that, for all its conciliatory policy toward China, she had conceded nothing. A spy was sent to ascertain the strength of China, but before he could return the impatient had had their way. The Amur was a Russian province with eleven settlements going up, and even a cathedral abuilding at the capital town.

The fact was that not in years had China been as strong. She was now under the great Manchu emperor K'ang-Hsi, a young man of peace and toleration, educated in part by Jesuits, for whom he had great respect. They were his advisers in many matters, including foreign affairs. As he once explained, he had refrained from war on the Amur out of consideration for Moscow, knowing it had not sanctioned the invasion. Should Moscow approve, he warned, he would strike. In 1682, hearing the news, he ordered two of his ablest generals to proceed with 36,000 men. He also wrote Moscow, saying the door remained open to diplomacy.

That letter unaccountably failed to reach Moscow for three years, by which time China had the Amur back in hand. Hoping that K'ang-Hsi was still of the mind he was when he wrote, Moscow hurriedly sent him envoys to ask for a conference concerning the Amur. A negotiator would be waiting on the Siberian border, a noble by the name of Fedor Golovin, who was dispatched from Moscow with a large diplomatic suite. When, a year later, Golovin arrived on the border he was met by a strange sight—thousands of refugees, among them Russians, fleeing Mongolia.

The Kalmyks were finally driving to subjugate their fellow Mongols in order to harness them for more world conquest. K'ang-Hsi acted swiftly, ending forever all danger from Mongolia by sending his troops to beat back the Kalmyks and take possession of the country, which was ultimately turned into a buffer state against the Russians, who were thus defeated in all the borderlands of China. But that is ahead of the story. The troubles caused Golovin to wait three years for the conference, which was finally held in the late summer of 1689 at the border town of Nerchinsk.

Golovin prepared carefully, erecting a great ceremonial tent for the negotiations, furnishing it with all the splendor he could muster, and arraying himself in sable and jewels. He had, as he well knew, few cards to play. The Amur was gone; Siberia could not support further war. On their arrival with a large army, China's delegates housed themselves in black Tatar tents. They were high-ranking Manchus, flanked by two Jesuits also in mandarin dress: Fathers Josef Gerbillon and Tomás Pereira, who would do the negotiating, all in Latin.

After much acrimony, which the Jesuits sought constantly to soothe, a treaty was drawn up, China's first with a European power, the Treaty of Nerchinsk, signed on the spot that September of 1689. It was to determine much of the history of the Far East for the next 150 years and to affect America as well. The Amur was made over in perpetuity to China. The Russians were left no right even to navigate the river, a deprivation the consequences of which they still did not foresee. The boundary was so drawn as to exclude them entirely from Manchuria, leaving them access only to the headwaters of the Amur. But they were granted their long-sought trade agreement. The promise was that any of them having the proper passports could enter China with certainty that business would be done.

This concession was won by no skill on Golovin's part. That the Manchus came prepared to make it is the indication in the Chinese sources. The course had unquestionably been urged on K'ang-Hsi by the Jesuits: give the Russians their tea, constrain them to keep relations good. The policy was to work admirably. It was China who, in the years ahead, would be capricious about keeping her part of the bargain.

The trade was soon under way. So profitable was it that Irkutsk, by virtue of its location on the route to Peking, quickly became the richest town and the capital of eastern Siberia. A whole new impetus was given the hunt for furs, forcing the opening of regions as remote and difficult as Kamchatka, the huge peninsula that looks out toward America. A few years after the signing of the Nerchinsk treaty, Kamchatka had its garrisons of yasak-gathering Cossacks.

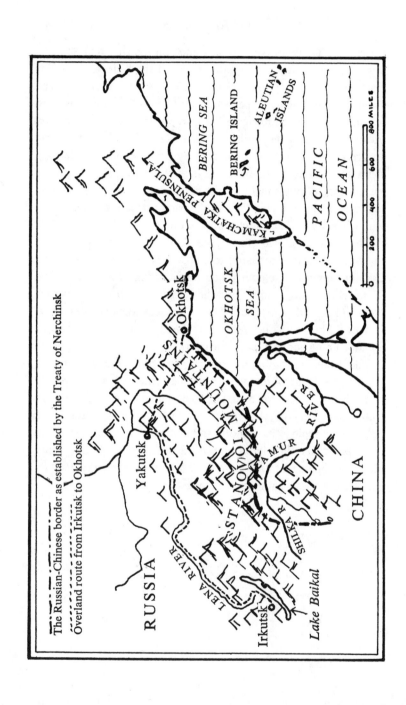

The Russian-Chinese border as established by the Treaty of Nerchinsk

Overland route from Irkutsk to Okhotsk

II

Columbus Despite Himself

It was revolution of a sort. Men went beardless; women were brought out of seclusion; the sexes could mingle in public. Foreigners were given places of honor. Secular books were printed for the first time in Russia. A whole new city was built to serve as her capital. The government was made over; the old bureau system was abolished. Muscovy was at an end. This was all nevertheless part and parcel of the past, the work of one man, the ultimate affirmation of the power that had come to reside in a tsar.

Peter the Great, who reigned for thirty-five years, was a giant of a man, nearly seven feet tall, and endowed with the will of an Ivan the Terrible. He came to power in 1689, the year of the signing of the Treaty of Nerchinsk. The fact that Russia had been defeated in the Far East was to him a welcome thing. His wish, to which he clung with passion, was for his people to turn from the Orient and retrieve their lost sense of belonging to Western Europe. He it was who laid down the policy whereby the agreement with China was to be long and faithfully observed.

Early in life Peter had learned to hate the backwardness of Moscow—the belief that Western knowledge might corrupt, the mistrust of foreigners, Germans in particular, the Orientalism denoted by the garb, and the view of shaving as a sin. Peter snipped beards and forced the nobles out of their wide-sleeved kaftans into Western clothing; then, finding he would never work much more of a change in Moscow, he decided to leave it only commercial importance and build the nation a capital where he could implement the ideas for betterment he kept jotting on the papers filling his pockets.

He wanted his city to be on the Baltic, where it could look out over salt water on Europe. First he had to force the nearby powers to concede him the space. His next war was with nature, which had intended no city to stand at the place he had won. Canals had to be dug to drain the marshes, thousands of piles driven to support the broad boulevards and the public buildings he envisaged. Saint Petersburg, it was called. Now it is Leningrad, renamed after another remaker of Russia, whose government chose to return to Moscow and its Kremlin, shrine to all that Peter detested.

Foreigners came to Saint Petersburg by the thousands to staff the institutions Peter devised, among them Russia's first Navy. For that he amassed 30,000 men and 800 ships, built a Naval Academy and, as one of the leading structures of Saint Petersburg, an Admiralty. Very often he reached for the pinnacle before he had the foundations laid. That was the case when, in 1723, he began importing German and other foreign savants for the purpose of starting an Academy of Sciences, although Russia had as yet no secondary schools, let alone a university.

Peter, whose curiosity was insatiable, worshiped science. He had felt greatly flattered when, on his visits to Europe, noted scientists paid him court. The geography of the North Pacific was then a field for speculative mapmakers, who projected lands that did not exist and who hotly debated whether America and Asia were joined at their northern extremities. Asked to settle this point, Peter sent two men to Kamchatka in 1719. Nothing was learned by that expedition, but Peter's curiosity had been whetted.

In December of 1724, as a consequence of having jumped into freezing water up to his waist while inspecting the work on a new canal for his beloved city, Peter was down with virulent pneumonia. For some reason his feverish mind fastened obsessively on that question about America and Asia. He thought of little else, saying it was something he had to know before he died.

As head of the full-scale exploring expedition which he ordered to the Siberian coast he chose, on the advice of his admiralty, a Dane in his naval service, one Vitus Bering, a brave, plodding, incurious man with no real interest in science. Peter wrote out Bering's instructions himself, and that was his last official act. He died, at fifty-two, in January of 1725. He was succeeded by his widow, Catherine I, who carried out the plan left by her husband.

Country wild beyond the imagination of any European armchair geographer, an unmapped welter of snow-capped ranges, dense forests, rushing rivers, and mosquito-breeding muskeg bogs, lay in the way of the traveler seeking the Pacific from interior Siberia. The final barrier, the Stanovoi Mountains, which rim the entire coast, called for climbs of four to five thousand feet to reach their passes. The situation, which came of the fact the Amur River was closed to the Russians, makes it something of a historical marvel that they ever established an overseas colony to the east, all men and supplies having to be transported to the coast through this geographic bottleneck.

From Irkutsk to salt water was a journey of 2200 miles and hardly feasible at all during the spring floods and fall rains.[1] In summer it took three months, in winter less—if, that is, the cold could be withstood. The first leg, the 1500 miles down the Lena River to Yakutsk, was made by boat or horse, depending on the season. Then came the difficult part, the 700 miles east of Yakutsk, to and across the Stanovois. No one went by himself. The travel was always by expedition, organized at Yakutsk. Reindeer were often used in winter. To get a heavy object such as an anchor across the Stanovois, dozens of horses were needed. Iron was accordingly scarce on the coast.

The route was still the one scouted by Cossack Dimitrii

---

[1] See map of the route, page 22.

Kopylov when, in 1639, he was sent from Yakutsk to see what lay across the Stanovois and, having followed the Okhota River down the eastern slope, was brought to that great bay, the Sea of Okhotsk.[2] On its shore now stood Okhotsk, a small fort surrounded by a tiny church and a few houses, all built of logs, with boat-building works nearby, and a wharf. Though ice-locked half the year, usually fogbound, often beset by storms, this was Russia's one and only port on the Pacific. Nor, for fear of infringing on the ill-defined territory of China as set forth in the Treaty of Nerchinsk, was there to be another for more than a century.

By boat from Okhotsk it was six hundred miles across the Sea of Okhotsk to the peninsula of Kamchatka, where some three hundred Cossacks were stationed at various forts. The unlettered may not have called it America but few on Kamchatka could have been in much doubt that the natives told the truth who said that to the east and not very distant, across the waters later to be named the Bering Sea, lay another continent.

The fact was apparent in a number of signs, including the size of the waves, which were smaller than those from the south, the direction, as the Russians knew, of the Kuril Islands and Japan. The question whether Asia and America are joined had been settled in the 1640s by a group of Cossacks who, in boats held together by willow withes, had explored the Arctic coast to its eastern limit. The report about that was unknown in Saint Petersburg because it was buried in the files at Yakutsk.

The Pacific presented the Russians with a whole new order of wildlife to be understood. They were very, very anxious to know about the sea otter, its habits, where it was to be found in greatest abundance, and how best to catch it. Its pelt outshone even that of the sable for richness and beauty.

The Chinese, as it turned out, already knew about this fur, having been introduced to it by the Spaniards of Mexico, who

---

[2] Pronounced O'hoatsk, the h strong and the accent heavily on the second syllable.

were doing some trading in it, though in no great quantity. The merchants of Peking were so avid for it that for one skin they paid the equivalent in trade of a year's income for a Russian clerk. But the hunters on the coast could so far do nothing more than watch for appearances of the animals, which were large, weighing up to eighty pounds. One day there a swarm of them would be, playing and frisking in the surf like so many friendly pups; then they would be gone—back to islands toward the east, the natives thought, which posed the question of the location of those islands. Had the people of Okhotsk been asked what sort of exploring the government ought to do, in all likelihood they would have suggested an investigation of the distribution first of the sea otter and next of the fur seal, about which there was also great curiosity.

In the fall of 1727, after spending a year and a half on the way, Vitus Bering arrived at Okhotsk with his officers, crewmen, shipwrights, and supplies, including the largest quantity of iron ever seen in those parts. Indeed so scarce had iron been at Okhotsk that the boats were held together by leather thongs. In spring Bering moved on to Kamchatka and across to the side facing America, where he put up quarters, built a small shipyard, and, the year after that, 1728, launched a little packet boat named the *Saint Gabriel*.

In July, Bering sailed north and made short work of his mission after that. In less than two months he was back, satisfied that the continents were not joined, but without complete proof. Nor, on his return to Saint Petersburg, where he arrived in 1730, was he able to say he had made any great effort even to catch a glimpse of America through the fog and rain, close though he had known it to be. His report was received with much criticism, notably at the infant Academy of Sciences organized by Tsar Peter seven years before.

Germans were at the moment supreme in the government. The Academy, with its predominantly German membership, could ask for almost anything it wished. The members, who were also predominantly young, as young as twenty-five, and still had too few pupils to keep them busy, were having a glorious time of it, endlessly debating the unsolved questions of the day. The result for Bering was that after three years he again found himself heading an expedition, made up this time of some nine hundred people, including scientists.

Proving the continents to be unjoined was the least of the tasks assigned the second Bering expedition. In fact that was almost forgotten amid a welter of new plans, some barely related, the project as a whole representing the most monstrous thing of its kind conceived up to that time or since. It was only part of it that nearly all of Siberia was to be explored and charted and Japan was to be investigated—and all with the added task of ascertaining the lay of America as far as Mexico.

Eight years later, in June of 1741, worn down by all the responsibility, even less interested in science than before, Bering finally sailed from Kamchatka for the purpose of finding America, doing so in a small, newly built square-rigger, the *Saint Peter.* She was accompanied by a similar vessel, the *Saint Paul,* commanded by Captain-Lieutenant Aleksei Chirikov, a man younger and abler than Bering. Their course was southeasterly; the plan was for them to explore together, but, to Bering's added gloom, they were soon separated in the constant fog and rain. After each had vainly searched for the other, they had to go it alone.

Bering, whose fears concerning food and water were not groundless, liked nothing about this vast, restless, slate-gray ocean with its capricious currents, swift changes of winds, and no lands where the armchair geographers had projected them. After weeks of wandering, on July 16 he saw America. It was a breathtaking sight. The clouds parted, and there, haloed in the bright sunshine, stood the peaks of the awesome Saint Elias range. But Bering shared none of the excitement aboard ship. To him the sight meant only that he could go home now. His work, he felt, was done. Only with difficulty did his companions prevail on him to see more. And so it was that he and Chirikov, working separately during that summer and fall of 1741, ascertained the configuration of the great shoulder of northwest America.

Tragedy in the form of scurvy, that old scourge of seafarers, struck at Bering and his men before they could return to base on Kamchatka, killing several of them, greatly weakening the others, and incapacitating him. Seeking refuge from the screaming fall gales, they put into a bay along a large island off Kamchatka, only to see the *Saint Peter* break up. Here Bering died in early December, giving the island his name. His survivors got through the winter by subsisting on the seals and the other abundant wildlife, including many otters. Next year, 1742, their strength restored, they built a boat from the wreckage of the ship and, looking like the wild beasts whose skins they wore, they made it to Petropavlovsk, the base built by Bering on Kamchatka.

From Chirikov, who had long since returned, Kamchatka had already learned about the Aleutians and the fact that sea otter swarmed in the offshore waters all down the coast. With the appearance of Bering's survivors came stupefying demonstration of the quantities of the pelts that could be obtained. In addition to the furs on their backs, they had many more in bundles, all highly interesting for their variety and quality: skins of the blue fox, the fur seal, and the sea otter—900 of these last, at their lowest valuation worth 90,000 rubles in trade with the Chinese. This was more than enough to have paid for a quarter of the cost of the entire expedition from the time it left Saint Petersburg.

Nothing else was to matter. The papers of the expedition, the charts, the logbooks, the thousands of pages of valuable observations, were thrust into files, many in the provinces. The wish at Saint Petersburg was to forget the enterprise that had been so badly planned and so often badly executed, and which had cost so much. Russians were again running the government. The

Germans had been tumbled from power by a palace revolt that had installed a new sovereign, a daughter of Peter's but intellectually no kin of his.

Tsaritsa Elizabeth, who was as decorative as she was good-naturedly unlearned, was willing to let the empire run itself. As for America, which Russia could now claim by right of discovery, that was too far away for Elizabeth. Her government would send no troops, put up no forts. This time development was entirely up to private initiative. The promyshlenniki [3] could have the field to themselves.

---

[3] For the definition of promyshlennik, see page 10.

III

The New Salts

Those armchair geographers who had argued that there had to be a link between America and Asia were not entirely mistaken. They reasoned incorrectly only in believing it to be farther north than it is, and in assuming it would be plain to see. It is there, a true geophysical link, a range of mountains running along the ocean floor. The tops of these mountains that show above water are the Aleutian Islands. The ship from Asia reaches the first of them something over four hundred miles east of Kamchatka and, by following the island chain, is brought presently to the mainland of America.[1]

On the geographic face of it, with the exception of those first four hundred miles, the course is an easy one to follow. Never is land out of sight. The islands number half a hundred, lie close together, and some are several hundred square miles in size, with rivers, lakes, and conspicuous mountains. Billions of sea-birds further mark their position, and there is the constant sound of breakers and seals. Even so, this is among the world's most dangerous regions to navigate, especially for sailing ships.

What is bemusing about the advance of the Russians along the Aleutians, island by island, is that at first and for a long time they knew only river navigation, and their early vessels, which were held together by leather thongs, were river boats. As a display of intrepidity the story partakes of the fabulous, but in

[1] For a visualization of the route from Okhotsk to the Aleutians, see map on page 39.

other respects it is not pretty. The first of the promyshlenniki to come to the Aleutians, where the Tsar was indeed far away, illustrate the view that ultimate frontiers draw the psychopaths.

Like a great boom the Aleutians separate the cold waters of the Bering Sea from those of the Japan Current, that vast cosmic swirl that comes up the Asian coast and goes down the American, imparting some of the warmth of the tropics as it moves. The consequence is that fog clings to the Aleutians like cotton, rain is frequent, and an altogether clear day is rare even in summer. In winter few ships dare put out because of the gales, which, howling with idiot fury, may change direction five times in as many minutes.

Yet, also because of the warmth of the Japan current, the climate is mild, with seldom a freezing day. To anyone coming from a place such as Yakutsk, the Aleutians were as South Sea islands—treeless, all the wood coming by drift, but greenly beautiful in many places, with grass that grows so long it overhangs the cliffs into the surf, in which it waves like hair. On Unalaska, if not on others of the islands, are two varieties of wild orchids.

Foxes abounded; the shoals teemed with sea otters. To the north were islands to be named the Pribilofs, the world breeding grounds of the fur seal. So numerous were they—millions—that on a June day their barking sounded like thunder above the surf. Then there was the great multitude of whales—but the wealth in whales the Russians were not to appreciate until too late. Their interest lay entirely in furs.

The natives, whose appearance caused the Russians to conclude they came originally from Asia, had lived for a sufficient number of centuries on the Aleutians to become perfectly adapted. Seldom did any of them prove happy when made to live elsewhere, even at such places as Hawaii. •Winter and summer they wore never a shoe and only two garments, an undershirt of sewn seabird skins, over it a long one-piece waterproof jacket of seal gut called a *kamleika*. Occasionally the men wore rain helmets carved from driftwood. The Aleuts were as amphibious

as human beings can be. Their canoe, to which the Russians
gave the name *baidarka* (diminutive for *baidara,* a much larger
boat), was a wonderfully unsinkable contraption made of skins
stretched over a light frame of carved driftwood. Double-bladed
paddles in hand, their clothing attached to their baidarkas in a
way to keep out the water, no matter what the weather, the
Aleuts thought nothing of journeying hundreds of miles.
Their dwellings were simple excavations roofed over with
driftwood and sod. When it came to storing food they were like
children, often suffering in winter as a consequence. Yet they
were not an altogether primitive people. They were quick to
learn and were very adept with their tools, which, having no
metal, they had to make of bone, stone, or wood. The women
could do the finest kind of sewing with their gut thread and bone
needles. When excited by anger, curiosity, or joy, they were
given to expressing their feelings in dance, moving together as in
a ballet. They were warlike, often raiding for slaves, but certainly, by contrast with such mainlanders as the Tlingit Indians,
the Aleuts were a singularly gentle people, friendly, kind, and
trustworthy.

In the summer of 1742, when Bering's survivors returned
with all those sea-otter pelts, one Emelian Basov was sergeant
of Cossacks at the fort on the Kamchatka River near which lay
the shipyard built by Bering sixteen years before for the construction of his first vessel. Due east, 115 miles distant, lay
Bering Island, presumably still with plenty of sea otter. He
would, Basov decided, spend a winter there himself.
A trader by the name of Andrei Serebrennikov put up the
money for the building of a boat, Basov got together a crew of
perhaps thirty promyshlenniki, and work was begun on a *shitik.*
The shitik, which originated on the Volga, was a sort of flatboat, almost keelless, so it could be easily beached, yet remark-
ably stable. It was built to be poled along, or towed from shore,
or sailed, having two masts sparred for single square mainsails.
Some shitiki were big enough to carry as many as fifty men and

several tons of freight. Basov's, when he launched it in the summer of 1743, was christened the *Kapiton*. As of old, everyone was on shares when, with Basov in command, the first promyshlenniki set out after furs across salt water.

Basov not only returned safely, he went back for a second winter on Bering Island, then a third and a fourth. Perhaps he then retired. He and his men as well should all have been rich enough. The number of skins from the second voyage is known: 1600 otter, 2000 fur seal, 2000 blue fox. The value: some 200,000 rubles. And that was from just one voyage.

Judging by the flurry of activity that followed Basov's first return in 1744, there had been a general waiting to see how he would fare with his river boat and the rest. Two, if not three, groups immediately set about building shitiki with a view also to hunting on Bering Island. And early next year the commander of Kamchatka gave permission to two traders, Chebaevskoi and Trapeznikov, to outfit an expedition for the Aleutians. And so still another shitik, no doubt the biggest so far, to be christened the *Eudoxia,* went under construction at the old Bering yard. The crew, which was made up of at least sixty promyshlenniki, among them local natives, was under one Yakov Chuprov. A young man who had been a crewman with Bering and had seen the Aleutians was chosen to act as navigator. His name was Mikhail Nevodchikov.

The *Eudoxia's* green timbers and leather thongs were in place by September; haste was then made to set sail, for that was the season of the offshore winds. Luck was with Nevodchikov. So steady did the wind remain, so fair the weather, that the *Eudoxia* made all of three miles an hour, and, after six days, on September 25, 1745, they sighted a mountainous headland rising abruptly from the breakers crashing at its base. This was Attu Island, the westernmost Aleutian. Passing to the north of it they sighted a fine valley high in rye grass but for some reason decided to go on to the next island, Agattu, where they threw out their wooden anchor, planning to go ashore next day for fresh water and to see how this would do as a wintering place.

The one certain thing about that historic first landing is that it went badly. Stories involving atrocities that were later brought out before the authorities are seldom clear. Morning showed the men of the *Eudoxia* a hundred natives on the beach, excitedly waving spears and arrows and probably performing a dance of welcome. That they were not hostile Chuprov ascertained when, after he had thrown them packets of trade goods—needles, perhaps, or knives—the natives threw back fresh-killed birds. It may have been that strange dancing that kept Chuprov nervous. At any rate he and the men with him had their muskets at the ready as they set out in the yawl.

If the Agattuans behaved like other Aleuts, they crowded around, curious about everything their visitors wore and carried. Chuprov gave them tobacco and pipes. The natives had no notion what to do with these but politely gave in return a stick ornamented with the head of a seal carved from bone. To them this called for another exchange, and they signified they wanted a musket, the use of which they did not know either. But Chuprov, who was tiring of this, refused with rudeness; the smiles faded from the faces of the Aleuts, some of whom moved over to take the yawl. Though the testimony is that only one native was shot, and in the hand, there must have been a deal more action than that before Chuprov and his men got back to the *Eudoxia,* for it was clear to everyone aboard that they had better go back to the first island.

The people of Attu had evidently heard what happened on Agattu. Far from performing any welcoming dances, they fled before the newcomers. Finally one Shekhurdin, a Cossack whose degree of conscience is indicated by the fact he later testified as to the misdeeds, captured two natives, whom he brought aboard ship and treated well, with the result that a number came out of hiding. They were given needles, thimbles, and the like; in return they sang and danced to the sound of bladder drums. Apparently they agreed even to the giving of hostages, something the Russians always demanded on encountering natives new to them.

Chuprov distributed the men at various camps all around the island, sea otter evidently having been sighted in pleasing abundance. When trouble broke out with the natives it was apparently over the obtaining of women, which should have been a simple matter of giving suitable presents. That was either not understood or brushed aside. At one camp fifteen males were shot down. When told this, Shekhurdin later testified, Chuprov sent the killers fresh ammunition.

After that, Chuprov's men doubtless did as most of the promyshlenniki who followed them to the Aleutians were to do. They beached their ship for the winter, built themselves habitations of driftwood at their various camps, adopted the Aleut dress, and adopted also the Aleut diet of meat and fish down to the blubber. They lived like sultans with the women and made the males do the hunting for them, paying them or not as they pleased, mainly in iron if they had it to spare, that being the commodity most wanted by the Aleuts.

So fine a time of it was had on Attu by the men of the *Eudoxia* that they stayed on through the summer and did not set sail again until September, although that was the season of contrary winds. Whereas the voyage out had taken only six days, the homeward one took six weeks and ended in shipwreck on an island off Kamchatka. The loss was twelve lives and all but three hundred of the otter pelts. This inglorious climax did not impeach the fact that, all things considered, the voyage had been a success. The rush for the Aleutians was on.

Attu's next visitors came on the *Saint John,* a shitik built and navigated by a trader named Andriian Tolstykh, who was also manager of his promyshlennik crew. He greeted the island chief with due respect and presented him with a copper kettle and a full suit of Russian clothing. He also offered generous terms for the privilege of staying the winter, with the result that he was helped to obtain 5000 otter skins worth 500,000 rubles.

Tolstykh was to shine as the most successful of all the voyagers in the early Aleutian trade, and the government was to reward him for his record with the natives by remitting his taxes, 10 per cent of each of his catches, yet his methods were adopted by few. Abuse prevailed. The leaders remained typified by Chuprov. One Russian text states that many of the promyshlennik crewmen were Siberian natives. To them perhaps the submissive Aleuts were objects of contempt. Following the *Eudoxia*'s pioneer voyage, Saint Petersburg gave authority over Aleutian affairs to the commander of Okhotsk, but he could exercise little control over a crew which had shipped out. His only weapon was the threat of punishment for reported misdeeds.

The government endeavored to spare the Aleuts hard liquor and venereal disease. The men shipping out swore before the Okhotsk commander that they were in good health within the meaning of a stern law of Peter the Great which decreed severe punishment for those knowingly spreading venereal infection. As for liquor, it was a government monopoly. Traders could not deal in it at will. Stills are known to have been run during winterings on the islands, but that was at the risk of heavy penalties. The only alcholic beverage allowed was kvass, which was brewed from grain, fruit, or anything fermentable and had long been used by the promyshlenniki as a preventative for scurvy.

Of less benefit to the Aleuts was the imposition of yasak, which came around 1748 by decree of Tsaritsa Elizabeth. It was directed that a Cossack collector go with every vessel. Yasak was a hard thing to explain to the Aleuts. They had never heard of tribute and fealty to a distant lord. To them the proposal was an insult to their intelligence, smooth talk intended to get furs out of them for nothing. Manifestly the Tsar was too far away to matter. Certainly little credence could be put in the allegation that tribute to the Tsar brought protection when it came from such yasak collectors as Gavril Pushkarev, who caused the deaths of twenty-three Aleut girls and committed other crimes.

In the early 1760s the natives of Unalaska and neighboring islands had had enough. They waited until five ships were in the vicinity, then struck, taking terrible revenge for past wrongs. The few Russians ashore who escaped death did so by hiding in remote places. Four of the five ships were destroyed.

A navigator by the name of Ivan Soloviev and his crew took it on themselves to punish the Aleuts in a manner calculated to be unforgettable. Years later a record of the affair, some of it from survivors, was compiled by the first historian of the Aleutians, Father Ioann Veniaminov, who was at no pains to conceal his indignation. On Unalaska eighteen native villages were destroyed systematically, as were all those on Umnak, all also on the island of the Four Mountains, and several on Unimak. Bonfires were made of native boats and other gear. Many of the natives, before they met death, were tortured to reveal where their companions had hidden themselves. Never again were the Aleuts to revolt. According to Veniaminov, on one occasion Soloviev had a dozen Aleuts tied in a row to find out how many bodies it took to stop a musketball. The answer: nine.

Thanks to the fact that among the Russians were also men such as Tolstykh, a number of Aleuts were won over, taken to Siberia, baptized, given Russian names, and taught the language, afterwards to serve usually as interpreters with the ships.

At a guess, about six ships a year had been putting out by the time the trade was ten years old. Only those that returned are on record. The loss was probably one in three. Longer and longer voyages had to be made every year in search of islands undepleted of furs; the sea otter learns to shun waters with too many enemies about.

The longer voyages called for ever larger and stronger ships with iron in them. The cost of transporting that commodity had forced the removal of shipbuilding from Kamchatka to Okhotsk, which had accordingly developed a respectable shipyard. Design had attained a certain sophistication. The Russians had learned to build sloops at Okhotsk and had developed another kind of vessel which, though called a galiot, bore little resemblance to the Mediterranean vessel of that name. The shitik was practically a thing of the past, with the development of the Okhotsk galiot, which could also be hauled up on a beach. It could have been capable of no speed. It was broad of beam, almost keelless, had a rudder as long as 12 feet, was usually about 80 feet in length, and had a single square gaff mainsail with an auxiliary jib. It had openings for sweeps—long oars worked from below the main deck—which were no doubt used in tacking or against heavy seas. Cattle could be transported on these galiots, 50 or 60 tons of freight, and up to 150 men.

The ships voyaging from Okhotsk traversed 1500 miles of fog-beset ocean before they reached the nearest Aleutian. The distance was accounted for by the crossing of the Okhotsk Sea and the rounding of the peninsula of Kamchatka, plus the 400 miles beyond. The hazards multiplied as the voyages went farther and farther along the 1200-mile length of the Aleutian chain. As if it were not astounding enough that any of those Okhotsk-built vessels returned, the only instruments they are known to have carried are the telescope and the compass. As

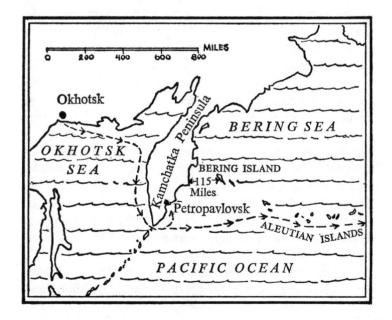

for charts, some came into being, compiled originally from the records of the Bering expedition, added to and corrected as time went on, but they remained the crudest of guides and were of course no use at all beyond the areas they covered.

The navigators had come to form a professional class with a monopoly of their trade. Their sole qualification was, however, their accumulated knowledge of the Aleutian run. None of them seems to have known anything about the science of marine navigation, least of all how to take a position when out of sight of land. A passenger aboard the galiot *Saints Zosima and Savatii* recorded what happened after she was blown 1200 miles out into the open Pacific. The crew, in line with the old promyshlennik custom when confronted with the incapacity of a leader, deposed the navigator. "Trust was then reposed in the omnipotence of God and in the Saints Nikolai, Zosima, and Savatii. . . . Their ikons were carried on deck as was that of the Mother of God, and we promised with tears that from whatsoever direction God would now send the wind we would follow it. Up to now we had sailed north and we had sailed south and we had come upon no land. Now we would simply follow the wind God sent us." Well, a wind came up from the south and remained steady, and presently Shuiak Island among the Aleutians was seen again.

Some of the discoveries of new ground were made simply because the navigators were off course. That was the case with the discovery of the Pribilofs, the navigator, after whom they are named, being in his cups at the time. He was in fact a notorious drunkard, as were several of the others. They were all nevertheless employed because they kept their number small by imparting their knowledge as it was gained only to each other. They were an arrogant lot, trying alike to the merchants forced to hire them and to the officials of Okhotsk. When a ship returned, two shares in the catch were given the Church in gratitude for safe deliverance.

Okhotsk, which was many times its former size, was a busy place winter and summer, what with all the shipbuilding. Inso-

far as the seagoing promyshlenniki could be said to have a place
of residence, it was their home and fast acquiring the name it was
long to have for quarreling and drunkenness. There were always
those who had drunk up or gambled away what they had made
from their previous voyage and waiting to sign up on the next.
There were also those who would never sail again, who had to
live on such charity as they could get because they had lost an
arm or a leg or had sustained a broken back. For that no man
was ever paid anything extra. As for medical attention, the
nearest physician was at Irkutsk. When a leg had to be cut off
or other surgery of the sort was called for, it was done by some
individual who drew on his practical knowledge of anatomy, the
anesthetic consisting of a large dosage of vodka aided by friends
who helped to hold down the patient.

In early June the merchants of Irkutsk who had an interest in
a ship due to return that summer began arriving at Okhotsk
with trains of packhorses laden with supplies for the next voyage. Excitement mounted in the town as June wore on. The
latter part of the month was the time to expect the first arrivals
of the year. The tension held right up to the minute a ship was
finally tied to the wharf. Few vessels putting into the miserable
roadstead of Okhotsk failed to sustain some damage in the
process.

No one came ashore until a government inspector had gone
aboard to count the bundles of furs before removing them to the
Commandry. There those accounted as yasak were separated
from the others, which were opened for counting, sorting, grad-
ing, and valuation, in preparation for taking 10 per cent as tax.
This was done in the presence of all who were concerned, including the crew. On this determination depended what each
man would get in terms of money. The financers of the voyage,
whose share was about 40 per cent, had one more expense, that
of getting their furs under heavy guard to Irkutsk. These days
the route was beset with outlaws and natives on the lookout for
unprotected shipments of furs.

The trade was now big business, of ever-increasing importance inasmuch as the land furs of Siberia were giving out. The merchants engaged in it, among whom were several of the traders who financed the early voyages, stood high indeed at Irkutsk. As a group only the promyshlenniki appear not to have gotten rich. Some may have held on to enough of what they had made to buy that piece of land and that livestock, but the record suggests they were few. Most of them went on until they were drowned or scrapped because of injuries. As is shown by the lists of those who shipped out, more often than not the same men made up the crews, voyage after voyage.

In 1763, with the sighting of Kodiak Island by Stepan Glotov and his crew, a Russian ship was on record as having sailed the length of the Aleutian chain. Twenty years had passed since Basov's pioneer voyage. The distance from Okhotsk was 2700 miles; from Saint Petersburg, calculating the twists and turns of the land route, nearly 9000 miles.

IV

The Man Who Would
Own America

Some three hundred miles south of Irkutsk, across the Mongolian border in a pleasant wooded valley, stood a community of peculiar aspect called Kiakhta. It was made up of two establishments, one Chinese, the other Russian. No longer did Russians wishing to trade with China have to take themselves and their goods by camel the 1300 miles to Peking, across Mongolia and its Gobi Desert. It was now the merchants of China who ran the caravans. All commerce between China and Russia was carried on at the border, two places having been designated for the purpose. Kiakhta was one and eventually became the only one, the other closing because of its lesser convenience.

Peking had not made the arrangement for trade at the border out of friendly consideration for the merchants of Russia, who indeed could no longer legally enter Mongolia or any other part of the empire of China at places other than the designated two. The arrangement represented a final effort on the part of China's Manchu rulers to exclude Russians from Mongolia and to turn it into a buffer state against them. Matters came to a threat of war in 1727, forcing Russia to sign a second pact with China, the Treaty of Kiakhta, whereby a boundary with Mongolia was established and closed, as had been done with the Amur Valley thirty-eight years before.

This second treaty, like its predecessor, the Treaty of Nerchinsk, had to do with trade, which Peking had not freely granted, despite the guarantees of the Nerchinsk pact. Time and again the commerce had been halted, at one point for five years. As of old, the Chinese wished they could exclude an outside world increasingly demanding to buy their goods, but that was only part of it where the Russians were concerned. The halts in trade were pressure on the Russian government to force its nationals to desist from trading with the Mongols and from aiding them to resist subjection to the Manchus.

The treaty proved ineffective; it was too unpopular in Siberia. At length Peking halted the caravans entirely, relegating trade to the fixed points along the border, which Russia agreed to aid in policing against smugglers. Full-scale operations began at Kiakhta in 1744.

By the middle of the century the average worth of the Kiakhta trade to Russia was four million rubles, approximately a hundred million present-day American dollars. The furs from America accounted for most of it. Prior to their discovery, such was the growing scarcity of Siberian peltry, furs had had to be imported from London in order to maintain the trade with the Chinese.

Kiakhta was to serve as the center of trade between the two empires for well over a century and to be missed by no traveler wishing to say he had seen all the significant sights of northern Asia. The Russian and Chinese establishments stood 150 yards apart. The Chinese called theirs Fortress Mai-mai-cheng. A moat surrounded a high wooden wall that enclosed an area nearly half a mile in length and over a quarter-mile in width. Back of it were sheds and corrals for camels. Within, along two streets gay with lanterns and bunting, were two temples, a theater, the residence of the governor, and a court of justice, all in Chinese style, several warehouses, and a number of structures used by the merchants both as dwellings and as shops for the display of their wares when the Russians came to do business.

The merchants represented business houses in various parts of China and came for stays of a year, alternating with their partners. They, their clerks, the officials, and others at Mai-mai-cheng made up a year-round population of 1200. There were no women. Chinese women were not permitted contact with foreigners.

The establishment of the Russians, whose only name for it was Kiakhta and who referred to its neighbor as "the foreign quarter," consisted of the usual wood-block Siberian fort surrounded by a number of log-built sheds, barns, and smithies for the hundreds of horses always on hand. Inside the fort were a church, a customs house, the residence of the governor and other dwellings, shops for displaying goods, warehouses, and barracks. Two military companies were in residence, on border-patrol duty. One of them, a contingent of Siberian Cossacks, was made up entirely of Tungus natives. The year-round population, which numbered about three thousand, counting women and children, consisted largely of merchants and their clerks, some of whom were empowered to deal on behalf of the government, which retained monopolies over commodities such as silk.

The dealings between the two camps were all by barter and required much visiting back and forth, with frequent exchanges of hospitality as well as samples. Several of the Chinese and Russian merchants came to know one another well over the years. Some of the Chinese even learned a little Russian but, according to observers, the Russians could never grasp Chinese. Mongolian, the common border language, was the medium. The barter, which went on the year round, was at its height in winter, when the frozen rivers made it easier for the Russians to bring in goods. In February Mai-mai-cheng held a fair. Kiakhta might then have a thousand visiting merchants from all parts of Russia. Much of what was bought from the Chinese was resold in Western Europe at a large profit.

Tea, of all grades and many kinds, constituted some 80 per cent of what the Russians bought. Next in volume came a variety of rhubarb root grown only in China, which was much wanted in Europe for the making of an intestinal tonic. Silk, raw as well as manufactured, came next. Also bought were gold and silver in bulk, cotton goods, porcelain, Chinese tobacco, rice, candies, ginger, and musk. The Chinese bought, in addition to the furs of every kind and grade the Russians had to sell, various European imports, glassware, hardware, talc, wool, leather, hides, cattle and, curiously, dogs.

All these commodities, on their way to or from Kiakhta, necessarily flowed through Irkutsk, which was the seat of the governor general of eastern Siberia and in all respects well past the day when, a hundred years before, it began as a fort for the collecting of yasak from the local Buriat Mongols. The prosperity of Irkutsk, which had 6500 residents, was evinced by such modern improvements as streets paved with wooden blocks and lighted at night. Were anyone to gain control of the supply of American furs, he would control the economy of Irkutsk. But no one appears to have feared that possibility. What did worry Irkutsk, and constantly, was the unpredictability of Peking where trade was concerned.

Exactly as of old, Peking from time to time halted the trade, ordering the closing of Kiakhta for periods ranging from days to months. Usually the action followed some border incident and was clearly meant as a warning or a punishment, but there were times when no reason at all could be discerned other than a wish on Peking's part to show it had the power. Protests were to no avail. Irkutsk could only pray that the next time Kiakhta was closed it might not be for long.

Irkutsk probably did not expect the change to have any very great meaning for it when, in 1762, it was learned that in faraway Saint Petersburg the palace guardsmen had dethroned the incompetent Peter III and had made his German wife sovereign with the name Catherine II. In her own very different way she was to be the first ruler of stature Russia had had since the death of Peter the Great thirty-seven years before.

There had been a time when no one would have predicted any very romantic future for handsome, buxom Catherine the Great. She was then a homely adolescent, a daughter, with no large prospects, of a minor German prince. Books were her world, works of philosophy, in particular on the revolutionary thought in the making in France. She was probably the best-read woman in Europe when, at sixteen, she married and came to live at the Russian court, where she blossomed. Her husband, who still played with tin soldiers, gave her no love, but there were ever so many others who were ready to tell her she was as beautiful as she was learned. And now, because of her popularity with the handsome young nobles of the guard, she was Tsaritsa, though she had not a drop of Russian blood. Catherine was happy to rule. Indeed she delighted in it throughout the thirty-four years of her reign, to the end savoring the romance of the station she had attained.

With it all she was a shrewd politician. She was determined to be a reformer but, as she well knew, she could not afford to alienate the element that had put her in power. Though her liberalism—of which she was to think less well, when the French Revolution came—called first of all for going against the nobility and alleviating the condition of the serfs, on the whole she left the latter worse off than they had been. She succeeded in doing little about simplifying the cumbersome machinery by which the empire was governed. Even when she had a clear field, she sometimes lost interest in what she had been trying to do. Consistency was not her chief virtue. She changed her mind when it suited her. She was capable of compromising her principles herself. Peter the Great was not more successful at stamping out dishonesty in the government, yet Catherine allowed her lovers, of whom she had some fifty, extraordinary license. Faults and all, she was nevertheless a great woman if only for the impetus she gave education, medical care, and much else of the sort, in which Russia had been woefully backward.

In foreign policy Catherine's attention was fixed almost wholly on Western Europe, with little left to spare for the Far East. She was given to boasting of the size of her domain, but at times her actions suggested she thought it too large for the number of people. The Russian disdain for distance was not

something she shared. Yet she took real if spasmodic interest in
Russian America and did more about it than her predecessors.
Though she never issued a specific decree claiming the region,
her actions and words asserted jurisdiction. Typically, on a document concerning the Aleutians which was addressed to the
governor general at Irkutsk, she added in her own hand the
order to "impress upon the hunters the necessity of treating
their new brethren and countrymen, the inhabitants of our
newly acquired islands, with greatest kindness . . ." Her government required the ships setting out from Okhotsk to carry
metal plates bearing the imperial insignia, which were to be
buried when new ground was discovered, and she approved a
number of expeditions to survey the discoveries.

Though at the time of Catherine's accession the advance on
America had been in progress nearly twenty years, no word of it
had reached the governments of the West. The assumption was
that nothing had followed the Bering exploration. Only the
ships of the Dutch, who alone among Europeans could trade
with Japan, came anywhere near the Aleutians, and they
seldom. Foreigners in Russia, especially the ambassadors, rarely
learned anything they were not intended to know. Evidently
they were allowed to believe that all the otter must be coming
from the Siberian coast. Catherine, who loved to startle the
ambassadors and to boast of the exploits of her subjects, let out
the truth, apparently building it up a bit. The nations which had
a stake in America were accordingly roused.

Spain had the sharpest reaction, ordering her viceroy in Mexico to prepare forthwith for defense and to occupy more of the
western coast. Upper California came quickly into being, as
Franciscan missions and military presidios were built, beginning
with San Diego in 1769. From time to time ships were sent from
Mexico to ascertain how the Russians were progressing and to
attempt the gaining of footholds in the distant north.

France, despite her revolutionary troubles, eventually sent an
inquiring expedition, that of LaPérouse. England sent James
Cook, her most famous explorer, who did more than merely see

what the Russians were up to. The charts resulting from this expedition were subsequently adopted by the Russians themselves, down to the English names bestowed on many places. The concern giving rise to these inquiries was at first based on no knowledge of the wealth in marine peltry. The motive of the Russians was not at all understood. Cook's men obtained a few hundred otter skins from the natives but did not appreciate their value until they put in at Canton, where for those few skins the Chinese proved willing to pay ten thousand dollars. Until then no Englishman seems to have known even that the Chinese were greatly interested in furs. There was almost a mutiny as Cook's men endeavored to have the ships turn back north. The story of the price paid them was underscored by a Captain Hanna who, on hearing it, directed his brig up the American coast. He bought 560 otter pelts from the Tlingit Indians, which he resold at Canton for a startling five thousand pounds sterling. After that, other ships were not long in following suit.

Irkutsk, which had been kept apprised of the Cook exploration while it was in progress, presently learned of the sale of otter pelts at Canton. The information came through the Chinese merchants of Kiakhta, who could not have been pleased either, since the news indicated that they would no longer have a monopoly on the sale of otter skins in their country. The merchants of Irkutsk probably never knew it was their loose-tongued sovereign who had hastened the day of foreign competition, but in any event Catherine could expect them to forgive her in view of what she did for them soon after her accession. She was a strong believer in laissez faire—then very advanced thinking—and she had emancipated the merchants in accordance.

As later generations were to see things, the merchants were given no great degree of freedom, but to them at the time it was revolutionary, so many had been the restrictions on them. Most had been tied to their towns; few had been privileged to do business in foreign countries. Now, within limits, they could function where they willed and had greater authority to manage their own affairs through their guilds. New fields were open to them, Catherine having abolished the monopolies, keeping only a few commodities, notably liquor, under state control. And she abolished yasak, thereby giving the merchants more furs in which to deal privately.

Catherine served notice that she meant to be consistent in applying laissez faire. The merchants must enjoy their freedom at their own risk. The government was not to be looked to for protection. In 1769, in answer to suggestions that she aid endeavors in foreign parts, she wrote, "It is for traders to traffic where they please. I will furnish no men, ships, or money. . . ."

Nowhere was the effect of the emancipation more evident than at Irkutsk. In two years the population more than doubled, increasing to sixteen thousand, so great and immediate was the influx of merchants from elsewhere to settle there, bringing with them their clerks and other employees, attracted in particular by the fact that private individuals could now handle such highly profitable Chinese commodities as silk. And with the newcomers, many of whom were from the area of old Novgorod, once the heart of the Russian fur country, came millions of rubles of new capital, much of it to be invested in ships going to America.

Into this heady atmosphere, in search of his fortune—probably in 1767—strode a young man, aged twenty, of handsome appearance, strong physique, and boundless ambition, whose name was Grigorii Ivanovich Shelikhov.[1] It is likely his status was that of merchant's clerk. He hailed from Rylsk, a small town in southern Russia, and that is one of the few facts known for certain about his early life. For a man who was to write as much as he did about himself, he was curiously reticent about some things. He was also an egregious liar. Even when he was alive it sometimes took considerable guesswork to deter-

---

[1] This is the spelling of his name according to his signature.

mine exactly what Grisha Shelikhov had done and how he had done it. There was, however, never any question that he was as able as he was anxious to rise in the world.

Among the few in Irkutsk who came to like him was a man older by several years who came from Kursk in southern Russia, which made them practically fellow townsmen. Ivan Larionovich Golikov by name, he had been a prominent citizen of Kursk and was in Siberia as an exile. His offense, which had to do with taxes, had not been so great he could not function at will in Irkutsk. So respected was he that he had been entrusted with the administration throughout the province of the government liquor monopoly, a highly profitable assignment. He was wise in the ways of finance, and it was through him that Shelikhov was to rise to the top.

For a time Shelikhov appears to have worked at the customs house at Kiakhta, just the place to learn the business end of the fur trade. He then set out for Okhotsk to learn the production end, the workings of which he soon knew thoroughly. His capital was evidently small. His first venture, undertaken in partnership with another young aspirant to riches, was the outfitting of an expedition to hunt in the nearby Kuril Islands.

After that he was in the trade with the Aleutians, at first in a small way, himself working to help build some of the ships, always with partners, sometimes several, with whom to share the risks. Knowledge he displayed later suggests that he may well have gone on a voyage or two. His desire was to know every phase of the business. No eye for costs was shrewder than his. Presently he was investing also on behalf of his friend Ivan Golikov, who was thus drawn into the fur trade.

Grisha Shelikhov was well on the road to wealth by the time he was thirty, in 1777. Success did not cure him of boasting. He could never tell the simple truth about an accomplishment of his. He always had to embroider. The fault seems not to have troubled his wife, whose antecedents are as obscure as his. By all indications she was a handsome woman. She and Grisha were well matched. Nataliia Alekseevna Shelikhova was as aggressively ambitious as her husband. She was intimately acquainted with his business affairs and could manage them when he was away at Okhotsk. They lived well and they entertained lavishly, cultivating in particular officials of the government. They disdained the traditional merchant garb, dressing in European style, Shelikhov going beardless. The conservative element of Irkutsk may well have said that the Shelikhovs showed where all this new freedom was leading.

Few of the merchants paid much attention to the world beyond their own, but Grisha Shelikhov was of a more inquiring mind. He had acquainted himself with the geography of the Asian coast. He understood the need to retrieve the Amur, at least for navigation; his thinking encompassed trade with Japan, the Philippines, and other known places in the Pacific. He understood also how weak in fact was Russia's claim to the Aleutians. When all was said and done, there were only temporary camps out there.

On hearing about the Cook exploration and, after that, about the sale of otter skins at Canton, he became very thoughtful. His thought deepened when it was clear that Saint Petersburg intended doing nothing. Had Her Majesty not said that it was up to the merchants themselves to protect their interests? What was needed out there in the Pacific was a permanent Russian settlement for all the world to see. Whoever established it could be certain of at least fame. That thought greatly intrigued Grisha Shelikhov.

Such a venture would of course be costly, enormously so. Supplies enough for at least five years would have to be accumulated. To make a truly respectable showing, the settlement should have cattle, sheep, and areas under cultivation, which called also for seeds and implements. Freighting all those things just to Okhotsk would be costly enough. Then there was the problem of the men. Two hundred should do, but they must be of a less restless bent than the average among the promyshlenniki, willing to sign up for five years or more, which would require giving them a share larger than usual. As for ships, at least three would be needed, both larger and better than those usually built at Okhotsk.

The high cost lay of course in the initial outlay. Once that was made up, a permanent base, if properly placed, should be highly profitable. The hunting operation would be continuous, the hunters establishing distant camps over a wide area. It ought to be on or near the American mainland, where few so far had successfully ventured. By all accounts huge Kodiak Island, convenient to the mainland, seemed the right place.

By 1781 Shelikhov's mind was made up, but, figure it every way he tried, he could not finance the whole venture himself. He went to Golikov, who interested a relative, and the three of them organized a partnership firm named the Golikov-Shelikhov Company. But the combined capital this represented was still not enough. Shelikhov put himself deeply into debt by borrowing 50,000 rubles. This colony of his was going to have to succeed. He would, he decided, head the expedition himself, at his side his wife, Nataliia, who seems to have been excited by the project from the first. There were those who would care for their three children during their absence, which might be for three or four years.

Shelikhov, whose talent as an organizer was great, was ready in two years, a monumental achievement, considering the problems of transportation along the 2200 miles between Irkutsk and the seaboard. The cattle, the seeds, and the rest of the supplies had been brought; nearly 200 men had been chosen and signed up for five years; three ships had been built, two galiots and a sloop. No doubt after a prolonged service in the little Okhotsk church—the Shelikhovs were very pious—sail was set in August of 1783.

Nataliia and her husband were on the larger galiot, which had been named *Three Saints,* short for *Saints Basil the Great, Gregory the Divine, and John the Golden-Mouthed.* The second galiot was the *Saint Michael Archangel*. The sloop, called for short the *Saint Simeon*, was *Saint Simeon the Friend of God and Anna His Prophetess*.

No sooner were they out of the Okhotsk Sea and past the Kuril Islands than they were struck by a squall, after which the *Saint Michael* could not be found. There was no sign even of wreckage. The loss of a ship was serious enough, but the *Saint Michael* also carried most of the tools. Deciding that her navigator, one Olesov, might have gone on to Bering Island, a rendezvous for ships in emergencies such as this, Shelikhov had his two remaining vessels proceed to that place. The *Saint Michael* was not there. Winter camp was made, in the hope she would appear, but she did not. In spring, no doubt after conferring with navigators Dimitrii Bocharov of the *Three Saints* and Gerasim Izmailov of the *Saint Simeon,* experienced hands both, Shelikhov decided to push on. The missing vessel might be waiting at Unalaska, which was another meeting place for ships.

Next the *Saint Simeon* disappeared in the fog as they sailed along the Aleutians. Shelikhov had learned better than to spend much time searching, and he went on, finding the *Saint Simeon* at Unalaska but not the *Saint Michael*. Nor had the men connected with the other ships in the vicinity heard anything about her. On the promise that any news would be sent on to Kodiak, Shelikhov again weighed anchor, after hiring twelve Aleut hunters, two of whom knew enough Russian to serve as interpreters.

By late July of 1784, a year out of Okhotsk, the *Three Saints* and the *Saint Simeon* were in sight of the mountainous ridge identifying hundred-mile-long Kodiak Island. After skirting the southern shore, they cast anchor in a capacious bay along a pleasing stretch of grassy coast. Here, Shelikhov decided, he would build his settlement. He named the place Three Saints Bay. The closest settlement of Europeans was the tiny presidio of San Francisco, founded eight years before.

Eighteen months later Shelikhov could begin to think of going home. He and his men, whom he had kept under the strictest discipline, had accomplished an amazing lot, despite the

shortness of tools due to the loss of the *Saint Michael*. Three
Saints Bay was a neat, well-built little village consisting of seven
or eight individual dwellings, a set of bunkhouses, a commissary, a counting house, barns, storage buildings, a smithy, a
carpentry shop, and a ropewalk. A dozen outlying stations had
been established, one on the mainland, fronting on Cook Inlet.

In the doing of these things, Shelikhov and his men were
aided by the natives of Kodiak—in itself a major achievement
on his part. The natives, who were considerably more warlike
than those on the Aleutians, had never before been won over,
and at first Shelikhov was met with great hostility. How he
handled them his writings do not make clear, so embellished are
they by boasts and absurd claims. Probably he was patient, gave
many presents, and paid for work done. However it was accomplished, the testimony of others leaves no doubt that he persuaded the islanders to become willing workers on his behalf; a
number of their dwellings stood close to the village at Three
Saints.

In February of 1786, two months before his departure, Shelikhov's faith in his luck was renewed by the news that the *Saint
Michael* was not lost. She was at Unalaska, where she had put
in the previous year after losing a mast on the way and suffering
other damage. Olesov, her navigator, was evidently no man to
be trusted with a bottle. After his ship had been repaired, he put
her on the rocks as he attempted to clear the harbor. So she was
still at Unalaska, undergoing further repairs. This news was
brought to Shelikhov by two emaciated men, the only survivors
of a crew of thirteen who, six months before, had been sent by
baidara to inform him. His relief on learning he still had all his
ships was not so great that he failed to decide to put the *Saint
Michael* in other hands.

For the man who would head the colony after his departure,
Shelikhov wrote out a lengthy and detailed series of orders, the
more complex for the fact this was among the documents he
meant to show the authorities at home. Discipline must be
maintained, the natives treated kindly, exploring continued, ever

more outlying stations established. As must never be forgotten, it was all on behalf of the fatherland.

The *Three Saints,* which was to hurry back directly she had fulfilled her mission of returning the Shelikhovs to Okhotsk, set sail in May. With her went the furs gathered these twenty-one months—no great quantity, hunting having had to take second place, but a number encouraging for the future. Shelikhov needed grounds for hope on that score. So far his colony had cost a quarter of a million rubles.

The Shelikhovs were a year reaching their home in Irkutsk and did not arrive until the early months of 1787, so many had been the delays and mishaps on the way. No doubt they were disconcerted to see how their son and two daughters had grown during their absence of nearly four years.

They were met by an accumulation of extremely bad news. The business of Irkutsk was at a virtual standstill. Two years before, Peking had again halted trade, and Kiakhta was still closed. (It was to remain closed for another five years.) Saint Petersburg, whose attention was occupied elsewhere, was at the moment not to be looked to for much help with Peking. Tsaritsa Catherine's arms had taken the Crimea, which meant that the last of the Tatar strongholds had been subdued after five hundred years and that Russia might presently have Constantinople, the goal central to her foreign policy. The nation exulted, but not Shelikhov, who had hoped immediately to interest Catherine in his achievement. She was away on a prolonged triumphal tour of southern Russia and her newly acquired territory.

Golikov was no longer at Irkutsk, which was another piece of bad news for Shelikhov, who needed greatly to consult with his partner. A year or two before, by an amnesty granted many exiles, Golikov had been allowed to return to his home in Kursk. Shelikhov wrote him at length, sending also a map of Kodiak and the adjacent territory their men had explored. Judging by Golikov's subsequent actions, his partner strongly stressed the desirability of interesting the government with no delay. They now had more than vanity as a motive. Let Kiakhta remain closed much longer, and their colony would unquestionably suffer for lack of money. In a case of as much moment as this to the empire, Her Majesty should be expected to set aside her assertions that the merchants could look only to their own means.

Irkutsk had a new governor general, Ivan Yakobii, whose acquaintance Shelikhov set out to cultivate. "Your great soul," Shelikhov wrote him, "will of course pay no heed to futile adulation, a fact well known to me from all I have heard. For this reason he would act wrongly who, laboring under the delusion that he could sway you by flattery, would make so bold as to trouble the high person of your excellency with fanciful or dishonest reports." Yakobii was charmed. He was also impressed when he had gone over the maps and other papers on which Shelikhov begged "an opinion." The result was that Shelikhov prepared, for transmittal to Saint Petersburg by this new friend, a lengthy list of benefits which he believed should be conferred on his company.

He asked for a government ship as a free gift, for the right to establish a private port on the Okhotsk Sea, for permission to open trade with Korea, Japan, India, the Philippines, and with the Spanish, as well as other colonists in America. He asked also for priests and deacons, for a military contingent to help guard his colony, and for naval men to aid in navigation.

He should, Shelikhov went on, be given also a corps of skilled workmen and engineers, a group of exiles who would institute farming, the privilege of employing men who for various legal reasons were not supposed to leave Siberia, approval of the employment of natives and of a plan to increase the labor force by ransoming slaves held by various native tribes. Another request was that the colony be freed from the jurisdiction of coastal officials and placed directly under the governor general, with the privilege of direct communication with Her Majesty. The two final requests were for money and honors. He asked for

500,000 rubles. Concerning honors he wrote, "It would be advisable to assure everyone who deserves it of recognition and distinction."

Yakobii approved of the entire document but did not hurry to send it to Saint Petersburg. Her Majesty was still away on her triumphal tour. The news brought by courier to Irkutsk constantly told how successful was the tour, how splendid, how well organized, in what style Her Majesty traveled, how impressed were the foreign ambassadors she had invited to accompany her. Shelikhov no doubt wished she would get it over with and come home. All he could do meanwhile was chew his nails.

Given this time to reflect, emboldened by the easy acceptance he had had from Yakobii, Shelikhov began developing a thought that must have been latent in his mind all along. He should also have asked for a monopoly, certainly within the area he had occupied, if not of the entire operation in America. Her Majesty was, to be sure, against monopolies. On the other hand she had made exceptions and she had expressed herself on the subject of mistreating the natives. There lay the argument, as Yakobii agreed. Threats and even punishment had failed to control the less disciplined among the promyshlenniki. No official was out there in the Pacific. The answer was to privilege a company of proven responsibility.

Shelikhov's fellow merchants, who had been watching his maneuverings with disquiet, were furious when they heard the talk of monopoly. One of them decided to establish a permanent post of his own in America. Another declared that if matters went much further he would expose Shelikhov's lies. As was his habit, Shelikhov had been embroidering heavily, even claiming to be the discoverer of Kodiak. According to him, the number of natives he had brought under Russia was fifty thousand, a figure off the truth by ten times. He was also claiming that he had conducted a school for the native children and that he had made converts to Orthodoxy so fervent they themselves had turned to missionary effort. Then something happened that surely left his opponents speechless. So fortuitous was it, so improbable, that he indeed seemed blessed with an irresistible destiny.

As Tsaritsa Catherine was on her way back to Saint Petersburg from her tour of southern Russia, the huge coaches of her train stopped for a respite at Kursk, the home of Ivan Golikov. It was the custom for sovereigns, when traveling about the empire, to make themselves accessible to people of many sorts. During the interview he obtained, Golikov produced the map and other papers Shelikhov had sent him. Catherine was acutely interested when she understood that a permanent base had been established. Before going on her tour she had taken two new steps with regard to the Pacific. She had approved another exploration, which was already under way. She had also considered a plan, which awaited her return for final approval and was a well-kept secret, for the stationing of a portion of the Baltic fleet in the Pacific, an act calculated to serve notice that Russia meant to protect her new lands in the distant East. Having interrogated Golikov closely, Catherine delighted him further by instructing him to inform Shelikhov that she wished to see them both in Saint Petersburg.

It must all be by God's will, Shelikhov surely concluded after reading the letter from his partner. Yakobii was equally delighted. By all means go immediately to Saint Petersburg, he told Shelikhov. He himself could, he added, be counted on to send whatever recommendations might be needed.

Their well-wishers were no doubt all on hand when the Shelikhovs set out in their three-horse sleigh in January of 1788; ahead of them lay a journey of 3700 miles. Post stations stood every 50 miles; the route was served by 3000 men and 10,000 horses. Everything went so well that within a few weeks, in February, the Shelikhovs were in Saint Petersburg, where Golikov soon joined them—if indeed he had not been awaiting them.

Her Majesty had not forgotten she wished to see them; they were expected by the officials on whom they called. But they would have to be patient. Her Majesty was still very busy with all that had accumulated during her absence. Besides, as a consequence of her recent conquests and her tour, Turkey had declared war. Shelikhov and his partner were instructed to draw up a petition for what they wanted and to file it in their joint names.

"Most gracious Majesty, we offer this petition most humbly," the partners wrote, "reverently kissing the dust under the hallowed feet of Your imperial Majesty . . ." Far fewer demands were made than in the document prepared for Yakobii by Shelikhov. Perhaps Golikov prevailed on him to omit everything but the essentials: a monopoly, armed assistance, the right to employ natives and the like, and, of course, the money. Shelikhov's original demand on that score was scaled down by more than half, to 200,000 rubles, and it was asked for as a loan.

That Catherine saw the petition is clear. She instructed her Commerce Commission to hold hearings on it. Nor was that a mode of shelving the matter. Shelikhov could not complain of the attention he was given by the chairman of the commission, who agreed that the halt in trade with China was sufficient reason to ask for the loan. As for the monopoly, yes, something of the sort might be conceded if, as Shelikhov claimed, his treatment of the natives was so much better than that of his rivals. Yakobii's recommendations were all that could be desired. "I think it evident that Shelikhov has been more concerned with the interests of his country than with personal gain. It would be only just to recompense his company for all it has done by giving it the exclusive privilege of the fur trade in the places its ships have explored. . . . As for the natives, it is better to entrust them to one whose work is known than to the many who will have only their own gain in mind. . . ."

The commission made up its mind within a month. Its report, drawn up in March, could not have been more favorable. The requests for a loan, for the monopoly, for armed protection were all approved. Her Majesty was urged to proceed with her plan to send a portion of the Baltic fleet to the Pacific. But that recommendation was soon idle, as war was declared by Sweden, which was persuaded to the course by the powers unwilling to see Russia defeat Turkey. Her Majesty was now busy indeed. This new war on a second front put Saint Petersburg itself in danger. Golikov and Shelikhov were to have to wait six months, until September, for their final answer.

Bridle their impatience though they had to, those six months appear to have been no unhappy time for the Shelikhovs. Nataliia, who dreamed even of elevation to the nobility, decided that some day she would live in this wonderfully elegant city on the Baltic. So sure of the outcome was her husband that on a visit to nearby Valaam Monastery he gave the fathers ten shares in his company, asking them to persuade the Church to establish a mission at his colony, which he promised to support. How he wanted to be remembered is to be seen in an idealized likeness he had had made of himself. It shows him in the clothes, the pose, and the accouterments of a gentleman explorer of, say, England or France.

There is no evidence that he ever got to see Catherine. The court calendar listing appointments of the sort is bare of mention. The blow he was given was as cruel as it was unexpected. It came in the form of a decree dated September 12, 1788, issued by the Senate, the body which, on instruction from Catherine and often with wording furnished by her, issued most decrees. It was clear, curt, and complete. "Her Majesty does not regard it as right to give exclusive privileges to the trade. The granting of such a concession would not be at all in agreement with the principles adopted by Her Majesty, which call for the abolishing of monopolies of whatsoever kind." Denied also, without explanation, were the requests for a loan and for armed protection. Shelikhov and his partner were given only one thing: an award of swords and gold medals bearing the portrait of Her Majesty and suitably inscribed.

Why Catherine refused in this categorical fashion has been much debated. The war on two fronts was a drain; Catherine had reason at this time not to irritate Britain; her interest in the

Pacific had never been paramount; as she herself said, Siberia had too few people for colonization schemes. Then there were the views concerning merchant activities expressed early in her reign, in the light of which, historian Frank Golder insists, she was bound to give the answer she gave. Yet she had considered altering her views in this case. Sometimes a happening is clarified if less attention is paid to what was said and more to the way it was said.

The striking feature of the decree is its cold curtness, in sharp contrast to the warmth previously shown Shelikhov. Then there is the evidence that Catherine did not allow him to see her. And that award of swords and medals—as awards then went, this one was so petty as to amount to insult under the circumstances. Even nobility had been conferred for less, and by Catherine herself. Everything points to the probability that Catherine, who had a temper, was made suddenly very angry and acted accordingly, abruptly disposing of a matter about which she had been of more than one mind.

Shelikhov himself hinted at the explanation in a letter in which he alluded darkly to what he intended doing to a rival who had ruined his case. The weapon of that rival would have been exposure of his lies. He was lucky to get off as well as he did. To Khrapovitskii, Catherine's confidential secretary, he had seemed likely to end up "in chains."

There was nothing he could say in reply. Having been given the answer, all that he and Nataliia could do was pack up and say good-by to Saint Petersburg. He must have shuddered as he thought of all the laughter he was bound to hear from his colleagues on his return to Irkutsk.

V

Saint Petersburg Takes Command

By 1791 Grigorii Shelikhov was looking old, much older than forty-four. Three years had passed since his return to Irkutsk from Saint Petersburg, and his situation had only grown worse. Simply making ends meet had become a problem, although his warehouse bulged with furs from his colony. Sales were small. For six years now Peking had kept Kiakhta closed. As for the markets in Europe, they were glutted with the furs the Chinese were not buying. His competitors could cut their costs; all but two of them had pulled in their ships off the Pacific. They did not have a colony to keep going in order not to lose the investment.

In hope of still obtaining a loan, he had worked ceaselessly to have his case reopened in Saint Petersburg. His efforts had resulted in the sending of two strong recommendations by a new governor general, but to no avail. Partner Ivan Golikov had worked to the same end in Saint Petersburg. Feeling that the Church would be their best ally, he had painted so touching a picture of the yearnings for Christianity on the part of the American natives that the Holy Synod had been moved to recommend to Her Majesty that priests be asked to volunteer. But that too had been idle. By the look of things, the colony would never be allowed even a priest by Catherine the Great.

Emphasizing the ill luck that had dogged him these three years, the summer's mail from Okhotsk had brought Shelikhov the news that he had lost his best ship. The galiot *Three Saints* had been wrecked at Unalaska while on her way to the colony with the first shipment of supplies sent in some time and a large contingent of new men, including a new manager, Aleksandr Baranov by name. He and all the other men were said to be alive, thanks be to God. They would surely find some way to continue on to the colony, but that did not solve the problem of replacing the ship. If only that Catherine woman had disgorged some money—but she had not.

At least that Catherine woman was not going to rob him of his place in history, about that Shelikhov was determined. He had written a book which a Saint Petersburg bookseller would presently publish, *The Voyage of Grigorii Shelikhov, Russian Merchant* . . . He was oblivious to the detectability of the lies it contained, to the possibility that it might one day disgrace his memory.

His luck bettered abruptly with the ending of Russia's seven-year tea famine in 1792. Peking reopened trade at Kiakhta. He could now exult over the fact he had kept his colony going. That gave him the jump over his competitors, who had pulled in their ships and would now need months in which to outfit themselves anew. Having plenty of furs to sell, he hurried to the border, re-registered at the Kiakhta customs house, where once he had been a clerk, then proceeded to renew old connections among the Chinese merchants returning to Mai-mai-cheng. He stood to be the richest merchant of Irkutsk once his debts were paid off.

There was more. He had acquired a powerful friend at court, no less a personage than Catherine's latest lover, twenty-three-year-old Platon Zubov, a former army corporal. Catherine, who was sixty-two, dotingly allowed him to exploit to the full the high station to which she had elevated him. He was making a business of extracting favors from her on behalf of individuals. Shelikhov, who seems to have been related to him in some fashion, was at last granted his monopoly. It was limited to his own colonial holdings but generous in scope. No competitor could henceforth operate within 500 versts (333 miles) of a present or future Shelikhov post. Other favors were showered on Shelikhov, who remained delighted until 1793, when he received a letter from Saint Petersburg that made him look old again.

Zubov, he read, had persuaded Her Majesty to approve three requests he had made in the past: for missionaries, for a labor force of exiles, and for the privilege of buying serfs for service as agricultural colonists at a place called Yakutat on the American mainland. He had, he learned, acquired thirty serfs and their families from a bankrupt estate and, as he well knew, he must use them only for the purpose he had stipulated or risk severe punishment. The concession was a large one on the part of Catherine, whose view had been that serfs should not be removed from the homeland.

He must have read the letter over and over unwilling to believe that his boastfulness could be responsible. The chance that his request would be granted had seemed small when he asked for serfs. He had simply been talking big, posing as the great colonizer, throwing in a catchy name. Yakutat, which was hundreds of miles from his colony, was so unfit for agriculture that any farming tried there would be both fruitless and costly. Then there was the news in the letter about missionaries, for whom he had petitioned in the expectation of financial aid from the government.

Only too clearly did he now recall his visit to Valaam Monastery during his stay in Saint Petersburg, his large donation to the fathers, his grand talk of supporting a mission. He would, he had said, provide everything, food, clothing, shelter; he went so far as to say he had already built a church. He had been taken at his word. He was, the letter stated, being sent no less than ten clerics who had responded to the call for volunteers from the Holy Synod finally permitted by Her Majesty, and all were from Valaam: the Archimandrite himself, Father Iosaf; four archmonks; an archdeacon; two monks; and two servitors. None had had experience with parish work or had any real notion of life in the wilds. The expense would be huge. In Shelikhov's view, the only thing of value he had been given was the exile labor force.

The exiles would be drafted from those in Siberia. The clerics and serfs would be coming from Russia in charge of a government official no doubt instructed to see that he, Shelikhov, kept his promises. The party would arrive in May. At least they had given him time to prepare. What with the new employees he intended sending the colony, he would have about 150 people to transport. Instead of tying up his fleet for the purpose, he had better buy and renovate a couple of old ships. There would also be a deal of freight. There were all the things that had to be bought for the fathers, including church furnishings. If only he hadn't said he had already built a church.

As he totted up the costs, which were almost enough to start another colony, a monstrous thought struck him. That government official would accompany his charges only as far as Okhotsk. And, since the grant of the monopoly, rival traders could not ascertain what went on in the colony. Letters of complaint from there could come only by Shelikhov ships, and he would be able to intercept them. The fathers would simply have to support themselves. On their departure they would be told that supplies enough for three years were being shipped with them. Let them discover the truth on their arrival. As for the serfs, Manager Baranov would have to mix them in with his labor force. No money was going to be wasted on useless farming at any such godforsaken place as Yakutat.

When, in April or May the following year, 1794, the official responsible for the priests and serfs coming from Russia arrived in Irkutsk, ahead of his charges, to see that all was in readiness, Shelikhov was all smiles and so was his wife. Nataliia had always covered for her husband. The official, a tall, lean, long-faced young noble of thirty, was Nikolai Petrovich Rezanov.

Rezanov belonged to a family that went back nine hundred years, but his branch had lost its wealth. His father, a man of great probity, was a career government official in the legal field.

He was attached to the judiciary section of the Senate, which in effect was the supreme court of the land. Irkutsk remembered him well for his service twenty years before as justice of its equity court. Nikolai had lived most of his life in Saint Petersburg, where he had imbibed the peculiar culture, French grafted on Russian, sponsored by Catherine. He was strongly liberal of outlook; he spoke French flawlessly; he was grounded in other languages, including Spanish; he was adept at the violin.

He had had military training in childhood and at eighteen, his birth entitling him to the privilege, he had entered a regiment of the Imperial Guard, the prime school in which to study the governing of the empire. Little went on at court not known to the guard, whose members were as often as not deeply involved in the intrigues, not a few of which stemmed from Catherine's spectacular love life. She liked having handsome young men about her and for other reasons favored the guard, well remembering it was this body that had put her on the throne.

Rezanov rose to the rank of captain during his five years in the guard, but he seems never to have felt at home in it. He was surrounded by associates, most of whom had much more money than he. He was restless, discontented, unable to decide where he belonged. He had firm friendships among the intellectuals and thought of becoming a writer himself, but that was no career for anyone of his station who had no money. When he resigned from the guard it was to enter civil service. He chose the legal field, following in his father's steps.

After a brief while in the provinces, gaining experience, he was recalled to Saint Petersburg on an assignment that suggests he had his father's reputation for probity. He was named assistant to a man Catherine had appointed to head the Bureau of Petitions, which she had sought to rid of the corruption that had always marked its operation. But her resolution lasted only until Platon Zubov became her lover. He seized on the bureau for the purpose of pocketing the bribes, causing the new director soon to resign after a violent quarrel with Catherine, which left Rezanov to deal directly with both her and Zubov. In 1794 he was on his way to Siberia, possibly by his own choice, the official in charge of the clerics and serfs going to Shelikhov's colony in America.

Rezanov, whose instructions must have included making sure that Shelikhov kept all his promises, saw nothing suspicious and apparently became a guest at the Shelikhov home. He was soon well acquainted with Anna, the second daughter, who was fourteen, then an entirely nubile age. She was a vivacious and spirited girl, judging by letters she later wrote. The atmosphere of the household was at the moment particularly conducive to thoughts of matrimony. The older daughter had recently been married, with a large dowry. Her husband, whom Rezanov liked very much, was Mikhail Buldakov, a rising and intelligent young merchant from north Russia who had settled in Irkutsk.

The Bishop of Irkutsk and his leading clergy were on hand for the arrival of the Archimandrite Iosaf and his monks. A great and special service was held in the cathedral for the success of the first Russian mission overseas, which was to be under the Diocese of Irkutsk. The real hero of the occasion was Shelikhov. This was his hour. He was extolled and he was blessed, and his opponents could only glower in silence.

Now came the journey to Okhotsk, which would take the summer, first the 1500 miles by flatboat down the Lena River to Yakutsk, from there east for 700 more miles, by horse, to and across the Stanovoi Mountains. Shelikhov could only be admired now. He was in his element. He knew every detail of the route and exactly how to manage even so unusual an expedition as this, which, counting the men handling the boats and the horses, must have been made up of some 400 people.

That journey was a tremendous experience for Nikolai Rezanov. Until then he had merely known, without realizing, how big was his country, how much history had been made even here, amid these awesome wilds, as was suggested by every little log-built town they passed. And he learned all about Russian America. During the long days they spent floating down the Lena, he sat and listened as Shelikhov, no man to pass up the ear of a government official, told of his colony and its problems. They were blind in Saint Petersburg, blind. The whole of Northwest America lay ready for the taking, but let much more time pass and it would go to the English. More men, more ships must be sent. This journey from Irkutsk to salt water, this long, tedious, difficult, expensive journey would be unnecessary, were the Amur open to navigation. Ships could be loaded within highway distance of Irkutsk and sailed all the way to the Pacific. The Chinese were known to be making no use of the river, yet never once, never once had Saint Petersburg sent them a mission to ask for the privilege. And one day Peking must be asked to allow Russian ships to trade at Canton. The confinement of trade at Kiakhta added to the problems of transportation. Ah, there was a great future for the rising young noble who would put his mind to these things, a great future indeed.

As usual, Shelikhov exaggerated when he spoke of his achievements and his colony, depicting his posts as little towns, smartly garrisoned, with an ever-expanding population of natives who, thanks originally to his efforts at instructing them, hungered for more education, even of the higher sort. Rezanov was not naïve, and surely he knew of this man's reputation for mendacity, but when they reached Okhotsk there appeared to be no further reason to be in doubt about him. The ships were waiting, as promised, to all appearances laden with supplies for the fathers, and with everything else that was supposed to be in their holds. Clearly Shelikhov was spending a fortune for his country, which had repaid him with insults. However crude and forward, he was a great man. Rezanov, who had been taught to ignore birth in his estimations of men, was to defend the name Shelikhov and to retain the picture of America painted for him until, years hence, he was to see it for himself.

It was October when they were back at Irkutsk, where Rezanov was urged to stay until winter would make easier going of the return to Saint Petersburg. In December or January he married Anna Shelikhova. That he loved her there can be no doubt, in the light of the grief he was to feel at her death. Her father saw to it that his new son-in-law would not lose interest in America. The dowry he settled on his daughter consisted of a substantial block of shares in the Golikov-Shelikhov Company. Legally those shares had to remain Anna's property. As a noble, Rezanov could not own them, vote them, or otherwise take part in the affairs of a merchant corporation. Aside from the income they would provide him and his wife, the meaning of those shares for Rezanov was that he could promote Russian America without laying himself open to suspicion that he had been bribed. Enhancing the value of his wife's property was an understandable motive.

The Shelikhovs could look on the marriage as a job well done. The happy couple, they presently learned, were well settled in Saint Petersburg; Nikolai had been given just the post he wanted, in the department of the Senate where his father had distinguished himself.

Half a year after the marriage of his daughter, in the late summer of 1795, Shelikhov died, apparently from a heart attack. He was only forty-eight; he had been under heavy strain. Worse was to come, as could be told by the first letters of the season from the colony, where the priests and the others had arrived safely.

Manager Baranov wrote scorchingly, demanding among other things that he be relieved. He, not Shelikhov, was being held responsible for their plight by the fathers, who had had to be made to help with the scrabbling for food, the large and unexpected number of new people straining resources to the utmost. The colony, wrote Father Iosaf, was a vicious and disorderly place, only his regard for Shelikhov prevented him from reporting the situation to the ecclesiastical authorities.

Since these letters were to Shelikhov, his widow could suppress them, but Nataliia could not evade trouble of another sort. Her husband's death had been the signal for his opponents to try breaking his company, which she now managed. They had organized for the purpose, forming a combine. The accumulated animosities of the years turned the battle into a personal feud.

Nataliia was charged with dishonesty; her credit was undermined; a lawsuit representing an old claim for damages on Shelikhov was filed against her. The noise reached Saint Petersburg, necessitating a written explanation to the Commerce Commission. The sarcasm suggests that the writer was Rezanov. "Many Irkutsk merchants have for years harbored a grudge with regard to the activities of the late Shelikhov, accusing him of having been the one to take away their trade in the Pacific Sea and of enriching himself in the area in which it was proper for only them to enrich themselves. . . ."

In 1796 Catherine died, at sixty-seven. She had willed the succession to her grandson Alexander, whose upbringing she had supervised and who shared her views. She hated her son Paul, Alexander's father, who in any case was unfit to rule. "Mad Paul," he was called. He may not have been psychotic, but erratic he certainly was, tyrannical, given to childish tantrums, filled with peculiar prejudices. He was against the changes made by his mother, declaring that when he became Tsar he would abolish them. And he became Tsar. Alexander, who was nineteen, refused to stand in his father's way.

The dismay that swept the capital at this turn of affairs was shared by Rezanov, who had looked forward to serving under Alexander, whom he knew well and liked. Now it was a question how long he would have any career at all. Paul had use for no one who had been close to Zubov, regardless of the capacity. But, protected by his close friend, Count Petr Pahlen, one of the few to whom Paul was listening, Rezanov not only kept his footing amid all the dismissals, he was even made head of his department in the Senate. Not that he could look forward to an easy time of it. The post called for direct and frequent conferring with His Majesty.

Paul was no Ivan the Terrible. Thoughts of prison and torture sickened him. All the same, anyone provoking one of his tantrums was liable to feel the imperial cane about his head and even find himself on his way to Siberia. Paul's moods were subject to unexpected shifts. Coping with him called for the greatest patience and tact. Rezanov was so disheartened at one point that he would have resigned, but for the fact he would thus have deserted the entourage built up by Pahlen, which was giving the government what stability it had. Rezanov went on, presently becoming one of the few Paul trusted to any depth.

Paul posed a threat to Russian America. He believed that no Russian should be abroad and that he should curtail the freedom his mother had given merchants. Rezanov made him feel differently by playing on another of his prejudices. Republicanism was a word to turn Paul livid. As Rezanov argued the case for continuing trade in the Pacific, it was necessary in order to "soften the manners of the savages by bringing them into continuous contact with Russians," which in turn engendered a liking for "the Russian way of looking at things, a way which ascribes the well being of a people to the monarchistic system. . . . Otherwise the trading nations envious of us, and which often take a peep into those regions, may, especially in view of the present unrest in Europe, lead those natives astray, gullible as they are, infusing them with the spirit of Republicanism."

While Rezanov thus brought the childish Tsar to a better frame of mind regarding merchants, those at Irkutsk heedlessly continued their noisy war on Nataliia Shelikhova. The combine against her now had an important and unexpected ally, to wit, Ivan Golikov, who was back in Irkutsk looking after his interests. Whatever had happened to embitter him against his late partner's widow, in putting in with her enemies he had split the old Golikov-Shelikhov Company down the middle.

Probably advised to do so by Rezanov, Nataliia proposed that they all unite, the friendly with the unfriendly, form one company, eliminate the cutthroat competition alike at Irkutsk and in the Pacific. She would, she said, throw in all her resources, which were still the largest in the American trade—her ships, her colony, her cash, everything. Her appeal proved fruitless; it was opposed in particular by Golikov, who would have nothing to do with her any more. A sharp command in the name of the Tsar came from Saint Petersburg, ordering the amalgamation along specified lines, in conformity with the practices of European organizations of the kind. The author was unquestionably Rezanov, who, as head of his department in the Senate, could issue such a decree. In this way the United American Company was formed in the summer of 1797.

Nataliia's name headed the list of nineteen merchants who signed the agreement, which also set forth the objectives of the new firm. "In the name of God Almighty," it began, ". . . we, the partners of the American and Irkutsk trading companies . . . as true subjects complying with the wish of His imperial Majesty, who, in approving our union, expressed the desire that we organize after the manner of foreign European companies and ordered us to follow their example in commerce and organization . . . our company, confirming the preliminary union, begs the Omnipotent Creator to give it strength and understanding to follow and to execute the intentions of His imperial Majesty. . . ." The objectives, first among which was the care of the mission "engaged in the propagation of the Holy Gospel," included shipbuilding in America, the fostering of settlements, trading with foreign powers, and many more. "We undertake to carry out all these projects with honor, truth, philanthropy, conscience, and in compliance with the interests of State, Society, and Company." The author was probably Nataliia.

Peace did not ensue. Some of the merchants who signed the agreement did so sullenly; there were those who refused to sign at all. Efforts to discredit Nataliia went on; the lawsuit against her was not dropped. To testify in the matter, she was called to Saint Petersburg. Rezanov's hand is clearly evident. The proceeding was in his department of the Senate. Nataliia was not only cleared of all charges; she had her dearest wish fulfilled: she, together with her children, was ennobled.

The following year it was clear to Rezanov that the United American Company was never going to work out. He was forced to proceed with another plan, far more ambitious, much larger in scope, which he had delayed advancing for fear, no doubt, of Paul's reaction.

This was the age of the colonial corporation, the Hudson's Bay Company, the Dutch and British East India Companies and several more. Typically they were stockholder-owned and privately controlled, yet were devices for imperialist expansion, ingenious instruments in that their degree of freedom to act was such that their home governments could at will claim or disclaim responsibility for their acts. They governed as well as exploited their domains, in theory preparing distant lands to come one day fully under the crown. Rezanov could say it was a tried and proven device, the models having only to be adapted to the situation.

As a professional administrator he had seen that the basic need of Russian America was for a government, no plans for which had ever been made in all this half-century of *de facto* occupation. Rezanov, who at one point rejected a proposal to declare the region a crown colony, was doubtless attracted first of all by the independence inherent in the idea of a colonial corporation. The twists and turns of Russian politics made that feature highly advisable. The corporation, if properly empowered, could cope with the related problems of the Far East as well as those of the colony, for which he had conceived some expansionist plans exceeding in boldness anything Shelikhov had had in mind.

The Russian-American Company, as Rezanov wished it called, should be able to maintain its own armed forces, treat with neighboring powers, trade where it willed. Within its domain it should own all property not of a personal kind, from ships to fishnets; it should control all exploitative activity, from hunting to mining. Its domain was seen by Rezanov as extending from the Arctic south to the 55th parallel and from the Siberian coast eastward to the American mainland and beyond, without limitation by any fixed boundary. The Company's privileges and duties were set forth in a charter to be in force for twenty years, after which the government could choose to renew it or take over the colony. Meanwhile, through the stockholder-elected board, the Company alone would administer the colony, appointing the officials and paying their salaries.

It would be a government within the government, hardly a concept to appeal to Paul, with his notions of preserving complete autocracy. There was, however, the argument that his mother at her least consistent would never have approved anything so contrary to laissez faire.

Paul consented to consider the proposal. News of it leaked to Irkutsk, bringing a number of merchants hastily to Saint Petersburg to register their protests loudly. They did not wish to cease their operations in the Pacific to become mere stockholders, and in their view this was an infringement on their historic monopoly of trade. Rezanov wanted the noble class as well to have the privilege of owning stock and otherwise taking part.

The merchants found a spokesman in Lopukhin, who was procurator general of the Senate and thus Rezanov's superior. He was also father of the woman with whom Paul was having what for him was an affair. At stake now was more than Rezanov's plan. His own downfall would be the outcome in the event Lopukhin prevailed. A power struggle ensued as the Pahlen faction lined up in support of Rezanov. It is to be wondered whether the issue was finally decided at all on the merits of the plan. In a complicated matter such as this, Paul's choice often came simply down to a decision on his part as to which set of advisers he most trusted. The intrigues brought to bear were such that when Rezanov found a letter showing that his wife had been writing a running account of the battle to her sister in Irkutsk he added the postscript, "For God's sake, tear up the correspondence."

It was Lopukhin who fell. The day following his dismissal from his post, on July 8, 1799, Paul signed the charter of the Russian-American Company. Companies not wishing to be absorbed had a year in which to withdraw from the Pacific, where Aleksandr Baranov was made governor.

Irkutsk had been decided on as the logical location for the

main office. What a miscalculation that was, in view of the dissatisfaction of the merchants, Rezanov began to learn the day the office was opened. What had been planned to be a happy celebration became so disorderly the authorities had to intervene. The first stockholders' meeting was even worse. Though the Shelikhov element held the largest block of shares and wanted the chairman of the board to be Mikhail Buldakov, Shelikhov's other son-in-law, insuring his election took an imperial order. And even after that Buldakov was forced out of office. Rezanov then threw up his hands and obtained another decree, moving Company headquarters to Saint Petersburg. Nataliia could now live at the capital, as she had always wanted to do. She retired after that. Her work was done.

On a night in March 1801, the fifth year of Paul's reign, a group of men entered his sleeping quarters, his trusted Pahlen among them. And when he refused their command to abdicate he was assassinated. His rule had become intolerable; under despotism there was no other course.

The accession of his son, Alexander I, was cause for rejoicing throughout the empire. He was young, handsome, kindly, and full of plans for reform. Rezanov was made Procurator General of the Senate, the nation's second most important administrative officer. And Alexander confirmed the Russian-American Company in all its privileges, in particular approving of nobles' taking part. He set the example, himself buying shares in the Company, designating the dividends to charity, as did others in the imperial family.

Rezanov was appointed sole intermediary between government and Company, with the title of Correspondent. His brother-in-law, Buldakov, was re-elected chairman of the board, which he was long to remain. To serve as Company headquarters, a fine structure was bought on fashionable Moika Quai. Grisha Shelikhov could rest comfortably under his opulent monument at Irkutsk. His two sons-in-law were carrying on very well indeed. There was just one thing: about the colony itself, little had been done so far.

VI

A Man of No Station

Shelikhov's name was not beloved at his colony in 1791. He had never been generous with supplies; he was, in fact, stingy when it came to the little things that made the life easier, such as tobacco and the like; and now it was three years since there had been any ship at all. Several of the 130 men were due to go home, and that was something else. They had worked out their five-year enlistments but had to wait for replacements. The current manager, who himself was due to be relieved, easy-going Greek-born Evstrat Delarov, could not say why there was no ship.

Two years before, the galiot *Three Saints* had sailed with furs for Okhotsk, and there, unless she had been wrecked, she still apparently was, as idle as the vessels of the merchants who had suspended their operations for the duration of the halt in trade at Kiakhta, which was now in its sixth year. Perhaps Shelikhov was broke. All that the colony knew for certain was that there was no flour with which to make bread, no new rigging for the two vessels left, the *Saint Michael* and the *Saint Simeon,* neither of which was in good condition.

The colony, which was now seven years old, had not grown. Some of the outlying stations had had to be closed for lack of men. On the mainland there was still only one, Fort Alexander on Cook Inlet, which had a bare twenty men. Many more natives now lived around Three Saints village; otherwise it was no bigger than it had been when Shelikhov put up the cabins, the bunkhouses, the commissary, and the rest of it. Cabbages were grown, and a few potatoes; cattle and sheep still grazed; this alone gave it the air of a colonial enterprise. Shelikhov's letters, when there had been letters from him, demanded more action, but what could be done without more men and means? Delarov, though he kept strict order, drove no one.

Three Saints village was roused one day in late June by the arrival of a sealion-hide sailboat in which were sixteeen haggard Russians wearing the kamleikas of the Unalaska Aleuts. One of them, a little man with a bald spot fringed by hair the color of flax, had pneumonia. He was in a delirium of fever and had to be carried ashore. Delarov, when he understood who he was, had him bedded in his own house. His name, the village learned, was Aleksandr Andreevich Baranov. This little man had come to replace Delarov as manager.

Presently two more sealion-hide baidaras appeared with thirty-three more men. By then the village had the story. The *Three Saints* had put out from Okhotsk under Navigator Dimitrii Bocharov the previous summer with Baranov, fifty-two other men, and supplies, only to go to pieces in a gale at Unalaska, where she had put in, late in the season, for water and meat. There they had had to winter, seeing no ship all year; Kiakhta was still closed. In spring the three baidaras [1] were built, and here, at Kodiak, the men now all were, except for five who remained at Unalaska to guard what little had been saved of the cargo.

The colony still had no tea, but at least Shelikhov was not broke and he had tried. What about this new manager? Opinions were divided among the men who had sailed with him. A brilliant man, said a few, well educated, though self taught. He knew minerals and textiles and many other things of the sort. Nor had he spent the winter sitting in a dugout. What energy! He had been all over Unalaska, examining it, getting acquainted with the Aleuts, learning their language, learning how to manage a baidarka, how to hunt otter. Navigator Bocharov, who

---

[1] It is to be recalled that the word "baidara" meant a larger boat than a baidarka.

spoke for the majority, was contemptuous. Shelikhov had given them a man wholly without experience at this life, a landlubber who had never put to sea before. He had been sick as a dog on the voyage out and yet he had asked to learn navigation. But then he might not last. He was old for this kind of life, forty-four. As he was showing, he had been unable to take even six weeks in an open boat, eating only raw fish and sleeping on wet beaches at night.

The object of all the curiosity, as he lay covered with skins in the manager's cabin, no doubt pondered his own future and may well have thought over the steps in his life that had brought him to this place. Even as a boy he had seen how backward was Kargopol, the town in northwestern Russia where he was born, the son of a storekeeper, in 1747. At fifteen he had run away to Moscow, which was a different world indeed, a huge city, still the business center of the nation, despite Saint Petersburg. The merchants and their families who lived in the foreign quarter came from places as various as Leipzig and Bukhara.

Amid that element of Moscow, like Peter the Great before him, he had learned to like and respect foreigners. As a runaway boy with no passport to show he was privileged to be away from his birthplace, he had not dared apply to domestic firms for work. He was given a job and a place to live by a kindly German merchant, whose language he learned. And he educated himself in other ways during the ten or so years he was in Moscow, reading avidly, liking best works on science.

It had been a mistake to return to Kargopol, to imagine that because he had acquired the capital to open a business he could be happy in such a place after Moscow. Things were worse after he married and had a daughter. The union was not a happy one. He could say he had always since sent home money for the support of his family. When he left Kargopol for the last time it was to go to Siberia, taking advantage of the freedom of movement given his class by Tsaritsa Catherine.

He had opened their eyes in Irkutsk when he gave the town its first factory for the making of glass, which had been an expensive imported commodity. He had simply applied his readings in science. Discovering that the raw materials were available, he had interested men with capital in going into partnership with him, and he had done well, receiving many a compliment for both his originality and his business ability. But he had walked away from that too, after about seven years.

With only his younger brother Petr, he had gone up into the lonely wilds north of the Okhotsk Sea in the Anadyr country, where he built trading posts to deal in sable with the Chukchi natives, who were feared by most traders. To finance the venture he had gone heavily into debt, even mortgaging his shares in the glass factory, the management of which he had relinquished to his former partners.

It was not that he had wanted to get into the fur trade for its own sake. He could have been in America by now, working for Shelikhov, who had asked him more than once to run his colony, saying he was just the man. He wanted none of Shelikhov, whom he mistrusted. He wanted his independence, to be free of employers and even partners. And he wanted something else, something indicated by the remoteness he had sought. A man of talent who was of lowly birth was doomed to endless frustration under the rigid caste system dominating Russian life in settled places. The richest merchant on whom no rank had been bestowed had to stand cap in hand before the privileged. Here in these wilds a man was as good as his abilities.

What traps men sometimes set for themselves! In less than a year he had faced bankruptcy. The Chukchi plundered and burned his posts. Never again would he view with tolerance the possession of firearms by natives who could not be fully trusted with them. Leaving his brother to look after what was left, he made his way down the coast to report to the commander of Okhotsk, Major Ivan Koch, whom he had known in Irkutsk.

It had happened that Shelikhov was at Okhotsk, seeing to the dispatching of his galiot *Three Saints* to his colony. He and Commander Koch were greatly worried over a report just received, warning of possible foreign aggression in Russian America. Sweden, which was at war with Russia, was understood to have sent a privateer. Koch, whose jurisdiction extended over the islands, wanted someone out there who could use his head.

And now, a year later, in the summer of 1791, here Baranov was on Kodiak Island, abed, recovering from pneumonia. Shelikhov had given him a five-year contract and ten shares in the Golikov-Shelikhov Company, enough and more to restore his credit and enable him to go on supporting his family in Kargopol, pay his debts, and refinance the Anadyr operation, which his brother would manage. Not that he had immediately accepted the deal. As he had discussed the matter with both Koch and Shelikhov, hearing the situation in the Pacific described, the danger from the privateer, the increasing number of foreign traders, the possibility that other governments might send further exploring expeditions—matters with which he was likely to have to cope—many a doubt had assailed him.

Whether or not Shelikhov's manager had a title, he was perforce the representative of the government out there. He must be judge and jury in the event of a crime. He must keep careful records of explorations, note the locations of the metal plates buried in proof of Russian claims to newly discovered places. He, Baranov, was a rankless commoner. How would he be able to give any orders, should Shelikhov, as he talked of doing, succeed in obtaining naval officers to sail his vessels? Koch, to whom he opened his heart, understood perfectly. He had given him papers appointing him his personal representative with specific authority over navigators. Baranov was deeply grateful to Koch for that. He had meant it when he swore to do his best for his country.

Wanting to get well quickly, he did so. He was tough and wiry, for all his slight build. In five weeks he was on his feet, conferring with Delarov and inspecting his surroundings. His work, he soon saw, was cut out for him. When, in spring, Delarov departed in the *Saint Michael* with the homegoing men, Kodiak would be left with a force of only 110 men and one vessel, the aging sloop *Saint Simeon*. She was under command of old Gerasim Izmailov, who, like Bocharov, only looked contemptuous when asked for lessons in navigation. So much for that authority Koch had given him over navigators. Even Delarov, who was the best navigator in the trade, cooperative though he otherwise was, only smiled when asked to impart his knowledge.

Most of the men were not very enterprising, Baranov noted. Shelikhov, by his policy of picking men he thought would give him no trouble, tended to get lazy ones. An exception was a young merchant's clerk with a wooden leg, whose name was Ivan Kuskov. Baranov, who had got well acquainted with him on the voyage out, made him his assistant, putting him in charge of the commissary.

When he was fully in command, after the departure of Delarov and the other homegoers, Baranov asserted himself vigorously, imposing virtual military discipline. He was liable at any time to inspect the bunkhouses as if they were barracks. He made a ceremony of lowering the flag of an evening, firing cannon and having the men stand at attention.

Cards and other gambling devices he confiscated. He ran a still in secret, as did Izmailov, but he would allow no one else to do the same. Kvass, made mostly of cranberries, was the only alcoholic beverage allowed the men. A big vat of it was kept always on the brew; a man could drink as much of it as he wanted on his off hours. Baranov was careful to give no cause for legitimate grumbling by forgetting any of the numerous holidays of the Russian calendar. On Sundays and church feasts he read the prayers and he organized the celebrations, joining in the singing and the dancing to the accompaniment of the few instruments the men had.

He regulated relations with the native women, a frequent source of trouble among the men and with the islanders. Prostitution he forbade. A man had to stay by the girl he chose, and she, in effect, became his wife, doing his sewing and otherwise looking after him. No girl could be taken without her consent and unless her parents were satisfied with the presents they were offered.

Three Saints village ran with half-Russian children. In the view of the natives, they belonged to the mothers. A strict rule forbade taking any of them to Russia in childhood. The Russian warmth of heart toward children caused many a man to find himself emotionally trapped by the time he worked out his five-year enlistment. His only course was to remain until his children were grown.

It was soon evident that Baranov had a way with the natives. He learned their dialects; he listened to their grievances; he never talked down to them. Without the fealty of the natives he would be virtually without manpower. At Unalaska he had noted their curious improvidence and their resulting disposition to attach themselves dependently to those who were kind to them. On that rested their willingness to work. Delarov had instituted the practice of hunting by means of large flotillas of two-man baidarkas during the summer months when the seas were calmest and the otter easier of access. Baranov intended to follow suit and to use the islanders also as aides in exploring. He toured Kodiak, visiting the villages, meeting the chiefs, bargaining, always promising that those who contributed would never be in want.

Presently he was able to count on 900 natives in 450 baidarkas for his first summer's operation. He had made some large plans, wanting the biggest drive ever made for otter and to establish two new forts. He was a man of contrasting moods. He was now at high pitch, filled with furious energy, obsessively determined to let nothing stand in his way. He took it as no setback when a tidal wave all but swept Three Saints village away. Instead he seized the opportunity to move the community to a better place on the island, which he had seen on his tour. He had everyone work hard at building the new village until May, when completion was deferred until the summer's work was over.

He wanted one of his new forts along the mainland to the south, the other on an island east of Kodiak, in vast Prince William Sound—a name bestowed by Cook. Before he settled on exact locations, preliminary explorations had to be made. The expedition south to the mainland Baranov put under the command of two of his best foremen, assigning them four-fifths of the native force. He took personal charge of the investigation of the Sound and its islands. When he set out in a baidara armed with a 3-pound falconet in the prow, he had in his train 180 islanders in 90 baidarkas, each artel having an accompanying Russian hunter. Camp was made on Nuchek Island in the interior of the great gulf.

The natives thereabouts had first to be cultivated before any fort could be built; it was necessary to have their trade and goodwill. Though no kin to the murderous Tlingits farther south, they partook of Tlingit ways and had to be approached with caution, as had been discovered by the foreign shipmasters who had visited this region. As Baranov called with his interpreters at the various villages of long, low log-built communal houses, he found himself involved in lengthy questionings as to the trustworthiness of white men. These natives had been given reason, by Russians as well as other Europeans, to be in doubt. But at length a beginning at a relationship was made when a leading Kenaitze chief pledged himself to support a fort, giving hostages, as was the custom. On his part, Baranov had had to promise to take the chief's daughter to wife. He may not have thought the price too high. Though not yet a full-grown woman, she was darkly beautiful of eye, features, and carriage. When he could install her at Kodiak, Baranov decided, he would call her Anna.

One day when he was back at camp on Nuchek Island, he was alerted to the approach of a large schooner bristling with guns and flying the English flag. She had come in from the open sea to the south. One of her three masts was broken, and she was making for well-forested Nuchek, evidently in hope of obtaining a replacement. Mindful of Koch's warning to beware of possible aggression, Baranov prepared for trouble. Then, as the imposing schooner cast anchor, he saw she must be one of Britain's famous traders. The name on her prow was *Phoenix,* CALCUTTA. Unable to contain his curiosity, trusting to his Aleut garb to make him seem a native until he might want to reveal who he was, he pushed out in a baidarka.

A ladder was thrown down in response to his gestures. Yes, she was a trader, as he saw when he was on deck. They were hauling out goods for his inspection. Judging by the arms they carried, they took no chances. Bullock-hide screens against arrows shielded the decks. He was hugely amused to see the jaws drop when he threw back the hood of his kamleika and revealed his unmistakably Caucasian hair.

He had to shake his head at English and the other languages tried on him. It looked as if signs would have to serve, until he thought of the half-forgotten German of his Moscow days, and the captain proved to know a little German too. Introductions could then be made. The captain was Hugh Moore of the British East India Company and a most pleasant man. The mate was Joseph O'Cain, a shrewd and genial young man who hailed from Boston. Baranov found that there was great curiosity about him when he explained he was head of the Russians hereabouts. Having asked if he could be of assistance, he ended by offering the help of his men in repairing the mast. That evening he was made to feel that Moore and O'Cain and not he were doing the favors. The East India merchantmen were well stocked for entertaining, with fine wines, cigars, and the like. And the *Phoenix* had a cabin boy who could serve in style, an amiable and intelligent Bengalese who spoke English fluently and was called Richard. To Baranov, who could be very emotional and had tasted not even bread since leaving Okhotsk, the pleasure was enough to make him weep.

And there was the joy of engaging in civilized conversation again. How he wished, said Baranov at one point, envious of Richard's fluency in English, that he knew the language or had someone who could interpret for him. But the halting German was serving well enough. Men who fully wish to understand one another always seem to manage. They were traders together, the same breed; they talked shop, each side having information highly interesting to the other. National cautions were laid aside. Moore and O'Cain freely answered questions about the way business was done at Canton and the habits of the shipmasters frequenting this coast. Of special interest to Baranov was the information that danger of foreign aggression was over, the situation which had made that possible having changed.

With entire candor he revealed the poverty of his resources, greatly astonishing his hosts, who had thought the strength of the Russians much greater. When he explained that the difficulty was transportation, he was asked whether he would buy if shipped the supplies he needed. His answer, of which O'Cain made a large mental note, was that, though he had not the authority to buy from foreigners, he was greatly in favor of it personally.

His hosts could only marvel as they saw the proof of his poverty in his equipment. Whereas they and their kind dared approach this coast only in strong, well-armed ships, he went among the savages in canoes, his muskets and falconets museum pieces by comparison with the arms aboard the *Phoenix*.

Five days the schooner remained at Nuchek while her crew and part of Baranov's felled, shaped, and installed a suitable tree as a mast. He was aboard most of the time, every evening dining with his friends, who had come to like as well as respect him, as he could see. This was putting him behind with his summer's work, but he could not tear himself away. He was consumed with desire to know navigation; not soon again might he have a chance to study a vessel such as the *Phoenix* or be visited by foreigners so willing to answer his endless questions about Pacific trade.

If, as he had been told, the Tlingits were so dangerous that the crews dealing with them had to remain ever on guard lest they be overwhelmed and enslaved, why was the risk taken? Why did the ships come so far north? By all accounts, otter abounded all down the coast. Were the natives of California and Mexico even more dangerous? No, but neither were they hunters of sea animals. In any event, the Spaniards would allow no trade along their coastline. The Tlingits, who were good hunters, having many pelts to sell, were entirely free to trade.

Spain, Baranov learned, in effect determined the movements of all non-Spanish ships in the Pacific by keeping her colonies closed to foreign commerce. Forbidden to enter a Spanish port even for food, the shipmasters entering the Pacific had all to make straight for Hawaii, where King Kamehameha welcomed everyone who observed his simple and just regulations. The King always had quantities of food to sell, ranging from taro and fruit to pork and salt. So much of a rendezvous was Hawaii that shipmasters left letters there for one another.

Why was Canton the only Chinese port open to trade? To that there was no reasonable answer. Peking had simply so decided. It was like Kiakhta. The nations dealing at Canton were as careful as Russia not to disturb relations, putting up with numerous and arbitrary rules, restrictions, venality, and the arrogance of the officials in charge of the port.

Canton, Macao, Honolulu, Batavia, Manila—Baranov heard the names wistfully. If only he had a *Phoenix,* he too could visit those glamorous places, buy food at Hawaii, sell furs at Canton —if Russia should ever be permitted to trade by sea with China. Peking's attitude so far was that Kiakhta was trade enough for the Russians.

At length the mast was in place; the farewells had to be said. With apologies for not having more to give, Baranov presented his friends with five silver fox pelts and some Aleut kamleikas. Moore had evidently been wondering how to offer to pay for the help with the mast. Baranov was presented with someone who, when he had learned Russian, would be his interpreter in English. He was given Richard, who seems to have been willing to join him. He would, Baranov assured him, be made rich.

The rest of Baranov's summer was not overly fruitful. No new forts were established, and the drive for furs did not have results commensurate with the expenditure of manpower. One reason was that he had been too sanguine, planning too many things, deploying his forces too widely. It was, he learned, useless to send Aleuts in baidarkas down the coast into the country of the Tlingits without an armed vessel. They would not go ashore; they hunted only inattentively. And so, Baranov was informed by the two foremen he had sent in search of a site for a fort along the mainland to the south, no effective exploring had been done and only a thousand otter had been brought back—not even two pelts per Aleut.

Baranov could hardly argue. He had encountered Tlingits himself that summer, a raiding party which had come in long canoes to Prince William Sound in search of slaves, catching him unawares one night on an island away from Nuchek. The battle had been at the cost of two Russians and nine Aleuts. The affair had further set back the summer's work, but the fact that circumstances had contributed did not allay his chagrin at having accomplished so little. He was saved from going into one of his black, discouraged moods by news that sent him hurrying back to Kodiak. A ship was in from home.

And what a ship, he saw as he arrived in the harbor fronting the new village he had begun to build back in the spring. *Eagle* was her name, and she was no ungainly galiot. She was a neat, trim little packetboat, built for speed and maneuverability. The man who had built her had himself sailed her to the colony. Yakov Shiltz, the Russians called him. He was James Shields, an Englishman who counted shipbuilding and navigation as only two of his many skills, and who, for reasons best known to his vagabond self, had joined the Russian army, where he had gained a commission. In the army with him had been five other Englishmen, each also a onetime sailor. An indefinite leave of absence had been obtained for them by Catherine's lover Zubov as one of his favors to Shelikhov, who had paid them heavily to go to Okhotsk, build him a vessel that would speed communication with the colony, then sail her there.

That night half-finished Kodiak village rang with the *praz-*

dnik staged by Baranov in honor of the Englishmen, who were the more welcome for knowing Russian. There was every reason to be merry. The news was that Kiakhta had been reopened. Hard times should be a thing of the past. Only Izmailov was disgruntled. Alongside the *Eagle* his aging *Saint Simeon* looked mighty shabby. Nor would he any longer be the only man in the colony who knew how to sail a ship. To Baranov's delight, Shields had been instructed to teach navigation. But the Englishmen were to stay only through the winter; they must return to Okhotsk in spring, Shelikhov had sternly enjoined. Their services were costing him heavily.

Baranov was given additional reason for satisfaction when, on considering Shelikhov's letter in detail, he saw that he was ordered to start shipbuilding. Shields would show him how to begin. Extra tar, rigging, and other essentials had been sent on the *Eagle,* Shelikhov wrote. Baranov's imagination conjured up another *Phoenix*. Then he began checking what had actually been sent on the *Eagle*.

It was soon clear that talk of shipbuilding at the colony was boastfulness for the record. Barely enough tar and rigging had been sent to maintain existing vessels. Nor had Shelikhov, prosperous again or not, been any more generous than usual with supplies of other kinds. He had sent his manager no token of esteem, not even a bottle of vodka. Baranov went into a rage when, having checked all the cargo, he was sure that he had been sent none of the personal belongings he had not had time to collect before he left Okhotsk. Twice he had asked that this be done. Something snapped in him. Shelikhov, in his own handwriting, had ordered that ships be built. Very well, the order would be followed. Shields and his five English sailors would remain in the colony as long as they were needed. He, Baranov, by the written instruction of Koch, gave the orders to navigators. Let Shelikhov scream over the expense when he heard about it.

Shields was so shocked by the order to stay that he and Baranov came to blows, the two of them "rolling on the floor and pummeling each other like a couple of *muzhiks,*" in the words of someone who disliked them both. Then they became "thick as thieves," and with good reason. Shields had been shown that he stood to become a rich man. He and his companions were promised a substantial share of the profits, with increases when explorations they might conduct resulted in opening new fur grounds.

Baranov spent the winter studying navigation and finishing the construction of Kodiak village. For himself he built a two-story house in which he installed Richard and Anna, the Kenaitze Indian girl. In spring he set out with Shields to find a likely shipbuilding site and decided on a bay along Kenai Peninsula. Here, when the summer's hunting was over, he moved most of the men and started work on a schooner like Captain Moore's, even to the three masts, the two decks, and the name —*Phoenix.*

He had to find ways to make paint, calking—everything that was lacking. Nothing deterred him. He was in one of his highest, most obsessive moods. He was going to be able to say he had built a schooner, and that was all there was to it. Before it was over he nearly had a mutiny on his hands. At length his *Phoenix* was launched, in September of 1794. She was no beauty, but she rode easily and well. Shields would be taking her on her maiden voyage to Okhotsk in spring.

The shipbuilding over, the men were all moved back to Kodiak village, where they were settling down in hope of a peaceful winter when the ships arrived with the 150-odd people Shelikhov had sent from Okhotsk that summer: the new men he had employed, the 30 serfs and their families, the labor force of exiles, the 10 members of the Orthodox clergy headed by the Archimandrite Iosaf. Baranov was as dumfounded as anyone at Kodiak, which was not half big enough for this influx. With the exception of Father Iosaf, for whom a shed was hurriedly converted into a dwelling, the clergy and all the other new arrivals had for the time being to be housed in the packed bunkhouses.

Father Iosaf had, of course, soon asked where the church was about which Shelikhov had spoken, and Baranov had had to ask blankly in reply, "What church?" Then he had the added discomfort of having to inform the prelate that, no matter what Shelikhov had said about sending sufficient supplies to maintain the fathers for three years, there was nothing of the sort. The fathers were outraged; now surely they knew who was lying and that it was not that great and good man Grigorii Shelikhov. Baranov had to give up, seeing that his every word only made him seem more of a thief and a brute.

". . . Only with the greatest difficulty did I persuade a few of the hunters to marry their concubines," wrote Father Iosaf in a letter to Shelikhov to go with the *Phoenix* on her maiden voyage to Okhotsk in spring. "I should write His Eminence the Metropolitan or the Holy Synod about Baranov's attitude in this matter but my regard for you prevents me. . . . I fail to find one good thing about the administration of Baranov." Father Iosaf was of course unaware that Shelikhov would soon be dead, and so was Baranov, who was also writing. "To me you show unlimited greed and cupidity." He demanded to be replaced. This was 1795; he had served his five years; he wanted no more.

The single problem of feeding everyone had been formidable that winter. The fathers, along with all the others, had had to be made to dig clams and catch fish. Kodiak village had been like a prison camp. Order had been maintained only by keeping everyone hard at work building more housing and constructing two new sloops under Shields' supervision. For nearly all the newcomers, adjustment to the life was hard. The new employees were a poor lot. "Where," Baranov asked Shelikhov in his letter, "do you get such men?" The exiles, some of whom had criminal backgrounds, had come so poorly equipped that on arrival several had not even a shoe. "Since coming to work for you I fear I have lost what I value most, my good name." He was the one everyone blamed for the situation, Baranov knew. He took care not to go about alone that winter, always to have with him Shields, Richard, or Kuskov. These three, the tattooed Englishman, the turbaned Bengalese, and the Russian clerk with the wooden leg, had come to form his inner council.

The serfs, who had been permitted Shelikhov by the government on his pretense that he needed them to found an agricultural colony at Yakutat, posed a heartbreaking problem for Baranov. Uprooted from some old and settled farming region in Russia, they were in terror of mountains, forests, savages, and the ocean. Yakutat, which lay in Tlingit country, was a large bay indenting the mainland, heavily forested of shore and island. Kodiak was a far better place for agriculture. But Baranov was resolved that Shelikhov's pledge would be kept. He would have nothing to do with the plan to use the serfs any way he saw fit. The government was certain to inquire as to what had been done with them; he intended to write no false reports. The chief of the Yakutat Tlingits had recently ceded an island in the bay, and there, Baranov had decided, the serfs would be settled, behind fortifications, with hunters to help guard them.

The decision was more easily made than enforced. The serfs, who had given more trouble than any other element, mutinied when the ship bearing them to Yakutat came in sight of the savage grandeur of Prince William Sound. Baranov, no doubt cursing Shelikhov anew, had to order the lash to make them go on. In this way was the first settlement established on the mainland south of Kodiak.

Figuring the summer would be his last in the colony, Baranov planned to spend it exploring on his own, wanting very much to see a number of places along the coast about which he had been hearing, in particular Sitka Sound. Though Shields had taught him to be a fair navigator, he had sailed no distance by himself, and he wanted the experience. The *Olga,* one of the two sloops built by Shields that winter, was for his use. She was small, designed to enter narrow passageways. When Baranov set out, it was with only Richard and Kuskov as crew.

The foreign ships visiting Sitka Sound in ever larger numbers each year appear to have come and gone for the season by the time Baranov arrived. He was greatly taken with the place when he had explored some of the intricate waterways and inspected the islands. Judging by the verdure, the climate, though rainy, was mild the year round, kept so by the Japan Current. The stands of gigantic hemlock and spruce guaranteed lumber for generations. The soil was good, game plentiful; the waters teemed with fish and otter. The position was a commanding one for hundreds of miles north and south along the coast. Because of high mountains at the back there could be no attack from the rear. A harbor fronting a large island was of a size to contain a whole navy.

This was, to be sure, the heartland of the Tlingits. Huge totem poles advertised the presence of their communities, which were made up of great communal dwellings housing dozens of families. The Sitkans were lords in the Tlingit confederation, tall, strong, and supple, hard muscles rippling under their bronze skins. They walked on the winter ice with bare feet; they bathed in freezing water. They had a culture hundreds of years old. They were clever artisans as well as shrewd traders. They were the Mongols of this region, independent, assertive, loving war for its own sake as well as for the booty and the slaves it brought them. Like most Indians, they held that vengeance for the acts of an individual could be wreaked on his entire tribe.

The place had, nevertheless, to be occupied one day soon if Russia was to dominate this coast. Baranov had made friends of the Yakutat Tlingits and believed the same could be done with the Sitkans. But that would not be up to him, he thought, not after Shelikhov got his letter. It was late in the season when he set the *Olga* on her homeward course, back over the 560 miles to Kodiak, which he and his crew reached in October, caked with salt and exhausted after the battle with the fall winds. He could now say he was a sailor.

The news of Shelikhov's death did not cause him to withdraw his resignation. His mind was made up, he wrote in his firm, well-formed hand. "The place has made me old before my time." At length, after the formation of the United American

Company at Irkutsk in 1797, he had his answer. In a warmly friendly letter Shelikhov's widow and some of her associates wrote that they wished he would stay but if he still insisted on leaving he would be replaced at once by the manager the new firm had installed at Unalaska. All he had to do was let the man know.

Confronted by this clear opportunity, he found he no longer wished to go, not altogether to his pleasure. As he wrote a friend, his business interests in Siberia were in serious need of his personal attention. He was emotionally trapped in the way so many of his men had been who had taken native women. In 1797, his fiftieth year, Anna had presented him with something he had never had before, a son, a fine, handsome boy who had lovingly been christened Antipatr after the saint on whose day he was born.

His responsibilities had grown greatly these seven years since he came to the colony. His domain was now of kingdom size, extending from Yakutat northward to Bristol Bay. Prince William Sound now had two posts; in all there were nine establishments under him, counting Kodiak, which had some forty buildings, including a church.

He had paid for most of that church, putting up 1500 rubles, but the fathers, with one exception, had remained bitter, Father Iosaf in particular continuing to work for his dismissal. And now, with the birth of Antipatr advertising the sinfulness of the head of the colony, the fathers were wrathful. Another element troublesome to him had come on the scene of late, reminding him of his days in Russia when, as the son of no more than a village storekeeper, he had had to accept the insults of the snobs among the well-born. Fresh from the Naval Academy at Saint Petersburg, three midshipmen had come to the colony, their services as navigators having been obtained by Rezanov. Like all naval officers, they belonged to the noble class and, on discovering that they had the only rank in the colony, they made themselves insufferable, forcing Baranov at length to write one of them that despite his humble birth he alone gave orders to navigators.

The worst of the midshipmen was Gavril Talin, whose talent as a navigator was demonstrated when he sank the *Eagle* with the loss of five lives and 22,000 rubles' worth of furs. He claimed that before leaving Saint Petersburg he had been secretly informed that Tsar Paul intended to abolish merchant rule and turn the colony over to the Navy, a prospect interesting to the clergy, who helped spread the allegation. Baranov, to quiet the uneasiness, denied that he himself knew anything of the sort. The angered Talin threatened to hang him from the yardarm if he set foot on a vessel he commanded. At least, Baranov could reflect, he had earned the loyalty of the old hands, who suffered equally from the insults of the midshipmen and had only token regard for the clergy, not half of whom were endeavoring to be real missionaries.

Baranov nevertheless remained disposed to stay, even when, in 1798, Father Iosaf was called to Irkutsk to be consecrated Bishop of Russian America. In that capacity Baranov's mortal enemy would be able to make far more trouble for him, if indeed he did not bring about his dismissal. The prelate left on the *Phoenix,* which was to be held over at Okhotsk for a year in order to speed his return. Another who sailed with the *Phoenix* on that voyage was Shields, who, after six years, had been recalled to military service in Russia. Baranov was deeply affected at having to part with the friend who had taught him so much and who had added many a valuable new furground by his explorations. Shields would be no poor man when he had collected what was owed him.

Far from thinking of leaving, Baranov began to plan on establishing a post at Sitka, for which there had come to be a certain urgency. The foreigners visiting Sitka were evidently now dealing in large quantities of firearms. Guns, passed from hand to Tlingit hand, were coming up the coast to Yakutat, endangering the Russians settled there and alarming the non-

Tlingit mainlanders, among them Anna's people, who had become so attached to Baranov they contributed a hundred baidarkas each season to the hunting fleets. A post, by signifying occupancy, would justify calling the sale of arms a hostile act.

Though he had now only one reliable navigator and, with the *Phoenix* tied up at Okhotsk, only one large vessel, in the spring of 1799 Baranov informed the colony that he was proceeding. There would be no hunting that summer; all effort was to be concentrated on the Sitka project. When he set out in the *Olga* with Richard as his right-hand man, he had a force of some 1100 men in baidarkas: 100 Russians, 700 Aleuts, and 300 mainlanders.

During the long, slow voyage, as the flotilla crossed a rough section of sea, endeavoring to finish before nightfall and the break of a threatening storm, thirty of the canoes with sixty men were engulfed. Baranov decided to weather out the night on a nearby beach fronting a dense forest. Everyone threw himself down, exhausted, but not to sleep for long. Suddenly spears and arrows came from the forest, and the blood-curdling sound of Tlingit war cries. As Baranov and the others with guns knelt and fired, a number of the panic-stricken Aleuts ran into the woods, into the arms of their attackers. "What saved us from total destruction was the darkness, which prevented our assailants from distinguishing friend from foe," wrote Baranov. In the morning twenty-six men were missing, killed or captured. Happenings of the sort were usual on the voyages of the baidarka fleets. The drive on Sitka continued.

He came in peace, Baranov told elderly Ska-yut-lelt, chief of the Sitkan Tlingits. His people at Yakutat had shown they were good and valuable neighbors. The mighty Tsar was lord over all this region; those who allied themselves with him could look to him for protection against aggressors such as the traders who were committing atrocities. The Tlingits were at this time greatly exercised by the acts of a Captain Henry Barber, an Englishman who enticed natives aboard his ship, then held them for ransom, sometimes murdering them when payment was not made quickly enough to suit him. Ska-yut-lelt ceded a site for a fort a few miles from the main Tlingit community, on the same island. Baranov and his men then settled down to a winter of work with ax, adze, and whipsaw.

They could not dawdle, they soon saw; fortifications must go up quickly. Ska-yut-lelt was being criticized within his own clan and throughout the Tlingit confederation for allowing white men to settle. The growing tension was indicated by a number of incidents. At one point Baranov had to go in force to the Tlingit village to obtain the release of a captured man. The work was practically finished by Easter. Never had Baranov built more solidly. A fortress had risen made of timbers two feet thick and measuring seventy by fifty feet at the base, with an upper story jutting out two feet farther. High watchtowers stood at two corners. Around this structure were grouped the cook-house, the smithy, and other outbuildings, including barns for domestic animals, all enclosed by a high, strong stockade. At a solemn ceremony, the place was put under the patronage of Saint Michael Archangel.

In April the foreign ships began appearing, with the arrival of five from the United States. And, sure enough, their cargoes featured rum and firearms, even cannon, relics of the Revolution bought cheaply from the government. The captains, all from Boston, listened politely to Baranov's protests delivered through Richard but would not desist. Arms were wanted most by the Tlingits for their peltry; arms they would have.

Resolved to report on these conversations, Baranov prepared to return to Kodiak. He was greatly in need of rest. He was fifty-three; his winter of labor in the rain had left him aching with arthritis. Left in the new fort were thirty Russians and four hundred Aleuts, twenty of them women, with Vasilii Medvedni-kov as commander. The homegoing men in their baidarkas were convoyed by Baranov in the *Olga*.

Meanwhile the *Phoenix,* Kodiak-bound under command of

one of the inept midshipmen, went down with everyone aboard, including Bishop Iosaf. With her, the first ship to leave Okhotsk for the colony in two years, would have come the news of the formation of the Russian-American Company in Saint Petersburg and Baranov's appointment as governor.

He saw tragedy enough on that homeward journey with the baidarka fleet: two hundred Aleuts died after eating mussels new to them. That brought to nearly three hundred the deaths attending the Sitka project. Then, borne by the Japan Current, came wreckage indicating that a vessel, probably the *Phoenix,* had gone down somewhere along the Aleutians. Having paused only briefly at Kodiak, Baranov continued on westward in the *Olga* to look for survivors among the islands, finding only evidence that it had indeed been his schooner. It was November when, in the teeth of the fall gales, haggard and sleepless, he again put in at Kodiak, to find that during his long absence his enemies had been very busy.

The least of it was that the priests had endeavored to persuade Anna to leave him, so confusing her with their accusations of evil that she concluded she should kill her boy, and nearly did. The fathers had also been doing something very dangerous at this time, openly preaching revolt to the natives, who were unpaid for their labors because of the shortness of supplies, and in a state because of all the deaths. It was, they had been assured, only a question of time until merchant rule would be abolished, and meanwhile they must refuse further service. Charging the fathers with treason to the State, Baranov arrested them. They in turn forbade him to attend services, with the result that the church was closed.

In this unhappy atmosphere the year wore into 1801, still without a ship from home. The natives remained unpaid; the Russians were in no better frame of mind. Then, in May, an American ship appeared at Kodiak, the *Enterprise.* Her mate was the Joseph O'Cain who had been mate on Captain Moore's *Phoenix.* Though that was now nine years back and meanwhile he had not been on the Northwest Coast, the shrewd Boston Irishman had not forgotten Baranov's disclosures of his needs. He had an interest in the cargo aboard the *Enterprise* and had persuaded his captain, Ezekiel Hubbel, who seems to have been new to the Northwest trade, to see whether the Russians might buy before he did any trading with the Tlingits. In that event they would avoid the dangers of dealing with Tlingits and be in Canton weeks ahead of their competitors.

The cargo consisted of arms, ammunition, cloth, molasses, and much else the Russians wanted very much indeed. Baranov, ignoring the fact that he still had no authority to buy from foreigners, embraced O'Cain like a brother. When the *Enterprise* left, it was with two thousand pelts in payment and on O'Cain's promise not to let another nine years go by before his next visit.

Kodiak relaxed after that, grateful to Baranov for his action. The Aleuts, paid, even talked of going out hunting again. Tension eased further as supplies began coming up from Sitka, bought there from the shipmasters. And things were well again between Anna and Baranov, who this year was presented with a second child, a beautiful, fine-featured little girl who was named Irina. Antipatr, who was five, was growing up to be a handsome boy.

Baranov may well have been of two minds about the fact that still there was no ship from home and it was now four years since they had seen one. News might mean he would have to leave, and that would now be a wrench indeed. Yet it was unsettling to have the colony neglected in this fashion. Was it forgotten in Saint Petersburg, perhaps because of the Napoleonic wars said to be raging in Europe?

In May, one Ivan Banner arrived at Kodiak in an Aleut-powered baidara. The ship in which he had sailed from Okhotsk had been unable to proceed beyond Unalaska, where the manager, when he understood the import of the news, had his Aleuts hurry Banner to Kodiak. For the first time Baranov heard about the death of Tsar Paul, the accession of Alexander, the Russian-American Company, and his appointment as governor with jurisdiction as far west as the Kurils.[2]

There was more to dumfound Baranov in the papers brought by Banner, a former government official now in the service of the Company, who would remain in the colony as an assistant administrator. He had, Baranov read, been given shares in the Company to the par value of 25,000 rubles. He had also been awarded the Order of Saint Vladimir. Said the accompanying citation, signed by the Tsar, "For faithful service in hardship and want and for unremitting loyalty." Baranov burst into tears.

The people of Kodiak were assembled in one of the bunkhouses to hear Banner read his announcements. A cheer surely went up from the old hands, who through the years had acquired a great respect for Baranov. He was, he said, donating a thousand rubles toward a school for the children. And he invited everyone to attend the biggest prazdnik so far staged in those parts.

News of another sort came in July, that year of 1802. It was brought to Kodiak by the *Unicorn,* the twenty-gun vessel belonging to Captain Henry Barber, the Englishman whose acts, more than anyone's, had caused the Tlingits to want revenge on white men. Baranov's greatest fears concerning the sale of firearms had been justified. The fort at Sitka was a mass of ashes surrounded by severed heads impaled on stakes. The massacre had taken place in June, Tlingits from several clans attacking in great force. Aboard the *Unicorn* were twenty-three survivors: twenty Aleuts, eighteen of them women, and three Russians. Barber, aided by American Captain John Ebbets, had extracted some of them by force from the Tlingits, who had held them as slaves. Ebbets, an honorable man, thought Barber only kind

---

[2] "Governor" seems the aptest word in English to convey the powers conferred, which were large, particularly with respect to foreigners. The title bestowed on Baranov and borne by all his successors was a special one, *Glavnyi Pravitel,* which has been variously translated, occasionally as Chief Factor, usually as Chief Manager.

when he volunteered to take the survivors to Kodiak. Barber now made his purpose clear to Baranov, demanding a ransom of 50,000 rubles. Pay, or he would blow Kodiak off the map, he threatened. He took the 10,000 rubles' worth of furs Baranov had on hand.

Stricken Kodiak heard more over the days that followed. Nearly half the baidarka fleet out that summer had also been wiped out. Yakutat had been saved only by the timely warning of a friendly Tlingit. Of the 450 people who had been at Sitka, only 42 ever turned up alive. The Tlingits had killed or captured nearly 600 people.

Retaking Sitka became the obsession of Baranov's life. How to do it was the question. Half the colony's arms were gone with Sitka; for transportation there were only two old schooners. Nor could the spirits of the men be revived so soon. The best Baranov could do for the time being was build two sloops and hope that somehow arms would come his way. A year later he was obliged by Joseph O'Cain.

Ebullient Joe was a captain now with his own ship, which he had named the *O'Cain*. Apparently on the strength of his claim to close friendship with the head of the Russians in the Pacific, he had formed a partnership with the Winships of Massachusetts and had with him as mate young Jonathan Winship, Jr. Included in the association was O'Cain's brother-in-law, Captain Oliver Kimball of the *Peacock,* whom Baranov could expect to see one of these days. O'Cain was full of plans for an alliance that would keep the colony supplied and even recruit workmen of the kind Baranov had said he needed: shipwrights, metalworkers, and the like. Too, Baranov's furs might be sold for him at Canton.

And, O'Cain went on, the cargo he brought he had amplified at Hawaii, where he had thoughtfully bought up all available munitions on learning there that Baranov planned war. Oh, yes, that was known all over the Pacific. Did Baranov not realize how famous he was? King Kamehameha of Hawaii sent his best wishes for victory. The cargo was certainly all that

Baranov had hoped for: arms in quantities with ammunition to match, along with tools of all descriptions and foodstuffs. There was just one hitch: he had not the furs to pay, having recently sent all he had to Siberia—1,200,000 rubles' worth. This was a poser for O'Cain, who was evidently in no position to extend credit. But he was never long without an idea.

He proposed that he be lent a body of Aleuts and their baidarkas, with which to hunt the abundant otter along California. The Spaniards patrolled their coast poorly; no hostile natives need be feared. They would go shares on the catch. Baranov could buy the cargo out of his share. When, finally, he agreed, it was with the stipulation that the Aleuts be paid $2.50 per pelt and their families $250 in the event of a death. All orders must be given the Aleuts through a Russian foreman.

When, four months later, O'Cain returned from California, it was with no lives lost and otter pelts to a number calculated to perpetuate his idea. The Company's share was worth $80,000, more than enough to buy the cargo. Baranov agreed to the alliance, but not in writing and with the reserved right to deal with others. O'Cain was satisfied. When he departed, it was with the Company's furs as well as his own, to be sold under the American flag at Canton. In his pocket was an order for more supplies and a list of the kinds of skilled workmen Baranov needed most.

Baranov set out for Sitka in September of 1804, his flotilla consisting of the two crude new sloops, two schooners and some three hundred baidarkas. Fortunately for the Russian cause, as events proved, before war was launched against the Tlingits a Russian frigate appeared, the *Neva,* which had sailed from Saint Petersburg the previous year in company with another former war vessel of the same type, the two of them bearing Nikolai Rezanov on a mission to Japan. The *Neva* was commanded by Captain-Lieutenant Yurii Lisianskii, who explained that when they touched at Hawaii they had heard of the Sitka trouble. He had been instructed by Rezanov, who had proceeded on to

Japan in the other frigate, to sail to the colony immediately for the purpose of giving assistance.

Baranov accepted the reinforcement but made it clear he would direct the operation. The *Neva* was an imposing addition to the force invading Sitka Sound. The Tlingits, who had never seen her like, agreed to a parley. Baranov told them he meant to build his next fort where they had their settlement and that they must evacuate the island. This demand was refused. The war had to be fought.

Baranov got a bullet in the arm and almost lost his life trying to lead one charge. At length he saw he had to leave strategy to Lisianskii. The Tlingits had presently to give up under the pounding of the *Neva*'s guns. The island, which was to bear his name, was now Baranov's. Archangel had been Russia's first port on seas of her own. The port to be built here, Russia's latest, Baranov decided to call New Archangel.

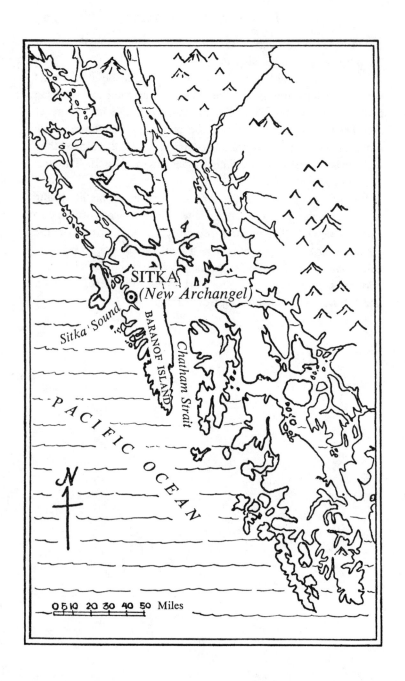

SITKA
(New Archangel)

Sitka Sound

BARANOF ISLAND

Chatham Strait

PACIFIC OCEAN

N

0 5 10 20 30 40 50 Miles

VII

Prince of the Promyshlenniki

In 1802, the year after the assassination of Tsar Paul and the accession of Alexander, Nikolai Rezanov was a very busy and happy man. He and Anna were expecting their second child. As Procurator General of the Senate, he was aiding the reform-minded young Tsar in reorganizing the government. He was absorbed also in the affairs of his creation, the Russian-American Company, which he alone represented in the councils of state.

His plans for the Pacific were large and growing larger. No longer would Saint Petersburg evade the problems of the Far East. Able diplomat Count Gavril Golovkin would head the mission to Peking, with the objectives of opening the Amur to navigation and of securing permission for Russian ships to trade at Canton. Less well advanced, but also definite, was a plan to gain admission for Russian commerce at Japan, which still traded with no Europeans other than the Dutch.

The feasibility of communicating with the colony by sea from Saint Petersburg was to be investigated. This plan was reaching large proportions. Two fine frigates, former war vessels, were being purchased from the British, one of them at Company expense and to remain its property. She was to be renamed the *Neva,* the other the *Hope.* They were to sail together for the Pacific, making a great celebration of the fact that the Russian flag was being carried for the first time around the world. Noted scientists would accompany the expedition; visits in the name of the Company would be paid at the world's famous trading ports for the purpose of establishing relations. The commander would be Captain Adam Kruzenstern, who had seen service with the British, had been at Canton, and had submitted proposals which had given Rezanov the idea for the great world tour.

Rezanov's ideas for the colony itself, of which his picture was still the one painted for him by Shelikhov, were many and varied. He hoped one day soon to give it an institution of higher learning. He planned on a great shipyard, as good as any in Europe. He saw territorial expansion as a simple matter. Unaware that a fort at Sitka had been both built and destroyed, he wrote to Baranov that he must advance down the south mainland, to the 55th parallel and beyond, even at the risk of encountering the British. He wished greatly he could visit the colony. He should meet Baranov personally, appraise him directly. There was question as to whether Baranov was the right man to be governor. His appointment had been made against criticism from naval officers and hostility from the Church, which had made serious charges. On the other hand, there were those who insisted he was the only man for the position. But when he might ever go to America, Nikolai Rezanov did not know. The Senate's procurator general could never be long away from Saint Petersburg.

Anna bore her child in October; twelve days later she died unexpectedly. Shelikhov's daughter was entombed with the noblest dead of Saint Petersburg. Her husband, broken emotionally and physically, could not be roused from his grief. He must be given a rest and a change, his friends decided, among them the Tsar. He was given leave to go on the world tour with the two frigates; he was named head of the mission to Japan, where the tour would culminate. From there he was to inspect his colony at his leisure.

Captain Kruzenstern was annoyed—this was bound to take some of the fame from him—but Rezanov was revived. He began collecting a tremendous array of gifts for the Mikado of Japan: 300,000 rubles' worth of gifts, ranging from a portrait of the Tsar by one of Europe's finest artists, to mirrors 15 feet long. He also began gathering the materials with which to found his institution of higher learning in Russian America: paintings, maps, models of ships, scientific instruments, books—1200 books, in languages including Latin, on subjects ranging from theology to mathematics. Where, Kruzenstern wished to know, were they going to stow it all? Rezanov brushed him aside. In his view he was now in command of the expedition.

On the eve of his departure in the summer of 1803, at a great banquet in observance of the fact that for the first time the Russian flag was about to be carried by sea, to the other side of the globe, he was toasted as "the Russian Columbus." His Majesty had named him his envoy to the world and had bestowed a rare title on him. He was now His High Excellency, Grand Chamberlain Rezanov, in rank the highest at court. The outlook for the tour was perfect. Napoleon had the world at peace for a change. Even Spain had agreed to the Tsar's request that his emissary be received at her colonial ports.

The glory was all at the outset. The tour produced little of importance to either science or commerce and was no pleasure cruise. Unseemly quarrels over precedence took place aboard the frigate *Hope,* which bore Rezanov, together with his diplomatic suite, and was commanded by Kruzenstern, who made it clear he was master at sea. Rezanov was exhausted by the time they reached Hawaii, where the unsettling news of the Sitka massacre was received and the *Neva* sent on to aid Baranov. Rezanov hoped he would not have to spend much time in Japan, as he proceeded there in the *Hope* with Kruzenstern.

The insularity of China was as nothing compared to that of Japan, which had once been open to the outside world. The Dutch were still allowed a scant trade because they had brought no missionaries. The inhospitality accorded foreigners was such that the shipwrecked were kept imprisoned until a Dutch ship could take them away. Nagasaki was the scene of Rezanov's defeat. It mattered not that he had brought with him, back to their homeland, a group of Japanese long marooned in Siberia.

Six months he waited at Nagasaki to see an official of importance, meanwhile treated in a fashion which, though exaggeratedly polite, was obviously meant to break his patience, to make him decide to leave of his own accord. Having asked to live ashore while he waited, he was ceremoniously shown to what amounted to a cage. When, finally, he was allowed to see a figure of importance, it was under humiliating circumstances and only to be told that neither his gifts nor his commerce were wanted.

He was ill as they left Nagasaki, having what appears to have been gastric ulcers. He seethed with formless plans for punishment. At his first opportunity, he vowed, he would send an expedition which would teach Japan that Russia did not take insults lightly. There was no use asking Kruzenstern to use his vessel and her guns in any such endeavor. Besides, Rezanov wanted to be rid of Kruzenstern, who was to take himself and his frigate back to Russia.

The *Hope* deposited Rezanov at the village of Petropavlovsk on Kamchatka. From there he would take another vessel on to America. With him would be his valet and Dr. Georg Heinrich von Langsdorff, a young German who had accompanied the tour as a naturalist and who was also a physician. No one was to write less enthusiastically than Langsdorff about Russian America, but at the time he was delighted by the invitation to see it with Rezanov, who feared he might need a physician in the months ahead.

It was as well for his morale that at Petropavlovsk it was not yet known that all his plans for the Far East had gone awry. The mission to China, which had been timed to coincide with his call on Japan, had been likewise a failure, Count Golovkin succeeding in getting no nearer Peking than Urga in Mongolia.

Petropavlovsk did know that Sitka had been retaken, and that was heartening news. He would, Rezanov planned, visit Sitka, make it his last stop on his journey through the colony, and he would winter there. He was filled again with eager anticipation as in June he set out to see the places first described to him so glowingly by Shelikhov. Together with his valet and Langsdorff, he had taken passage on a Company brig, the *Maria,* which had put in at Petropavlovsk on her way from Okhotsk to the colony with men and supplies. She was heavily laden, her cargo having been amplified by Rezanov's baggage, which ranged from his violin in its case to the boxes and boxes of books and the other materials for his institution of higher learning.

He saw the colony at its nadir, a fact not borne in on him until he was well along on his journey. Much of what he saw was shocking. Baranov had nearly all the able-bodied men with him at Sitka, helping him rebuild. The few Russians at the island stations were mostly the disabled, and the condition of some of them was wretched in the extreme. Nowhere was there a physician to care for them, much less a hospital. The Aleuts, who of late years had seen their numbers steadily decrease, were low in spirits. They had come to furnish practically all the manpower, the whole country never having had more than 250 Russians at any one time, and, what with the reputation for travail and bloodshed the colony now had in Siberia, it was ever harder to sign up new promyshlenniki.

The colony was by no means an organized whole as yet. The six-year-old Russian-American Company, which in Saint Petersburg had seemed so beautifully organized, was here only a name so far in many places, a name heard for the first time a bare three years before. What with the task of retaking Sitka, Baranov had had his hands too full to do any widespread organizing, to visit more than a few of the posts which had formerly belonged to competing merchants. There was want, owing to the fact that supplying the colony from Okhotsk had always been a problem, and now additionally for the reason that a new system of distribution had not been worked out. Langsdorff assumed that everything he observed was the set state of affairs. ". . . It is revolting to a soul of any feeling to see these poor creatures [the natives] half-naked and half-starved. . . . Nor are the Russian promyshlenniki any better off."

To all outward appearances, Rezanov was enjoying a triumphal tour. He was the lord of the Company and the nearest thing to a tsar ever to visit these parts. At Unalaska, during a walk of some distance he had to make, the Russians ran ahead of him with boards which they laid down over bogs and streams in order to keep his boots dry. That was a great marvel to the barefoot Aleuts. They were to talk about those boards for three generations. Rezanov played up to his part, granting audiences, listening to complaints, conferring medals on the meritorious, at one point severely punishing a man guilty of mistreating natives; but inwardly he was ever lower in spirit. What a liar Shelikhov had been. The very basis of the colony was insubstantial. There would come a day, and soon, if things were not done, when the fur-bearing animals would be gone.

His very first stop on his journey had been at the Company station on the Pribilof Islands. It was the breeding season for the fur seals, which annually migrated to these islands for the purpose. He had been revolted by the evidence of wasteful slaughter, alike by foreign shipmasters and by the resident Aleut and Russian hunters. A man could walk among the creatures and kill any number with a club. The herd, though it still seemed to number millions, had been cut down by 90 per cent in the scant 20 years since the discovery of the islands. The sheds were filled, the rocks covered, with rotting, useless pelts, much of the killing having been done merely for the sex glands of the seals, which the foreigners sold in dried form to the Chinese for the making of a rejuvenating drug. Rezanov took what seems the first conservation measure in the history of the fur trade. The slaughter, he commanded peremptorily, was to cease forthwith.

"These islands [the Pribilofs] would be an inexhaustible source of wealth for us were it not for the Bostonians," he wrote the Tsar from Unalaska. The Company, he suggested, should patrol these waters. ". . . It is very necessary to take stronger hold of this country, else we shall leave it empty-handed." The colony, he went on to tell Alexander, "can never be fully developed so long as bread . . . has to be shipped from Okhotsk." He stressed that point in his letters to the Company directors, in whom he earnestly sought to instill his awareness of the realities. "On the fur trade alone the Company cannot subsist. It is absolutely necessary to organize without delay a business of general character, a trade with other countries to which the road is open from the colony."

Nowhere did he see a school or a church until he arrived at Kodiak, the sight of which must have been the final straw. To his Saint Petersburg eye, the main settlement of the colony was no more than a village. Ivan Banner was in command during Baranov's absence. Rezanov approved of him, but not of the clergy, who were still gathered mostly here and seldom visited the outlying stations. Remembering the trouble their machinations had given him in Saint Petersburg, he was bitter when they presented him with their complaints against Baranov. He now knew how greatly Shelikhov had fooled them too, but, he told them, they could have done more for themselves. They had volunteered to be missionaries, and as such had been largely failures. He directed them to learn the native speech, take a leaf from the Jesuits, follow the example of the single one of their number who had allowed himself to make an adjustment. This was saintly Father German, who taught the school founded through the generosity of Baranov. Rezanov urged the natives to send their children to Father German; and to Banner's wife, the only literate woman in the colony, he suggested she take the girls into her home and teach them European housekeeping.

Along the shelves in an unused building he ranged the books he had brought, many of them beautifully bound, the ship models, the maps, the scientific instruments, the relics of his belief that the colony was ready for higher learning. There seemed nothing else to be done with them. It was August when, having again boarded the *Maria,* he left Kodiak for New Archangel on Sitka Sound.

Baranov, who had been expecting Rezanov for months, hoped he was still coming. He wanted to give notice, to ask to be relieved before another winter rolled around. And he wanted Shelikhov's high and mighty son-in-law to see for himself what had been entailed in the retaking of Sitka, to know how hard they had all had to work for the past year, the four hundred Aleuts and Russians making up New Archangel. Not that it was much to look at as yet. They had so far been able to build only for strength, not beauty. When, in fall, they began erecting shelter, every man had had to keep his musket near at hand. And that was the way things had had to be through the winter. The Tlingits had remained quiet, but vigilance could not be relaxed. The colony had not had the protection of the guns of the *Neva,* which had wintered at Kodiak and had now departed, taking the furs.

Had it not been for foreign friends New Archangel would have starved. Provisions had been short when winter began, and little hunting or fishing could be done for fear of lurking Tlingits. The sloop *Ermak,* which had been built for the retaking of Sitka, was sent to Hawaii to buy food, question though it was whether so crude a vessel would make it and back at that season. God was with her crew. She returned laden with pigs, taro, bananas, yams, and coconuts, for none of which King Kamehameha would take payment. He was, he had said, glad to help brother monarch Baranov in his time of need.

Then, in spring, the Yankees came, among them Captain Oliver Kimball, O'Cain's brother-in-law, who brought supplies in the brig *Peacock* and some of the skilled workmen O'Cain had promised to recruit. Jonathan Winship also came, bringing more supplies, in the brig *O'Cain,* the unlimbered guns of which dispersed a number of threatening Tlingits. Making the same deal with Winship that he had made with O'Cain, Baranov allowed him the Aleuts under a Russian foreman with whom to poach otter along California. The Company's share of the catch was worth $30,000. Thus, along with everything else, business had been kept going. Rezanov could be told that on her departure the *Neva* had taken furs worth nearly half a million rubles.

The position of New Archangel was a strong one. As a former military man, Rezanov should be able to see that. The feature was a high, broad, flat knoll on which the Tlingits had had their village. It had been wrested from them because it commanded all the approaches and overlooked the fine harbor. The knoll was now crowned with a rough bastion mounting twenty guns, together with a few cabins. Stairs led down to the main part of the settlement below, which was enclosed on the landward sides by a strong stockade and consisted of cabins, bunkhouses, a commissary, and other structures, including a barn for a few cows. There were also some pigs left over from the batch sent by Kamehameha, two goats donated by a Yankee skipper, and the usual number of dogs around all Russian establishments.

And now his work was done, Baranov planned to say. He would go live at Kodiak in retirement. Rezanov would have to concede he deserved a rest. He was fifty-eight, and to have had to spend another winter ax in hand in the cold and wet had left him so crippled with arthritis that to relieve the pain he was practically living on hot rum. Ivan Kuskov should be appointed. He was young and strong; after fifteen years in the colony he was thoroughly seasoned and proven responsible; he would do a good job of finishing the building of New Archangel, of which he had been second-in-command throughout the recent harrowing year.

Baranov, who was in one of his lower moods, had reasons for wanting to resign in addition to those he meant to indicate. He was a man of rank now, word of his elevation having come as he planned to retake Sitka. According to the Table of Ranks devised by Peter the Great, he was a collegiate councilor, a civil-service designation theoretically on a level with admirals and colonels. He was entitled to be addressed as Excellency. And still the arrogant among the naval officers in Company service had flouted him. Birth alone mattered to them. In their view he remained a trader.

In a fit of drunken rage, one of the officers had beaten the wooden-legged Kuskov for refusing him more liquor than his ration from the commissary. Baranov had been helpless to stop or punish the man. With his title of governor he had been given no specific authority over the officers, of whom there were now six in the colony. They drew wartime pay and served the Company without loss of rank, yet the work of most of them was slovenly. Only two of the six now on hand had proved themselves able and had behaved like gentlemen. On every count, Baranov felt, he had had enough.

It was late August when Rezanov appeared with his valet and his physician. Perhaps he had been prepared for Baranov's appearance and was unsurprised. The gnarled little man was evidently sensitive to the fact he had gone quite bald. On state occasions he wore a black wig, which was kept on by means of a kerchief tied under his chin. He showed his guest to a cabin atop the knoll and in his honor gave the community a two-day holiday. For the prazdnik that ensued, Rezanov perhaps broke out his violin, a gesture which would have endeared him at this place. There had been some music of late, furnished by a Yankee sailor off one of the ships who had a violin and a clarinet. Later in the winter, as is on record, the Tsar's chamberlain was to play duets with Seaman Ed Parker.

Baranov got all the reaction he could have wanted when he told of his wish to resign. Rezanov was horrified. He was now satisfied that only this man could bring the colony to prosperity. Evidently Baranov was persuaded to tell everything troubling him. "His name is famed the length of the Pacific," Rezanov wrote the directors. ". . . and yet, though heaped with praise by foreigners, here he has to drink the bitter cup of disappointment. The directors should approach the Throne in a body and ask new honors for him. Something has to be done to shield him from further insults. . . ."

Rezanov left no doubt as to his meaning. He penned a blast the Navy was long to remember. His words had the added bitterness of his own experiences with naval men. "It may be the fault of the training and education given our naval offi-

cers . . . in any case the Company will suffer losses because of
these men, and our country may even lose the American colonies. It is hard to make them forget by persuasion their unfortunately false standards. It is like trying to educate someone
afresh. . . . The contempt which those of the privileged class
feel toward traders makes them all masters here. . . ."

Baranov melted. He agreed to stay. His powers were enlarged, Rezanov giving him entire freedom of judgment in his
commercial relations with foreigners. To ease his problem of
paying for cargoes, credit was arranged for him at European
banks. At a number of round-table discussions of the colony's
needs, Rezanov promised a medical staff and a hospital, pensions for the faithful, the advancement of education for both
sexes.

To him the most important thing at the moment was territorial expansion. His old confidence in this respect had evidently
been restored by his acquaintance with Baranov. His ideas were
as reckless of distance as those of any old-time promyshlennik.
His expansionist blueprint he laid before Baranov and Kuskov.
All movement must be toward the south, to the entire neglect of
the north for the time being. The American seaboard lay open
before them as far as California, and perhaps even that country
was penetrable, in view of the known weakness of the Spaniards. Two immediate objectives were designated: a post on the
Columbia River, another just north of San Francisco. The posts
should be placed with an eye to the agricultural possibilities.

Hawaii, that most strategic of Pacific positions, was made
another objective. Baranov was to cultivate his friendship with
the King, win him away from the British, attempt to gain at
least a trading station for the Company on the islands. The time
was short for the doing of all these things; hence the need to put
them foremost. Napoleon would not forever keep Europe distracted. Few British ships were now in the Pacific, which was
one reason the Americans could advance their trade so vigorously. The endeavors of the Americans to supplant the British

were to be aided, a policy having the support of Saint Petersburg.

The winter that ensued seemed designed to discourage Rezanov. It was the worst in years. Savage, unremitting gales lashed the coast. A Company ship went down with all hands, the saddest loss of its kind since that of the *Phoenix*. The seas also swallowed up half a baidarka fleet. And the Tlingits, who had remobilized themselves, moved to exterminate the Russians along the entire mainland.

The ten-year-old settlement at Yakutat was wiped out; only ten people survived the massacre, and they were enslaved. The same fate might have been met by the forts on Prince William Sound had it not been for the loyalty to Baranov of Anna's people. The Tlingits took a defeat at their hands. The trouble reached as far north as Cook Inlet, one of the forts there sending Baranov a hurried call for reinforcements. He could spare only ten men, in view of New Archangel's own danger.

Baranov kept his cannon loaded day and night. No one went about without a gun, Rezanov wrote. Hunting and fishing were out of the question. Because of the weather, no vessel could be sent to Hawaii for fresh food, the supply of which fell so low that in February scurvy swept the community, incapacitating sixty and killing eight. Rezanov could stand the place no longer. The Columbia River, he announced, had forthwith to be explored. He would head the expedition himself, go in the *Juno*. The *Juno* was a fine, large, well-armed schooner he had bought from a Yankee skipper the previous fall, paying a large price. His purpose had been to use her in punishing Japan, a project he had hoped to set in motion when summer arrived. But now he seemed to have forgotten that plan as he talked of exploring the Columbia in the *Juno*.

Baranov refused him the ablest men. Of the thirty-three allowed the *Juno* as crew, several had scurvy. And of course little fresh food could be spared the expedition, the survival of which accordingly depended on the speed with which the Columbia could be reached and entered, and game or fish bought from the natives. In the hope she might even bring back a cargo of food, the *Juno* was laden with trade goods, cloth of excellent manufacture, wearing apparel, finery, and tools, from gimlets to axes. Some of the gifts originally intended for the Mikado were stowed aboard, pieces of cloth-of-gold, fine muskets, and the like. The *Juno* set sail in late February. With Rezanov were his valet and Langsdorff. The captain and the mate were Lieutenants Khvostov and Davydov, the two ablest of the colony's naval officers.

The Columbia was a difficult river for sailing ships to enter because of the bar at the entrance and the nature of the winds and currents. Crossing the bar required great effort on the part of the crew. The *Juno*'s scurvy-ridden crew could not make it. When eight of the men died, and of the living only a dozen were still able to work the ship, it had to be decided that further attempts would be suicidal without fresh food.

The nearest haven was San Francisco. Rezanov had with him his credentials as Russia's ambassador to the world, but whether the documents were still valid was a question. They were three years old and, according to the little he had been able to learn of late regarding the situation in Europe, coalitions for and against Napoleon were again in the making, with Russia and Spain possibly opposed. But the chance had to be taken. This crew would never make it to Hawaii. Besides, Rezanov wanted very much indeed to see California.

He and his officers planned carefully, going by the copies they had of explorer George Vancouver's charts of the coast, which included San Francisco Bay. They would enter quietly, before daybreak, make quickly for an anchorage as close as possible to the presidio. Rezanov, though he alone of his party knew any Spanish, would stay aboard ship during the preliminary parleys ashore, which would be conducted by Davydov and Langsdorff. Both knew French, and surely someone at a place as important as this to Spain would know that language.

That night Rezanov no doubt prayed that this would not be another Nagasaki.

María de la Concepcion Argüello, who was nicknamed Concha, was fifteen years old, a daughter of the commander of San Francisco and a rare beauty. Her distinctiveness in this respect was acknowledged by her own people, who were used to handsome women. Her teeth were perfect, her long-lashed eyes large and lustrous, her smile was ravishing, her figure flawless. Nor was she spoiled, having been brought up in a family of thirteen children. Her disposition was pleasing, her manners charming. Yet her suitors were bound to be few, confined to the small number of single officers at this and other presidios, in her case California's only eligibles.

Although it was now nearly forty years since Madrid, alarmed by the Russian advance in the Pacific, had ordered the occupation of Upper California, virtually the only establishments were still the missions of the Franciscans and the presidios of the military, both supported by Spain. No towns had risen worthy of the name; there was no industry; the ban on trade was strictly enforced. Much grain was grown and cattle raised, mostly by the missions, but the effort was largely idle, there being no market for the surplus. Spain maintained the country because of continued fear of aggression. Fortifications had been ordered strengthened following the news of the formation of the Russian-American Company.

No more than a handful of foreigners had ever been allowed ashore at San Francisco, which was the end of the Spanish world, its farthest outpost. Counting the fathers at the nearby mission, the people of Spanish blood numbered perhaps sixty. The houses, including that of Commander Argüello, who had risen from the ranks, were modest, of whitewashed adobe with puncheon floors and homemade furniture. But the life was undemanding, and most of the people were satisfied.

Not so Concha. She was given to saying about California that it was "a beautiful place with a warm climate, much grain and cattle, and nothing else." Her restlessness may have been imparted to her by the Franciscans, who had been her teachers. They were all from Spain and disapproved of the laws keeping the country closed. California was isolated even from Mexico, which was always slow to send supplies, keeping the fathers chronically short of tools and everything else they needed to carry on their work.

The views of the fathers regarding the advisability of trade were not shared by Argüello or his close friend, the governor, elderly Don José Arillaga, a pious man who liked to say that in all his years he had never violated his oath to uphold Spain's laws. No foreigner was ever going to have his permission to trade for even a trifle. He dutifully passed on Madrid's frequent expressions of fear that aggressors might be on the way, meaning, above all, the Russians. So frequent had the warnings been that, to his annoyance, they went largely unheeded. He had been at pains to impress on everyone the latest word he had had, which was that owing to new moves on Napoleons' part Russia and Spain were likely to be at odds.

Now it happened that both he, the governor of the province, and Argüello, the local commander, were away from San Francisco on March 28, 1806. The two of them had gone to Monterey for a brief stay. In this rare circumstance command had been given to Lieutenant Luis Argüello, who was twenty-one years old, friendly, amiable, and as anxious to see a new face as even his sister Concha. Apprised early that morning of the twenty-eighth that a ship with a strange flag was in the harbor, he gathered up a number of soldiers and, accompanied by Father José Uria, he galloped down to the beach, where they were joined by two men rowed over from the ship. One was obviously a naval officer, the other a civilian. The latter, after trying various languages, enraptured Father Uria when he proved able to converse in Latin.

When Luis galloped back to the presidio it was excitedly to tell the family they would have guests for morning chocolate. That ship out there had brought the famous Russian world-traveler whom Madrid had ordered hospitably received. Yes, Russian. Yes, Luis remembered everything the governor had said, but when had the Russians ever attacked? Besides, Father Uria approved. There would be three guests: the great man himself, one of his officers, and a very, very erudite German scientist. The household went into a fever of preparation, with Concha no doubt telling her brother he could have given them a little more time.

When the guests arrived, all eyes promptly went to the central figure and stayed there. Rezanov was a head taller than any of the Spaniards; he was dressed in a fashion to take the breath away, a rich fur cape hanging from one shoulder, his tunic adorned with decorations set with jewels, one of them ablaze with diamonds. At forty-two, he was still lean of face and figure; his carriage was still that of an imperial guardsman. Concha Argüello had never even imagined anyone like him. As for her effect on him, in more than two years he had seen no woman of any beauty at all to his taste. As he bowed to kiss her hand in acknowledgment of their introduction, surely she sensed that, habitual though the gesture obviously was to him, this time it was not casual.

Only later did he realize how fabulously lucky he had been to arrive at a time when both Governor Arillaga and Commander Argüello were absent. Had either been on hand, he would probably not have been allowed even to come ashore. As things were he had a week in which to make friends, his men aboard the *Juno* meanwhile regaining their strength on the fresh food obligingly sent at his request. And much of the week he spent at the Argüello home, exhibiting all his charm and courtliness, playing his violin, talking most of all to Concha, who seems to have had no trouble understanding his halting Spanish, which indeed she helped him improve rapidly. She wanted most of all to know about Saint Petersburg, and he, nothing loath, created in her a desire to hear even more. Probably it never occurred to him that he was following the old Russian custom of uniting with the women of newly penetrated lands.

Also during that week he visited the nearby mission at the invitation of the Franciscans, who made no secret of their views on Spain's laws against trade. He was given facts as to the amount of grain and beef that went to waste for lack of buyers. He excited everyone by passing out samples showing the quality of the goods aboard the *Juno*. An idea had formed in his mind by the time Governor Arillaga returned, accompanied by his old friend, Concha's father.

The atmosphere was now stiff and formal. Directly he could do so, Rezanov laid his idea before the old governor, who proved still to have no certain knowledge of war between Russia and Spain. He had, Rezanov said, come to discuss trade, in witness whereto he had brought a sample cargo. He admitted the needs of his colony and pointed out that California had its needs too. They should depend on each other. That was the road to peace between them. However, for the moment he was asking for only one cargo of foodstuffs to be taken to New Archangel as a sample. They could afterwards institute discussions with their respective home governments.

Arillaga had a bad time of it over the days that followed, as the Franciscans and the womenfolk belabored him to give an affirmative answer. But, through discussion after protracted discussion, he went on stubbornly saying he could never break his oath to uphold Spain's laws. Meanwhile Concha and Rezanov were drawn close. Indignant over the situation, she let him know what was said out of his hearing and gave him advice. His decision to ask her father for her hand came suddenly. It was now or never, by the way things looked.

A great family uproar ensued. No one suspected that more than a polite flirtation had been taking place, so discreet had been the courtship. Argüello angrily made his daughter go to confession. Her answer to the commotion was stormily to declare that she had committed no sin, that she loved the Russian and would marry no one else. The Franciscans helped restore peace. The real issues were then discussed, the formidable religious and political considerations in the way. It was out of the question for Concha to change her faith or Rezanov his. At length he agreed to wait for a Vatican dispensation and to seek the approval also of the King of Spain. On that understanding the betrothal was held.

It then dawned on Argüello that his daughter had done very well for herself. He told his prospective son-in-law to consider himself already a member of the family. Arillaga then threw up his hands. For an Argüello relative, he said, he would permit the trade. Men went briskly to work emptying the *Juno*'s hold of her cargo and filling it with foodstuffs ranging from beans to wheat. Nor did it matter when the courier from Mexico City finally brought definite word that war raged in Europe, with Russia and Spain in opposed alliances.

When, after six weeks in San Francisco Bay, the *Juno* set sail again, bound for New Archangel, her guns exchanged salutes with those ashore. Waving farewell were Arillaga and all the Argüellos. Concha was soon at work making beautiful raiment for her wedding. She felt she had to hurry. Her beloved had said he believed he could surmount all the difficulties and be back in two years.

And in truth, as his actions were to make clear, Rezanov was confident, supremely so, that all would go well and quickly. A man even less inclined than he to credit omens might well have concluded by now that destiny was at work, so fortuitously had everything occurred. His friend the Tsar would unquestionably aid him, given a favorable turn in the situation with Spain, which could come at any time, so rapid were the shifts in European politics these days. As for the Vatican, it would surely see the advantage to peace in this marriage, which would amount to a dynastic alliance, one uniting the Russians and Spaniards in the New World. What nation had it in its power to object, if Spain agreed? He, Nikolai Rezanov, had designed a new political map for America.

Time proved to be on his side. He saw New Archangel again in June. By acting quickly he could cross the Pacific to Okhotsk and even be in Saint Petersburg before the fall rains stalled

Siberian travel. Baranov, wearing his wig, was on the beach to greet him. New Archangel had revived, thanks to the Yankees, Joseph O'Cain for one, who had brought supplies in spring. Not that the winter was forgotten. For that too many lay dead in the little graveyard nearby and too many of the living were toothless from the scurvy.

Little new building had been done. Unfinished lay the small vessel which Baranov had agreed to build as a tender for the *Juno* when Rezanov had insisted on organizing a punitive expedition to be sent against Japan this year. Baranov surely stared at him in disbelief when he understood he was still of that mind. Such an expedition could only be a waste of precious manpower, with nothing to be accomplished other than the shooting up of a few Japanese fishing villages. Yet Rezanov was obdurate. Incredibly, he decided to stay at New Archangel until that tender was built. California had done nothing to ease the memory of his defeat at Nagasaki.

It was September before he brought the *Juno* and the tender to Okhotsk, where they were to be finally outfitted before proceeding against Japan. He wasted further time seeing to that. Lieutenants Khvostov and Davydov, whom he had placed in command, were not happy about this worthless assignment. He had a pang of conscience when they had departed. He wrote them a note, apologizing and withdrawing his orders, but it was too late to stop them.

September now neared its end. Rezanov was well advised to wait for winter before attempting those grueling 2200 miles to Irkutsk, which he remembered, having traveled them both ways with Shelikhov twelve years before. But the news reaching Okhotsk portended a break between Spain and Napoleon. Rezanov was all on fire to proceed. He hired the Cossacks and the horses and set out, gambling on reaching Yakutsk before the fall rains came down.

He failed. Drenched, chilled by the freezing winds, he fell so ill he had to be bedded in a native hut. No longer did he have a physician with him, Langsdorff having long since gone on ahead. Rezanov was five months reaching Irkutsk, where he arrived in February, looking like a ghost. Still he refused to wait for better weather. Seemingly he had to make up, at all costs to himself, for the time wasted on that rancorous expedition. As he pushed on with his Cossacks he fainted and fell from his horse. A hoof struck him in the head. On a day in early March of 1807 he was buried in the cemetery of the town of Krasnoyarsk.

California legend has it that his betrothed did not learn of his death for forty years. Concha Argüello knew within six years at the latest. She put away forever the beautiful clothes she had been making, leaving them to be handed down in the family from aunt to niece. The suitors she rejected included a prominent American. At sixty, when the Dominican sisters established the first convent in California, she joined them. She, to whom the world had been promised, lies buried at Benecia with the nuns of her order.

VIII

Kremlin on the Pacific

During the spring of 1806, while Rezanov was in California, Baranov came to a new decision to retire. He spoke of it to Joseph O'Cain, evidently mentioning also his old wish to see something of the world before he died, when, around April, the Irish Bostonian put in at New Archangel with supplies. The ship in which he came, the *Eclipse,* was a new addition to his fleet. He was prospering mightily; he owed it all to Baranov; he showed his gratitude by inviting him to visit Boston. Baranov accepted. From New Archangel, O'Cain was going next to the Orient. Baranov entrusted him with 300,000 rubles' worth of furs to sell for the Company at Canton, the Chinese goods taken in exchange to be delivered at Kamchatka. From there O'Cain was to return the following year and take Baranov to Boston.

Something else happened to solidify Baranov's intention of retiring. His Russian wife was dead, he learned. He wrote the chairman of the company's board, Mikhail Buldakov, begging his aid in obtaining a writ legitimizing his son and daughter by Anna. Could that favor be done him, he would be enabled to live with his American family in Russia, where he could now look forward to having some standing by virtue of the rank that had been conferred on him.

When, in June, Rezanov returned from California, he was met by Baranov's positive statement that he would stay only through the next eleven months, until May of 1807, evidently the time around which he expected to see O'Cain again. Rezanov failed to talk him out of it this time. As he was requested to do, he saw to it the directors would be informed in time by sending them a letter marked for urgent delivery. Apparently it was understood that Kuskov would become governor, unsure though Rezanov was that he could fill Baranov's shoes. In fall, after Rezanov's departure, Baranov put Kuskov in full command of New Archangel and went to Kodiak, where he had not been in nearly three years.

He needed a rest; he wanted to set his affairs in order and get reacquainted with his family, which had remained at Kodiak in the care of Father German and Ivan Banner. Irina was now four. Antipatr, who was nine, attended Father German's school. Anna had been baptized and had become very devout. Baranov, who was greatly concerned over the future of his children, must have been overwhelmed when he learned the results of his plea for a writ making them legitimate. Buldakov had taken the matter up directly with the Tsar and had described the mother of the children as "the daughter of the Prince of Kenai." This appellation for the Kenaitze Indian chief who had fathered Anna was incorporated in the decree that was issued legitimizing the children, in effect ennobling them as well. The best schools would now be open to them. When he returned from Boston, Baranov appears now to have planned, he and the family would go to Russia.

How definite were his plans was indicated by Richard, who, after fourteen years at Baranov's side, returned to his native Bengal, no doubt a rich man. But Baranov's hopes were shattered, beginning with the one of visiting Boston. O'Cain was dead. His fine new ship had been wrecked along the Aleutians en route from Kamchatka. It could have been no comfort to Baranov that his good friend had died on his way to do him another service. The year 1807 also brought the shocking news of Rezanov's death, an event certain profoundly to affect the Company. Baranov waited to hear more.

In 1808 he finally had a letter from the directors on the subject of his resignation. Clearly the death of the man who had always told them what to do had left them confused and uncertain. They had, they wrote, been unable to agree on a successor. He was begged to stay on for the present. Not that their fear of making a change at this time was unjustified. The most experienced hand should be guiding the colony. The Napoleonic wars still raged, Europe was torn apart, the days ahead were very uncertain. The problems concerning shipping were in particular enormous. Baranov had the best acquaintance with the foreign traders on whom the colony must depend almost entirely.

Rezanov's expansionist plans had also to be pursued. Otherwise damaging though the Napoleonic wars were, they continued to furnish Russia with her opportunity in the Pacific. Attention should be paid with no further delay to Hawaii and to the founding of posts on the Columbia River and close to California. Baranov had the fullest knowledge of the way to organize these things. Everyone likes to be told he is indispensable. He was now sixty-one and greatly troubled by arthritis, but, like an old general called out of retirement at wartime, he prepared to return to New Archangel, where he had not been in twenty months.

He must have been mightily pleased to see what his onetime commissary clerk had wrought during his absence. Kuskov had practically finished the building of New Archangel, replacing much that had had to be put up in such haste that first winter. The solid fortifications mounted sixty guns. The palisade, which had lost its rude look, had imposing gates. No church had been built as yet, but among the several well-constructed buildings was even a bakery. Streets had been laid out and lined with wooden sidewalks. Flowers grew around the individual cabins. A beacon had been placed at the harbor entrance; a pilot was on duty day and night to guide incoming ships. And there was a shipyard, small but growing, the crew of which included some twenty Yankees. It was managed by one Lincoln, a shipbuilder who had been recruited by O'Cain. The place rang with the sound of hammers on anvils and of whipsaws turning logs into boards. Lincoln had already built two new vessels, one a three-master, and had rebuilt an old one. The yard was at the service also of visiting vessels in need of repairs.

Kuskov's triumph was, however, the constructing he had done on the knoll. Like the eminences around which Russian towns of old had been built, it was crowned with a kremlin. The forward part of the broad, flat knoll was laid out in a parade ground centered by a staff flying the flag of the Russian-American Company, which had been granted in 1806. Facing this was an impressive two-storied structure built of great square-hewn timbers. It was the residence of the governor and the central administration building for the colony. "Baranov's Castle," it was always henceforth to be called. The furniture, which included a piano, had been imported from Europe. There were a banquet hall and a library, which was hung with good paintings and lined with 1200 books in many languages. Travelers who saw it and knew about things of the sort were filled with wonder that such a collection should be in so remote a place. It had been brought down from Kodiak, where it had merely gathered dust. Here at New Archangel there was at least ornamental value in the relics of Rezanov's dream of giving Russian America higher learning.

The Tlingits had not given up hope of recovering the site of their old home, but Kuskov had kept them well in check. He had his garrison in good form. He could hardly have been pleased to learn that he was not to govern the colony after all, but he agreed to head the expedition in search of a site for a fort near California, on the understanding that in the event of success he could consider the region his domain. He left on his mission that fall of 1808. At almost the same time an expedition was dispatched in search of a fort site in the region of the Columbia.

How to comply with Rezanov's expansionist blueprint as it related to Hawaii was considerably more of a problem for Baranov, who wanted no misunderstanding with King Kamehameha. The Company had come to want, in addition to a station in Hawaii, land for a food-growing plantation and a share in the rich trade in sandalwood, a commodity for which the Chinese were paying high. The utmost diplomacy was called for. Kamehameha, though he welcomed the shipping of all the world, had allowed no permanent foreign establishments. He was no simple-minded barbarian to be easily cozened into doing what he did not wish to do. He was a very great man, whose chief concern was the welfare of his people. Only in the light of that consideration could he be made to see the benefit of any new proposal. Even England, though he leaned toward her and had Britons as his chief advisers, had carefully refrained from infringing.

Baranov himself would probably have been his own best emissary. Kamehameha had conceived a great admiration for him, as a result of all he had heard of his pertinacity in the face of privation and disaster. He sent his regards by almost every northbound ship, and Baranov had received gifts, among them a great fan of exotic feathers signifying the height of royal esteem. He had a standing invitation to visit the King, who had spoken often of visiting him. Why, then, he did not go himself is a mystery the greater in view of the emissary he chose: Lieutenant Leontii Hagemeister, commander of the *Neva,* which was now fully in the colonial service.

Hagemeister spoke English, which may have been one reason he was chosen. Evidently he had managed to conceal the contempt and distrust he was later to manifest with regard to Baranov. Also, evidently, he indicated that he understood the delicacy and importance of his mission, on which he departed in 1809.

By that time Baranov had thoroughly re-established himself at New Archangel. He was giving every indication of intending to remain governor. A son of one of his sisters, Ivan Kuglinov, who had been trained as a merchant's clerk, had come to the colony to serve as his secretary. He had had his family brought down from Kodiak. Antipatr and Irina were put under the tutelage of Abram Jones, another O'Cain recruit. Jones, who seems to have been about twenty-five, could sail a ship and had had a superior education. He had been in the colony three years; he had become fluent in Russian; now that Richard was gone, he was Baranov's interpreter in English, and he was practically a member of the family.

New Archangel was fast becoming a busy port. Some fifty ships a year now visited the north Pacific, and rare was the vessel not in need of some repair after a long voyage. New Archangel had the only facilities north of Hawaii. Half a dozen brigs and schooners were often at anchor, awaiting the services of Lincoln and his shipyard crew. Then there were the sealskins from the Pribilofs to bring the traders. The Company was now in entire control of that popular commodity, which could be bought only through Baranov. Too, some traders had come to prefer to buy otter skins from the Russians and avoid the dangers of dealing with the Tlingits. Those who went on dealing with the Tlingits and did so in liquor and firearms could expect no favors from Baranov. Russia was conferring with the United States on the firearms issue and would do so again, but Washington was not soon to concede that American cargoes should be limited in any way. Baranov was never to have more power in this area than he himself could exert by denying offenders his regard.

He had important commissions to give those who had earned his trust. One was the selling of Company furs at Canton, which had become regular practice. Regular too had come to be the practice of poaching otter along California, which could not be done without Aleuts and their gear. Baranov commissioned two or three shipmasters a year to engage in it. The returns ran as high as $100,000 a voyage. For all these reasons, many a shipmaster called at New Archangel, if only to pay respects. Although the relationship had cooled somewhat since the death of O'Cain, the Winship brothers, Jonathan and Nathan, still did much business with Baranov. Among other famous captains of the period who had his friendship and respect were George Washington Ayers, Joseph Meek, John Ebbets, and William Heath Davis.

Baranov loved his role as host to New Archangel's visitors.

He meticulously saw to it that the foreign flags, on entering the harbor, were greeted with the proper salutes from his guns. Special friends were saluted again as they came ashore or went back to their ships. He proudly showed off his castle and tendered banquets in a style that became legendary. The guests were expected to eat and drink heartily. The word-picture drawn of him by Washington Irving derives from reports of the masters who came to know the old man at this period: ". . . a rough, rugged, hard-drinking old Russian; somewhat of a soldier, somewhat of a trader, above all a boon companion of the old roystering school with a strong cross of the bear. . . ." Recalled John Ebbets ruefully: "They all drink an astonishing quantity, Baranov not excepted. . . . It is no small tax on the health of a person trying to do business with him."

A feature of those evenings was the music, which one Russian officer called "very good." Evidently New Archangel had acquired musicians enough to make up an orchestra. Some years before, Baranov had turned his own hand to composing. The result had become the colony's patriotic hymn. It was sung at the dedication of new posts and other occasions of moment. It has been titled "The Spirit of Russian Hunters," but in the colony it was known simply as "Baranov's Song." He was given to calling for it before a convivial evening was over. Along with his other traits, he was something of a romantic.

His hold over the colony was complete. His commands were as law at the farthest posts. He was accorded respect even by the naval officers, thanks to Rezanov's blast on the subject. Many an old hand had sworn that if Aleksandr Andreevich was ever dismissed he would leave too. He had pulled a number of them out of hopeless debt by squaring their commissary accounts out of his own pocket. He was also paying for the education of many of their sons. The conviction was solid that without him the growing prosperity of the colony would be at an end. Nor had he ever stood higher in the estimation of the native world. The Aleuts looked to him for everything. Even the Tlingits had come to regard him with a species of affection.

Their chiefs, on occasion, ceremoniously brought him gifts, indicating that, though they still hoped to oust him from the region, there was nothing personal.

He gloried in all the evidence of devotion to him. Only one thing pleased him more, and that was the way his children were growing up to be a pair of fine youngsters. And with his acceptance of the twin roles of patriarch and tsar had come complacency. He was not as well acquainted as in former years with all the men. Some of the newer arrivals he hardly knew at all. He had the impression that there was no longer anyone who hated him. And why should anyone hate him? Conditions were better; he alone had wrought the change; there should be no cause for unrest. Apparently it never occurred to him that the new men had to take it on faith that conditions were better. It was still a hard life. To some of the new men he was a tyrant and nothing more.

The violent revolutionary spirit stirring in the world was beyond Baranov's understanding. Impatiently he waved away the information, when first warned, that a plot against him was in the making in the New Archangel garrison. This was in the summer of 1809. Nine men had formed a secret society, the name of which appears to have been the Order of Ermak. A manifesto, setting forth grievances, had been written in the standard revolutionary language of the period. The plan was to seize a ship, take all the women of the settlement, and sail to Easter Island, there to found a republic. The society was conducting a membership drive, in hopes particularly of enlisting the Yankees working for the Company.

As the first step in the uprising, Baranov was to be assassinated, together with his family. It was apparently that which made him think all of it preposterous when he was warned. Why should anyone wish to kill Irina and Antipatr? They had harmed no one. Then some of the participants themselves decided they had better tell him. After that he deigned to investigate. The plotters were raided as they were holding a meeting. Though they hastily thrust their papers into the stove, they did not succeed in burning them all. Those half-burned documents told Baranov that he had been judged an inhuman monster, guilty of tyranny, murder, and the sale into slavery of helpless peoples. For these crimes he must die, and, lest his breed flourish, his family. Abram Jones was to die too, evidently having been found guilty by association.

All the romance was gone for Baranov, and he was gripped with fear for one of the few times in his life. Perhaps it was the doing of that word "assassination," so connotative of the gruesome in history. In vain he was assured that the conspiracy had not been widespread and that it had all been stamped out. He had his family packed off to Kodiak in the care of Jones, keeping only his nephew Kuglinov at New Archangel with him. And he wrote his will, an act which his kind in those days put off until they were at death's door. His wording was bitter: "Since my life is in constant danger not only from the hostility of wild tribes but from men often unwilling to submit to discipline, since my strength is exhausted and my health dissipated battling the hardships I have had to endure, I feel that that natural time, the hour of my death, is for me more uncertain than for most men, therefore I make my will." Father German and Company chairman Buldakov were named guardians of his family, who were left the bulk of his estate.

He also wrote the directors. Angrily he asked them when they intended replacing him. They were reminded how long ago he had asked to leave. He had been staying on what amounted to a temporary basis, he felt he had done his duty, and, he implied, if no action was taken soon he might simply go. The letter was marked for urgent delivery overland from Okhotsk.

After that, sitting in his castle, now empty of the sound of children, he got drunk and stayed drunk all winter, the winter of 1809-1810. He sank into one of the longest and blackest periods that ever possessed him. He could be roused to look after only the major chores of his office. Rezanov's expansionist plans he neglected completely. Hagemeister had made a mess of his mission to Hawaii, behaving arrogantly, allowing himself to be heard to say that what Russia could not gain by diplomacy she would take by force. Kamehameha was hurt, bewildered, and angry, as Baranov learned from Jonathan Winship and others. Yet he did nothing. He sent neither explanation nor apology, and Kamehameha, left to draw his own conclusions, strengthened his ties with Britain. Kuskov was proceeding with his explorations close to California, but nothing had been heard from the expedition sent to the Columbia region, which meant it had probably come to grief. Baranov did nothing about that either. Russia was in grave danger of losing her opportunity in the Pacific.

IX

The Tragedy of Anna Petrovna

The exploring expedition which set out from New Archangel in the fall of 1808 for the purpose of locating a site for a fort in the Columbia River region was under the command of a naval officer by the name of Nikolai Bulygin. With him was his young and attractive wife. Anna Petrovna Bulygina was to have the distinction of being the first white woman to set foot on New Albion, the name, borrowed from the English, by which the Russians denoted the vast stretch of coast between California and Russian America.

The leader of the promyshlenniki assigned to the expedition was Timofei Tarakanov, one of Baranov's most experienced men. Tarakanov was probably born in eastern Siberia, a descendant of the old promyshlenniki, and had been in the colony at least ten years. He was with the garrison of the first fort built at Sitka in 1799 and was one of the few not killed on the spot at the massacre in 1802. Captured, taken to a Tlingit village, he witnessed the death by torture of two of his comrades. He was the last man to be rescued by Captains Ebbets and Barber.

Unfazed by the experience, he made himself one of the colony's foremost dealers with the Tlingits, whose speech he learned. He had an ear for the speech of all the natives, who generally respected him highly, the Aleuts in particular. When the practice of poaching otter along California was instituted, he went on a number of the voyages as foreman of the Aleut crews, having the respect and liking also of the American skippers. He was inventive and resourceful, having great skill with his hands. Though classed as a hunter, he could have qualified as a carpenter or metal-worker. He could also, as he had demonstrated, center a target with a Moscow musket at two hundred feet. He went with the Columbia River expedition in the capacity of supercargo. He would have charge of activities such as trading and other dealings with the Indians.

The expedition departed New Archangel at virtually the same time that Kuskov and his men set out for the purpose of reconnoitering the region just north of California. Neither party was to build a fort. They were both to return and report before final action would be taken. The Columbia-bound vessel, commanded by Nikolai Bulygin, was the *Saint Nicholas,* a fine little brig acquired from the Yankees. Aboard were twenty people: seventeen men, four of them Aleuts, and three women, Aleuts with the exception of Anna Petrovna, whom Bulygin "loved more than himself," in the words of Tarakanov, who was to give a first-person account of what occurred. His narrative was preserved for publication, thanks to the interest in history taken by a ranking naval officer.[1]

Bulygin, who had been in the colony about two years, was better liked than most of the naval men. He had proved himself able and was considerate of others. The indications all are that he and Anna Petrovna had not been married long. She was popular, was probably about eighteen, and plainly had a zest for adventure. What Tarakanov may have thought of having her on such an expedition, his narrative does not say. He had no words of criticism for superiors. In the event of shipwreck a young white woman was likely to create special problems. Much of the coast they were to survey was rocky; all of it was wild, beset by fog and rain and peopled by savages known to take slaves. But Bulygin obviously had entire confidence in his skill as a navigator. Besides, the *Saint Nicholas* was taut and strong, and they had Vancouver's excellent charts. And, should some accident befall them, according to plan they would make for Gray's Har-

[1] See citation under TARAKANOV at the end of this volume.

bor and await Kuskov, who was scheduled to meet them there with his party in December.

They traded as they went, at the Queen Charlotte Islands and down Vancouver Island. Every Company operation, including exploring, was expected to pay for itself. As of old, the men were on shares; what they made depended on the year's take of furs. They lay to and fired a gun when totem poles showing above the dark, wet forest indicated a village. As many as a hundred canoes at a time would put out from shore, bringing otter. Since the Americans often visited these parts, the natives had guns. Tarakanov would allow only three of them aboard at a time.

Their progress was further delayed by storms alternating with periods of no winds at all. They were becalmed for four days off the Strait of Juan de Fuca, which they did not try to enter, repelled, no doubt, by the dense fog forever shrouding the entrance. Few vessels ventured in, despite Vancouver's clear indication of the passage. On a night late in October they anchored near Destruction Island, so named as a memento of the experiences of previous mariners with the Indians of the adjacent mainland, the Olympic Peninsula of the present State of Washington.

Disaster struck with dumfounding suddenness. Everything went wrong at once. Bulygin had thrown out three anchors to hold the *Saint Nicholas* against a strong sea current, but a stiff southeaster came up, adding so much pull on the cables that they snapped, one after the other, cut by sharp submerged rocks. A foreyard broke, ending hope of maneuvering the brig against the wind. On the morning of November 1 she was on the mainland rocks. So precarious was her situation that Bulygin ordered her evacuated and camp made on the beach, despite the rain, which at that season at that place comes in off the ocean in torrents, drawn inland by the high, cold Olympic Mountains.

Guns were issued as the tents went up, Tarakanov telling everyone to keep a sharp lookout for Indians. Enslavement at their hands was to him a fate "a hundredfold worse than death itself." Indians were not long in coming out of the thick forest fringing the beach, "a multitude" of them suddenly appearing, half naked and barefoot. To Tarakanov's relief they had no guns, only spears, which showed how seldom this section of the coast was visited by traders. These were Quillayute Indians, unrelated to the Tlingits and more primitive, but speaking a language sufficiently close to those known to Tarakanov for him to understand it.

They were merely curious, not hostile. They had a village nearby, as Tarakanov learned from the chief, who was affable. On learning that whites were in the vicinity, they had come running over to have a look. Their curiosity was unbounded. They were all over the camp, examining everything, fingering whatever attracted them. They tried to make off with some objects, provoking tussles. "Bear with them," Tarakanov advised. "Get them out of here peacefully." But someone lost his temper, perhaps hitting one of the Indians. They backed off, offended, throwing spears and stones, felling Tarakanov and drawing blood from Bulygin. Guns began going off. Three of the Indians were killed before the others withdrew into the forest.

The rest of the day passed in futile attempts to salvage the *Saint Nicholas*. In the morning Bulygin announced that without further delay they would start walking to Gray's Harbor, which lay less than seventy miles to the south. They should be there in plenty of time to meet Kuskov in December. The warmest parkas and the best sealskin mukluks were issued. Every man was given two muskets to carry and a pistol. Slings were made, in which to carry kegs of powder, bags of shot, axes and other tools of the kind, provisions, trade goods, and the most valued of their personal belongings. Because the Quillayutes were likely to loot the brig, everything which might serve them as a weapon was thrown into the water. Then they set out, at their heels the dog who was the pet of the expedition. One who no doubt relished this as adventure was Filipp Kotelnikov, a youthful student who had come on the voyage.

As events were to show, the Quillayutes had been holding

angry council at their village, debating how to avenge the three deaths and the wounds inflicted on them. They had not failed to notice how the whites protected that woman of theirs who had blue eyes and yellow hair. She would fetch a fine price from some wealthy tribe. When the sentinels appointed to watch the movements of the whites ran in with word they were on the march, fifty warriors ran after them to see where they were going and to harry them with spears and stones. The word went out all over the peninsula; Indians came running from miles around. In view of the direction the whites were taking, they would presently come to the Hoh River, which they would find too deep to wade. It was decided to set a trap for them there.

The heaviness of the constant rain gave Tarakanov and his companions one of their greatest problems as they slogged on, hugging the shoreline and avoiding, as much as they could, the forest with its hidden throwers of spears and stones. Loaded down as they were, it was difficult to see that the firing mechanisms of their muskets were kept dry at all times. The rain was coming down in sheets when, on November 7, they reached the Hoh River, which they soon saw would take boats to cross.

On the opposite shore stood a village made up of a number of large huts with dugout canoes moored nearby. Also there, watching intently, were some two hundred Indians. Only later was Tarakanov to realize that a quarter of them had been his party's pursuers. After a parley he conducted through cupped hands, two of the canoes were brought over, one large enough to carry nine in addition to the paddlers, and a smaller, for four passengers. Several trips would have to be made to get everyone and all the baggage across, but that was as well. They should not all be on the water at the same time.

Bulygin was giving the orders. He and Tarakanov would be among the last to cross. The ladies would go first, Anna and the two Aleut women. They, the student Filipp Kotelnikov, and the Indian paddler shoved off in the small canoe. The nine men who followed in the larger had their muskets at the ready to give protection when the women reached the opposite shore. But in midstream their paddlers unplugged holes that had been cut in the bottom and jumped overboard, leaving them to a hail of spears and arrows from the Indians ashore. Their muskets were too drenched to shoot back. They could use them only as paddles in a frantic effort to get back to safety, at the same time stopping the upwelling water with their feet. Meanwhile Anna and those with her were paddled across and whisked out of sight.

Bulygin could only rave and curse. In the sluicing rain he had allowed his musket to get too wet to spark shots, and so had all the men on his side of the river, including Tarakanov. They could give no cover to the men trying to paddle clear of the spears and arrows. When their canoe was pulled in, not one of them was unwounded. The Indians, having heard no shots, concluded that they could wipe out the whites and moved upstream to cross over for the purpose. By the time the attackers were on them, Tarakanov and the others had their arms dried and cleaned. Even so it took an hour to drive back the Indians, two of whom had guns. Manifestly this exposed position on the riverbank had to be abandoned. Carrying the seriously wounded in their arms, leaving behind much of their equipment, including the tools for repairing guns, they set out for higher ground.

When they had gone only a little way, one of the wounded begged simply to be set down in the brush. He could not endure the pain, said Khariton Sobachnikov, who was dying of the arrowhead in his belly. It had to be as he asked. All wept as they laid him down in a secluded place, bade him farewell, and prayed God to have mercy on his soul.

For nearly a week they plunged on through the forest in increasingly disorganized fashion, finding no campsite that offered an adequate food supply. They had used up their provisions; they lived on the few mushrooms they could find and on tree fungi. Finally they were constrained to kill and eat the dog. Meanwhile another of the wounded had died. Bulygin was no fit leader in a situation such as this. He was so unacquainted with woodcraft he did not know how to use an ax or shoot down a bird. And the thought of what might be happening to his wife had him in such a state that "it was impossible to look on him without compassionate tears." At length he asked Tarakanov to take command, confessing that he knew not how to get them out of their desperate situation.

Tarakanov asked to have the request in writing and, scrupulously following promyshlennik practice, had the men vote on it. He was unanimously elected leader. Taking the necessary risk of exposing the fact they were still in the vicinity, he led a raid on a small Indian village for its dried fish. The harrying they received after that decided Tarakanov to abandon the coast region. They would, he told the men, go up the Hoh River and into the mountains. There they would winter and think out what to do next. It was too late even to think of resuming the attempt to make Gray's Harbor. Kuskov could not now be met in time.

They had not gone far up the Hoh when two chiefs caught up with them. Presenting a mass of whale blubber for sale, they asked also how much would be paid for the white woman. Bulygin, when this question was translated for him, "was beside himself with joy." He contributed even his epaulets to the pile of trade goods and the personal valuables given up by all the men, the Aleuts included. But the chiefs were unsatisfied. They also wanted four guns. Tarakanov's reply to that was that they had to see Anna first. The chiefs had to concede it was only reasonable to prove they would not be selling a dead body.

Anna was brought from the opposite shore of the river in a canoe, but only about halfway. Bulygin had to talk to her across several yards of water. They "were drowned in tears and could hardly speak. She tried to comfort him, saying she had been well treated and had met with no harm." Her words were no doubt belied by her appearance. Those who had been captives of the Quillayutes for any length of time were usually gaunt, exhausted, and filthy. The chiefs now resumed negotiations, repeating their demand for four guns. When Tarakanov conceded no more than one broken musket, they ordered Anna taken away and they departed.

Bulygin, when he understood what had been said, was beside himself with anger. Ignoring the fact he had given up the leadership, he ordered the men to pay the price. Tarakanov tried to reason with him, pointing out that that meant giving up a quarter of their usable guns. Owing to their lack of tools for the making of repairs, they were now all down to one good musket apiece, and more were bound to go out of commission. Besides, any guns given away would be used against them. Bulygin only repeated his orders, adding a tearful plea. Tarakanov then sharply told the men that any who complied need no longer consider him their comrade. He prevailed. In bitter silence the march up river was resumed.

Some ten weeks later, in February of 1809, they came back down the Hoh in a crude boat with a friendly Indian as their pilot. Tarakanov, who had pulled them through the winter with no further casualties, had proposed they build the boat in the hope of making it out to sea. They should be able to reach Destruction Island, where passing ships could be signaled, or they might even attain the Columbia, which was being visited by the Americans. They would see how things went when they reached salt water.

Bulygin was again in command. When the proposal to build the boat was made he came out of the stupor that had possessed him and asked to be reinstated. Tarakanov had been agreeable. They would need his skill as a navigator. Bulygin seemed wholeheartedly of the opinion they should now all devote themselves to getting back to civilization, until they neared the village on the lower river where they had been tricked. He then announced he intended making an effort to find out what had become of his wife.

The men were angry. This was foolhardy. No longer did they have enough guns or ammunition to risk battle. But Tarakanov persuaded them to obey, and luck seemed with them for a change. Two Indians were easily captured and held on the boat in wait for their people to make the next move. One of the two was a woman whose husband proved to be of tribal importance.

Very concerned about his wife, he begged for four days' time, during which he would try to bring back the white woman, who had, he said, been given in tribute to a chief of the Makahs, a tribe living on the Strait of Juan de Fuca.

Bulygin decided to do his waiting where his two hostages would not be easily taken from him. Leaving the boat pulled up on the riverbank, he made camp on a cliff a mile distant. There, together with the men and the captives, he waited eight days. Word then came that a delegation of Makahs had arrived and were at the river, waiting to parley. To ascertain the truth of this, Bulygin sent Tarakanov, who went well armed with several men. It was all as reported. The Makahs were there, waiting, fifteen of them, headed by an obviously wealthy old chief named Utra-Makah, who wore a European shirt, trousers, and a fur cap. All of them seemed prosperous and above most of the natives thereabouts. And with them, "to our joy," was Anna Petrovna.

She was not the woebegone girl they had last seen the previous fall. Indeed her appearance was a great surprise. She looked healthy; she was clean; she was warmly garbed in good fur clothing and moccasins. And she had a different air. She was a person of power and influence among the Makahs. Though Tarakanov did not later say so in as many words, clearly she had become a favorite wife of the chief who had acquired her. What she had to say, when the greetings and expressions of surprise were over, "struck us all like thunder. . . . We listened with horror and bitterness. . . ."

Speaking "decisively and firmly," she refused to leave her present situation only to go wandering again in search of escape with no certainty of finding it, enduring more privations and dangers. What they should do, she told Tarakanov, was join her, voluntarily give themselves over to the Makahs, a kindly people who would treat them as well as she was treated. She could give assurance on the point; she had made the arrangement. They would be at villages on Juan de Fuca Strait, where two ships had of late put in, she had heard. When another appeared they would not be hindered from asking the captain to take them home. Tarakanov told her he would have to go talk to Bulygin.

It took Bulygin some time to believe the story and when he did "he was like a madman. He seized a gun and rushed away with the intention of shooting his wife." But he could not go through with it. He halted, burst into tears, asked Tarakanov to go talk again to Anna, who was to be told how close she had come to getting shot.

Her comment was sharp. "Tell my husband I have only contempt for his threat." Death did not frighten her, she said. What did was the risk of enslavement "by an evil and barbarous people." Having offered an arrangement by which they would all be safe and perhaps soon find their way home, she had no more to say.

Again Tarakanov hiked the mile back to the cliff and reported to Bulygin, who listened closely, stood a moment in thought, then collapsed. He was put to bed, crying helplessly and saying he wanted to die. The men wanted to get back to the boat, be on their way. Only Tarakanov gave thought to Anna's proposal. It was eminently worth considering, in view of her information that ships were now visiting the strait. As for the treatment they would be accorded, Anna should know what she was talking about. All things considered, joining her seemed a safer gamble than trusting themselves to that boat they had built. That evening he told the assembled company that he for one wished to surrender himself to the Makahs.

A rancorous discussion ensued, some charging Anna with the intention of betraying them, for love of her chief, apparently. In vain they were reminded that, after all, she was a Russian. The majority, from Ivan Bolotov to Savva Zuev and Kasian Zyrianov, voted to continue on with the boat. Only four sided with Tarakanov: his close friend Kozma Ovchinnikov, two of the Aleuts, and Bulygin, who was evidently letting his thinking be done for him. It was agreed that the party should split, though not in enmity. They would all pray for the safety of one another. Next day Tarakanov took the two Indian captives back to their people and conferred with the trousered Makah chief, who assured him that everything would be as Anna had promised.

When she and those who had chosen to go with her had departed for the Strait, the others relaunched the boat, their destination Destruction Island. They came to grief at once, the boat striking a rock and sinking when barely past the river's mouth. They all made it back to shore but had lost all their arms and ammunition. They were quickly captured by the Quillayutes, who sold two of them, an Aleut and a Russian, as far away as the Columbia. The Makahs bought some of the others, who thus rejoined their former companions.

The Makahs lived in wooden communal dwellings which provided no privacy and forever smelled of stale smoke and rancid fish oil, but by comparison to their neighbors to the south they lived richly, and their hospitality was at first all that Anna had said it would be. Tarakanov and Bulygin were made the property of the kindly Utra-Makah, who treated them entirely as guests, not slaves. His village, to Tarakanov's gratification, had a clear view of the Strait to the fog-shrouded entrance. Vessels venturing in would immediately be seen. Anna was at another village until her owner obligingly bought Bulygin, whereupon they were together again, in a manner of speaking. The captives scattered through the various villages included one John Williams, though who he was and how he got there, Tarakanov's narrative does not say.

Spring wore into summer; no ships appeared. The Indians, whose mood could change quickly, tired of maintaining so many captives in what, to them, was luxury, and put them increasingly to work. They also began to "pass us from hand to hand," by sale or as gifts to friends and relatives. Even Anna found herself sold to someone else at another village. Again she and her husband were apart. Presently the captives were nothing but slaves, made to work interminably in all weather and given the worst of the food, usually revoltingly unfresh fish.

Only Tarakanov appears to have been retained by his first owner. He managed it by making himself too useful and interesting to Utra-Makah to be got rid of. With tools he made himself, he fashioned dishes of wood and toys for the children and invented a device with which to signal in time of war.

In August Anna Petrovna died, apparently a suicide. Tarakanov, who details how others met death, in this case was laconic, stating only the fact and the month. She had reason to despair. August was the last month when a ship could reasonably be expected that year. None knew better than she how hideous was the situation into which she had led her husband and compatriots. Her last owner "was such a barbarian he would not permit her body to be buried and had it simply thrown into the forest." Bulygin gave up trying to live after that. He "went into a decline," succumbed to an infection of some sort, and died in February. Dead too was Tarakanov's close friend Ovchinnikov. They might all be dead if no ship came this year either.

The season was approaching when the ships sailing to New Archangel would be passing not many miles out from that cursed fog hugging the entrance to the Strait. Tarakanov put his inventive mind on the problem of signaling those ships. A kite! A kite would rise well above that fog and be judged the work of only a European. He made one of some thin material stretched over a wooden frame. His string was twisted gut. The Indians marveled, saying that he had found a way to reach the sun. There was even talk of making him a chief.

Tarakanov, a pious man, surely dropped to his knees when, in May of that year of 1810, a vessel materialized out of the fog. And she was one he knew, the Boston brig *Lydia,* commanded by Captain J. Brown. And when Tarakanov was aboard, who should clasp him in his arms but Afanasii Valgusov, whom the Quillayutes had sold to the natives on the Columbia, where Brown had ransomed him. As for the Aleut sold down the Columbia, he had been rescued the previous year by Captain George Ayers of the *Mercury.*

After some haggling, Brown offered the Makahs for each of

their captives, including John Williams, five blankets, twelve yards of cloth, a saw, a mirror, two knives, five bags of powder, and five of shot. Word of the price went out over the Olympic Peninsula so quickly that in four days the gaunt survivors were being brought in from as far away as the Quinault River. Some owners of captives tried to hold out for more than the standard price, but Brown put a stop to that by seizing one of them and putting him in the *Lydia*'s brig. Counting Williams, Brown rescued thirteen souls, including the two Aleut women, all who had survived the expedition, with the exception of the young student Kotelnikov, who was known to be alive but was at some place too distant for the Indians to trouble to find him. Seven were dead of the twenty who had sailed with the *Saint Nicholas*.

The rescued saw New Archangel again on June 9, 1810. They had been away twenty-one months, fifteen of them in captivity. To the clerk assigned to him for the purpose, for he was illiterate, Tarakanov began dictating the report telling of the fate of the first white woman to set foot on the shores of the Pacific Northwest.

X

Second Wind

The year 1812 was drawing to a close, and the occupant of the residence of the governor at New Archangel was still Aleksandr Baranov. For three years now he had awaited that successor he had so angrily demanded of the directors following the discovery of the plot to assassinate him. Not that the directors were to blame for the long wait. They had acted soon after receiving the notification, appointing a new man and sending him on his way at once, but he had died before he could reach the colony. And when the news of that reached Saint Petersburg, another had been quickly appointed. Now he was on his way, due to arrive in the early months of 1813.

Meanwhile Baranov had gone on living in loneliness at his castle, the only family member he kept near him his nephew and secretary, Ivan Kuglinov. He insisted that Anna and the children remain at Kodiak, though the plot had been practically forgotten by nearly everyone else. His mood had remained black. He was lethargic, saying that at sixty-five he was too old to be anything else, that after all he had been in the colony twenty-two years, that were it not for the rum he could not endure his arthritis. His eyesight, he said, was going. His glasses no longer helped him. Kuglinov read him the documents on which he had to act.

The rum had never before affected his ability to guard his tongue, but now he was letting himself talk freely, doing so on at least one occasion to the Company's most dangerous enemy.

This was Captain Vasilii Golovnin, who came to New Archangel in 1810 as commander of the first Russian war vessel to visit the Pacific waters. Golovnin was a leader in shaping the opinion growing within the Navy that it should control the colony, and he was on the lookout for information detrimental to merchant rule. Gratuitously Baranov volunteered the damaging item that a physician had never been sent to the colony. Golovnin, astonished, asked how the directors could be so remiss. According to him, Baranov answered, "I do not know whether they trouble themselves even to think about it. We doctor ourselves as best we can, and if a man is so wounded as to need an operation he must die." Recorded Golovnin in commentary: "And that is just one example of the 'wise' management of the Russian-American Company."

Throughout these three years Baranov had taken no active part in advancing Rezanov's expansionist plans. New moves, he said, should wait on his successor. That was his justification for his continued failure to repair the damage done by Hagemeister to relations with Hawaii. Nor had he sent a second expedition to the Columbia, with the result that the region had gone to the United States in 1811, with the establishment of Astoria, John Jacob Astor's colony. The rich and powerful Astor, king of the American fur trade, had proposed a far-reaching commercial alliance, sending as his representative to discuss the matter with Baranov the latter's good friend Captain John Ebbets, but he too was told that everything had to wait on a successor.

One part only of Rezanov's plan had been brought to realization, the part relating to the region north of San Francisco. Ivan Kuskov had succeeded in establishing his post, which Americans were to call Fort Ross. He had the construction nearly finished; he was laying out his acreage in grain, vegetables, and livestock; he hoped soon also to be trading with the Spaniards for foodstuffs. Only in a negative sense was any of this due to Baranov. He had not opposed Kuskov's stubborn determination to have that domain he could call his own.

Baranov was given a profound shock in January of 1813.

The news was brought him that the second man sent to replace him had also died on the way. The man had been aboard the *Neva*, which was wrecked in a storm almost within sight of New Archangel. Though never a pious man, Baranov was no unbeliever. It struck him now that all along God had seen to it he was kept at his post in America. The evidence was impressive. His first resignation had been meaningless because Shelikhov was struck down before he could act upon it. His second proved meaningless because of Rezanov's death. Father Iosaf, who had been the likeliest to succeed at having him dismissed, had gone down with the *Phoenix*. O'Cain was lost as he had been coming to take him away. And now there were these two recent deaths. He had better give up, Baranov decided.

As is evident, he informed the directors of his decision, advising them to send him no one else. He turned pious, planning a church and asking for the first time that a priest be sent New Archangel. His arrangements to stay on as governor were made

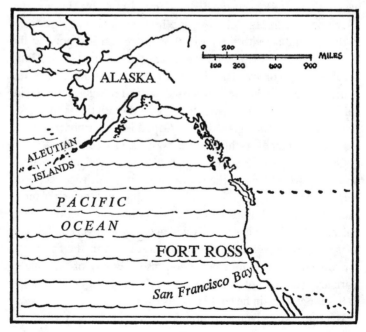

for permanence. He had his family return to live with him at the castle, with the exception of Anna, who seems to have preferred to go on living at Kodiak. Through friends in Europe he sought a governess for Irina, who was eleven. A German woman eventually came in response. Abram Jones went on tutoring Antipatr, who was sixteen and hopeful of qualifying for the Naval Academy at Saint Petersburg. Baranov came completely out of the lethargy that had possessed him of recent years. He forgot what he had been saying about his age, his arthritis, his eyesight. Strength comes with a conviction of God's sanction.

He recovered his old decisiveness none to soon for the good of the Company. The trade of New Archangel all but vanished in 1813, the news having reached the Pacific of the War of 1812 between Britain and the United States. Few American ships dared risk seizure by leaving the safety of neutral ports. And the news had come of Napoleon's invasion of Russia. Until that conflict was over, no ship from home could be expected. For a change Britain was on Russia's side, but that was not entirely advantageous to Baranov. He could not, for the time being, resume pressing for a realization of Rezanov's plans. The Columbia region was now under the British, who had taken Astoria. Hawaii was best left alone because of Britain's influence in that quarter. One complication Baranov brushed aside: he had no intention of considering the Americans his enemies because they were at war with his country's momentary ally.

Policy and strategy were both up to him. No answers to questions could be expected from Saint Petersburg in time to be of use. As of old, he made capital of misfortune. The situation afforded the Company a chance to acquire a first-rate merchant fleet. As he surmised, many a shipmaster idling at Canton and other neutral ports was rapidly going broke. To the lone American who made it past the gantlet of the British to New Archangel that spring, he let it be known he was in the market to buy or lease ships and to hire their captains and crews, who would be safe under the Company flag.

The word spread with a speed astonishing in view of the

immobilization of shipping. By summer's end three ships had made it past the watchful British, their captains ready to make a deal, and more followed. Baranov bought two of them outright, one an exceptionally fine three-masted schooner made of teak-wood. The others he put under lease, one a vessel belonging to Astor, who had directed his men to seek the protection of the Russians. He had seven vessels capable of high-seas voyaging at the close of 1813, and four for coastal navigation. More were to be acquired before the War of 1812 was over.

With no delay Baranov put each of his new masters and ships to work, sending them to the Philippines, Indonesia, Hawaii, and California. Fort Ross became an important port of call, Kuskov needing trade goods for his dealings with the Spanish. He was buying grain in quantities enough for Baranov to trans-ship some of it to Siberia. The otter-poaching along California was kept up, with the difference that the Aleut crews now worked under the Company flag. Baranov's one major loss due to the War of 1812 was the use of the American flag for the selling of furs at Canton. For the duration he had no alternative to sending all his furs to Okhotsk and thence to Kiakhta.

At the close of 1814, two years after his decision never again to resign, he could look back over his most profitable period. Despite the heaviest buying of ships in the Company's history, the high wages paid the American captains and crews, the loss of two ships, and the loss also of 800,000 rubles' worth of furs consigned to Okhotsk, the Company could pay a dividend of 1,250,000 rubles, a good round sum for those days.

The colony learned by the Pacific word-of-mouth news serv-ice how completely Napoleon had been defeated, how disas-trous for him had been his attempt to conquer Russia, but no first-hand account was received until November of 1814, when the first ship to come directly from Saint Petersburg in four years arrived at New Archangel. She was a vessel in keeping with the feeling of triumph in the air, a fine frigate bought from the defeated French and renamed *Suvorov* after one of Russia's historic military leaders. And everyone aboard her, from her captain, whose name was Lazarev, to her surgeon, whose name was Schaeffer, had seen action of one kind or another against Napoleon. They had all had a hand in bringing about the victory.

Never had more cannonading been heard in Sitka Sound. The guns of the fort saluted the *Suvorov* upon her arrival; she answered; then she was saluted by the other ships in the harbor and she answered them. It lasted for days, the cannon of the fort booming every time shore was visited or left by the brilliantly garbed and decorated officers. They were banqueted again and again at the castle, and the sailors were feasted in all the homes of New Archangel. Every man was asked to tell over and over about the battles in which he had fought. And so the colony presently knew almost as much about the war as these heroes, but many of them went on reliving the war just the same. It would be some time before they would allow themselves to think of much of anything else, notably the fact that the *Suvorov* belonged to the Company and that they were now all working for a merchant enterprise.

Some of the officers, among them Captain Lazarev himself, were highly amused by New Archangel. They jollied Baranov, plainly considering him a quaint old boy not worth taking seriously. Within Lazarev's circle the belief had grown strong that the Navy would presently have the colony. It was some time since Baranov had had to contend with the arrogance of his country's naval men. In the interval, having decided he was in America by God's will, he had worked a change in himself amounting to a difference in character. No longer was he in the least the man who had felt he could do nothing the time Kuskov was beaten by an officer. He considered the festivities over when Lazarev asked that a native girl be found for him, indicating that he expected to spend the winter idling in port. Baranov ordered him to take the *Suvorov* to the Pribilofs and bring back a load of sealskins.

The order touched off a contest that lasted through the winter, the *Suvorov* meanwhile remaining at New Archangel.

Apparently Lazarev thought it great sport to bait Baranov, publicly jeering at him and defying his authority to send the *Suvorov* anywhere. When warned that he would be reported, he replied that he intended to do the reporting and would say enough to have Baranov hanged.

In spring he finally went to the Pribilofs for the sealskins and on his return took on other furs for transportation to Saint Petersburg, but so great was the haggling between him and Baranov that in July the *Suvorov* was still at New Archangel. On the correct surmise that the War of 1812 was over, a number of American shipmasters had appeared. Lazarev, who spoke English, worked further mischief by advising some of the visitors to do things in a manner contrary to Baranov's advice and generally talking in a fashion to raise doubt as to who was now in command of the port.

The situation reached the explosive stage when Tlingits hawking fish and game were sold a keg of gunpowder aboard the American brig *Pedlar*. Not in years had an act of the sort taken place in plain view of New Archangel. The man responsible, Wilson Hunt, had every reason to know Baranov's violent feelings on the point. He had negotiated with him on this very issue as a representative of Astor, who shared the feeling. Hunt was, moreover, beholden to Baranov for protection through the recent war, the *Pedlar* having been under the Company flag. But Hunt had no personal liking for Baranov, and he was one of those who had been listening to Lazarev. Under the circumstances, his act was a gratuitous insult. Apprised of the occurrence, Baranov decided to remove all uncertainty as to who was in command. He ordered the seizure of the *Pedlar* on the grounds that a hostile act had been committed.

Word went out to all the ships in the harbor that any moves to help the *Pedlar* would be met with fire from the fort. To insure compliance from those aboard the *Suvorov*, the guns of the fort were trained full on her. Baranov's men took possession of the *Pedlar*, lowering her flag, spiking her guns, and removing her ammunition. Wilson Hunt escaped to another American vessel, where Baranov left him in the custody of her captain.

Some fifteen vessels were in the harbor that day, their rails no doubt crowded with men tensely watching what went on. There was drama enough. Lazarev, when he saw the guns of the fort trained on him, trained his on the fort. The counterthreat failed to influence Baranov, and throughout the afternoon's proceedings the frigate and the fort stood ready to pound each other to pieces. That evening, when the tension had subsided, Baranov dictated an order to Lazarev to begin on the morrow to discharge the cargo he still had aboard and otherwise to finish up his business. And there would be letters to be carried to Saint Petersburg, including a full report of all that had occurred.

At dawn Baranov was awakened with the news that the *Suvorov* had quietly weighed anchor and was heading out to sea. In a towering rage he ordered everyone in the settlement to grab muskets, pistols, whatever could shoot, pile into baidarkas, yawls, whatever could float, and go after the frigate. But she was already too distant to be reached even by the cannonballs sent whistling after her.

Left behind was the *Suvorov*'s surgeon, German-born Dr. Egor Schaeffer, who had not been a popular member of the ship's company. To Lazarev the loss was good riddance. And, in truth, Dr. Schaeffer was not a stable personality. He was not a man to be trusted far. But Baranov saw none of that.

Some time before, expressing distaste for Lazarev's behavior, a sure way to please Baranov under the circumstances, Schaeffer had asked to live ashore and was now ensconced at the castle, where he had been the pleasantest of guests, deferential and entertaining. Baranov had one blind spot when it came to judging men: he tended to equate erudition with integrity. Schaeffer could discourse for hours on science. He had a degree in natural science as well as medicine; he was an accomplished botanist; he was familiar with a number of languages, including English. Baranov was soon thinking of Schaeffer in relation to a very special problem.

Hawaii was much on Baranov's mind these days. It was clear

that Kamehameha had still not forgiven the Hagemeister episode six years before and Baranov's failure to explain or apologize. Company ships were doing a brisk business with the islands; Baranov even received an occasional greeting; but the greetings were perfunctory, the gestures of a polite man. The King had never resumed sending gifts or talking of exchanging visits. He was also wont to tell his foreign visitors that he had always been friendly to all nations and that, though he had rules such as the one against foreign settlements, surely that was no reason why anyone should have said that what his government could not obtain by persuasion it would take by force, a clear reference to Hagemeister.

Tempting though it may well have been to Baranov at this late date to leave well enough alone, he was still constrained to consider how to fulfill the Company's desires for a trading station on the islands, land for a plantation, and a share in the rich sandalwood trade. And lately a situation had arisen that could not be ignored. Russia had been given cause for complaint. A Company ship with a rich cargo had met grief on the island of Kauai, a part of Hawaii over which Kamehameha had never entirely succeeded in extending his sway. It was ruled by a bitter rival of his, Kaumualii by name, who also called himself a king. He had seized the ship and the cargo; Kamehameha could do nothing. By all the reports Baranov had had, he would have to use force on Kaumualii to obtain reparations. But Baranov wished to pursue no such course without approval from Kamehameha, who would be understandably wary. It was a serious and delicate situation.

It struck Baranov that in Schaeffer he had the perfect emissary, one who might even undo all the harm done in the past and obtain for the Company everything desired on the islands. The King had always especially welcomed scientists, and a physician he would regard as a priceless gift, having lost the one he had had. Moreover, as a botanist Schaeffer would be the ideal man to run a plantation. When told all the circumstances, he was eager, understanding what glory would be his in the event of success.

His instructions were many. He must conduct himself with the utmost circumspection. He was not to bring up the matter of the ship and cargo until certain he had the confidence of the King, whose foreign advisers were also to be cultivated. In the event it was found that great force had to be used on Kaumualii, reparation might consist of his very domain. Kauai Island was not under British protection, was rich in sandalwood, and was said to have fine sites for plantations. Baranov extended Schaeffer large credit on the Company, appointed him a special agent, gave him gifts to present, and, so sure was he of Schaeffer's success, told him that in spring he would have at his disposal two ships and a work force of sixty men. Schaeffer sailed for Hawaii that fall of 1815.

His reception was all that could have been desired. Kamehameha, who had grown old and portly, was charmed by him and pleased to have Baranov's message of friendship. Schaeffer was approved as a resident Company agent, given a place to live at Honolulu, and permitted to botanize throughout the islands. Yet he chose to view as a menace Kamehameha's longtime prime minister and interpreter in English, ex-sailor John Young, who gave him the one routine caution that His Majesty wished no foreign settlements.

Deciding to try settling the matter of the ship and cargo by direct negotiation, Schaeffer visited Kauai Island, finding King Kaumualii unsurrounded by foreign advisers, able to understand English up to a point, and so disposed to be agreeable that Schaeffer obtained a reparation amounting to 40,000 rubles. Kaumualii, he found, wanted very much to cultivate him, and he was entirely willing to be cultivated, having decided he had got as far as he ever would with Kamehameha. What emerged from his long talks with Kaumualii was wildly, explosively at variance with his orders.

Kaumualii gave the Company, through Schaeffer, the permanent right to maintain a trading station and land for a plantation, for this purpose giving indeed "a whole province," with the natives to work the soil, and the port of Hanalei. The Company also obtained a monopoly of all the sandalwood. On legal grounds, at any rate, Kamehameha could not object; the domain was not his. But there was more, a great deal more. Kaumualii was to be aided in making himself king of the greater part of Hawaii in place of Kamehameha. This was set forth in a "secret treaty" written by Schaeffer, who was to be dictator. In return for Russian aid, which was to consist of ships and arms, the subjected islands were to be placed under Russia, with large privileges guaranteed the company. In a formal, written declaration, Kaumualii acknowledged himself a vassal of Tsar Alexander.

Schaeffer informed Baranov only partially of these developments. He had decided to work directly through Saint Petersburg. In August of 1816 he wrote Company headquarters, sending the letter via Canton by American ship and arranging to withhold the facsimile from Baranov for several months. With the letter he sent a copy of Kaumualii's declaration of submission. Schaeffer asked for speedy approval "and to have sent here from Saint Petersburg two good ships with reliable crews, well armed. . . ."

Without waiting for a reply, apparently in the entire certainty his coup would be hailed a work of genius, Schaeffer proceeded to consolidate his position on Kauai, having received the two ships and the sixty Aleuts and Russians Baranov had promised to send him in spring. He laid out his plantation, for which he had gained additional acreage; he put up buildings; he erected fortifications. Then, suddenly, it was apparent that Kamehameha had learned the full truth, which was not being kept very secret on Kauai. Kaumualii received a peremptory order to expel Schaeffer. Kaumualii only laughed, and so did Schaeffer.

The foreign shipmasters were not amused. They were now denied the sandalwood of Kauai, and to know the truth of what was going on they needed only to see the forts going up and the

Russian flag above. The Pacific rocked as word spread that Russia seemed to be showing her hand in Hawaii at last. Shipmasters long friendly to Baranov gathered grimly in support of Kamehameha, who was as sad as he was angry. Kaumualii grew uneasy. No aid was evident from Saint Petersburg. Schaeffer, apparently unmindful of his increasing danger, allowed himself to become tyrannical, causing some of his own men to hate him and alienating the islanders.

To no evident regret on his part, or that of his subjects either, Kaumualii finally consented to the expulsion of Schaeffer in May of 1817, just a year after making his first agreement with him. Schaeffer tried making a stand, but the island population was too much for him. He and the men were forced to make their way as best they could by a leaking ship to Honolulu, where the populace went up in arms on learning that Schaeffer was near. He might have been killed but for the American captain who gave him passage to Canton.

In this humiliating fashion the book closed on Russian hopes in Hawaii, which was now best left alone. All that Kaumualii ever got from Saint Petersburg was an array of gifts, including a scarlet cloak, and a polite refusal of his offer of vassalage. Not that all the Russians left the islands immediately. A number had to remain eight months after Schaeffer's flight to remove Company property and otherwise clean up. They were in charge of Timofei Tarakanov, who demonstrated that, for all his illiteracy and humble status as a promyshlennik, he was a first-rate diplomat. When he and the last of the men departed, around January of 1818, it was to the regret of the islanders, and Kamehameha had been brought to see that no harm had been intended by Baranov, who was sent expressions of renewed friendship from his old friend the King. But beyond the relief to his feelings, there was to be no meaning in it for Baranov. His enemies had gained the upper hand.

XI

Accolade

Everything about it suggested luxury. It was a beautiful building even for Saint Petersburg, a city striving to outdo the world in elegance of architecture. And it had the smartest of addresses: 72 Moika Quai, a part of town where Tsar Alexander himself was wont to take his daily stroll. Formerly a private mansion, it retained an air of leisure despite the comings and goings of liveried messengers and the line of carriages forever out front. Its importance was indicated by the insignia in gold relief adorning its façade, the double-headed imperial eagle, which no other business firm could use. It was the headquarters of the Russian-American Company.

The decor within upheld the city's reputation for living on the most lavish scale in Europe. The executives, the secretaries, the translators, accountants, and other members of the exclusively male staff worked amid opulent surroundings. Rare rugs, costly furniture, objets d'art graced the foyer, the showrooms, the offices, the board room where the directors met and the stock-holders periodically gathered, gazed down upon by Founder Rezanov from his portrait. On occasion the directors met in conjunction with the State Council, a committee of three stock-holders high in government service, one of. them appointed by the Crown. This was the advisory body in political matters, the link with the government once represented by Rezanov alone.

The head of the organization was handsome, urbane Mikhail Buldakov, who had successively been re-elected chairman of the board ever since 1800, and the year was now 1817. He had come some distance since the day he migrated to Irkutsk as a young merchant in search of his fortune, which he found when he married Shelikhov's oldest daughter. The Company had become the foremost factor in the fur trade of the world, for the time being surpassing the far older Hudson's Bay Company, its only comparable rival. Branch-office buildings were maintained at Moscow and Irkutsk, warehouses at several other places, and agents abroad.

Profits had been such that nearly half the income had been going for the upkeep of 72 Moika Quai, without depriving the stockholders of dividends, which at times had run as high as a third of the cost of their shares. For themselves the directors had voted salaries of 15,000 rubles a year, with 25,000 to the chairman, plus bonuses as high as 100,000 rubles. But no such largesse had ever been voted the source of the wealth, namely, the colony, which no present member of the board had ever troubled to visit, Buldakov not excepted. The colony still had no physician, no real program for education, none of the Company-financed benefits planned by Rezanov, who had not lived to lay down regulations compelling the directors to spend the money. At the time he designed the charter he had been concerned more with defining the Company's privileges than its duties.

It now looked as if the directors might have to pay for their negligence. Of late they had been meeting with increasing frequency and anxiety to discuss a most unsettling prospect: the loss of the colony. The charter, which dated from 1799, had a twenty-year limit. The period would be over in 1819, two years hence. Before then the government must decide whether to renew the charter or allow it to expire and make some other arrangement for the governing of the colony. The Navy was bidding for the privilege.

The Russian Navy had never had much peacetime sea room, and thoughts of the Pacific, where it could have large freedom of movement and the excuse of guarding Russia's one overseas possession, had been on its mind since the time of Catherine the

Great. It had been a galling thing to see the waters of Russian America turned into a merchant's lake with the creation of the Company. The resentment had been such that very few officers had ever accepted the Company's generous terms for service. Now that the Company's charter neared its end, the naval politicians were busy indeed, the more so for the fact that the Napoleonic wars had left the Navy at maximum strength, with no future as things were.

The tactic was to expose the shortcomings of the Company. In this endeavor the leading spokesman was a man singularly devoted to advancing the Navy, one of its best speakers and writers, a master of invective, and no respecter of merchants in general. And Captain Vasilii Golovnin knew the colony, having visited it twice, each time gathering detrimental information, notably on the lack of physicians. There was no refuting what he had to say on points of the sort. He also went back over the past, having acquainted himself with the writings and doings of Shelikhov, who was held up as prototypic of merchant rule: ". . . As the shopman in the marketplace makes the sign of the cross and calls on God to witness why he sells goods a few kopeks dearer, so Shelikhov used the name of Christ and our sacred faith to deceive the government. . . ." Golovnin's harshest words were for Baranov, whom he declared to be in need of investigation for criminal wrongdoing.

Attacks on Baranov were also attacks on the charter and the directors, who alone were vested with the privilege of naming colonial governors. Buldakov in particular had been insistent on keeping Baranov all these years, against opposition from the Church as well as the Navy, for reasons that came down to his ability as a profit-maker. But self-preservation was now uppermost in the minds of the directors, and Baranov himself seemed to be trying to make it easier for them to think of deposing him at last. The end of the Schaeffer affair was not yet known, but by all indications the man was not someone to whom Baranov should have extended all that credit on the Company. There was also Baranov's conduct during the Lazarev episode, which had given the Navy fresh ammunition. However badly Lazarev had behaved at New Archangel, the fact remained that Baranov had fired on one of his country's own ships. It was to be wondered if he was still in his right mind.

The fate of the Company seemed sealed when the government announced that it would defer the question of a new charter until 1821 and meanwhile have a thorough inspection made of the colony. The man chosen to do the inspecting and write the report was Vasilii Golovnin. The glum directors were moved to consider a compromise. The thought was to keep intact the structure of the Company, with the colony given over to the Navy, and affairs at 72 Moika left under the present administration. The step could be taken immediately by naming a naval man to Baranov's post. The price was the aid of the Navy in seeking a renewal of the charter, which would be rewritten in a manner to satisfy the critics.

The Navy, which had no mechanism of its own for making the colony pay, may itself have suggested the peculiar union. At any rate it was agreeable, the more so, no doubt, for the reason that the association was likely to be profitable. The colony's naval governor and his aides would be made Company stockholders and, in addition, would be paid high salaries. Business matters would be in the hands of a civilian administrator. As its replacement for Baranov, the Navy chose the officer who, in Company service eight years before, had ruined relations with Hawaii, namely, Leontii Hagemeister. He now ranked as a captain-lieutenant, by virtue of his war record, and stood high in the estimation of his colleagues, though why so poor a diplomat should have done so is a mystery. Perhaps his familiarity with the colony was the reason he was chosen.

The day the board met to vote on the appointment, Buldakov's conscience could hardly have been easy. As he was well aware, though they had never met, Baranov considered him a close personal friend, one in whom he had the greatest trust, as he evinced when he named him co-guardian of his children in his will. The matter before the board should have been simple enough. Baranov would be seventy this year; no excuse for retiring him needed to be given. By voting him a generous pension the directors would have met their obligation. But Hagemeister would not let things be done that way. He wished to go to the colony under secret orders, which he would reveal when he thought proper.

Hagemeister was a complete believer in the allegation that Baranov had embezzled a large fortune, presumably on deposit in foreign banks. When Baranov had been exposed as a crook and the money recovered, he would then be told he was no longer governor. Evidently Baranov had once done something which had left Hagemeister revengeful. It was so ordered by the board. Baranov's "fitness to remain in office" was to be investigated, after which Hagemeister was to appoint himself or someone else. The majority of the directors seem to have feared what he would find; Baranov was voted no pension, not even a letter of thanks.

Baranov had become a wisp of a man, stooped and frail. Sometimes he felt so unwell he stayed abed all day. Yet, as always, he carried the entire load of the administration with only the assistance of his nephew Kuglinov. He had become very religious. The previous year, 1816, in response to the request he made three years before, a priest had finally been sent to New Archangel. The piety Baranov began manifesting when he decided it was by God's will he was in America found full expression after the arrival of Father Aleksei Sokolov.

Providing a church had been his absorbing interest through the winter. Characteristically, he had not looked to the Company to furnish the money. He had an old ship hauled up on land and remodeled for the purpose. He had also devised many of the furnishings, giving every detail loving care. The shipyard foundry had cast the bell; the blacksmiths fashioned the eucharistic vessels from Spanish silver. The vestments were Chinese silk, on which he had Aleut women do such fine beadwork that it looked like heavy painting on the cloth. He had called the day the church was dedicated the happiest of his life.

June brought him the news of Schaeffer's expulsion from Kauai. He was glad. The episode had done much to age him. He called Schaeffer "that traitor," but he blamed himself. He had chosen the man. It made him sad to learn how Kamehameha felt and how many of his old American friends regarded him with suspicion. But he was more philosophical about it than he would have been in years gone by. After all, he was not the Almighty and able to foresee everything.

June also brought him a rumor from Okhotsk that he was about to be replaced, and by Hagemeister. He waved it away. That kind of thing had been heard for years. And these days, with the approach of charter-renewal time, wild stories of all kinds should be expected. Hagemeister! That showed what preposterous things they would hear. And in the event of any change, he would be first to know. Buldakov would unfailingly inform him.

Whatever his end might be, it could not be in dishonor, of that he was sure. He had a realist's awareness of the worth his country should put on his achievements. By means he had often had to devise himself, he had put Russian America on the political map, formally enlarging the empire by nearly a third. There were now twenty-four posts, not counting Fort Ross, dispersed as far west as the Kurils, some of them one-man stations, to be sure, but nevertheless evidences beyond challenge that the territory was Russian.

He had done it all with no more than a handful of men from his own country. In all his twenty-seven years in the colony, he had never had more than four hundred men from Russia at his command at any one time. Moreover, few of them had stayed as long as fifteen years. His stable personnel, numbering perhaps a thousand, consisted of natives and part-bloods whose education had been largely by his personal generosity.

As he had paid for the founding of a school at Kodiak, he

had done the same for the one at New Archangel. He, and not the Company, had also been paying most of the expenses of the gifted boys, among them the son of the Tlingit chief, who had been sent to Russia for advanced work in navigation, accounting, and other fields. He had spent his money on the colony as if on a beloved woman. A number of his shares in the Company had gone to such men as Kuskov when they had threatened to leave. He had spent a small fortune getting many of his men out of hopeless debt at the commissary. And there had been the large sum he spent importing cattle for the benefit of the Aleuts, his gift to them as a people. But then, the directors were certain to see to it he would never be in want.

For Anna, who had gone on living at Kodiak, he had provided a trust fund. He wished he could assure the future of his children with equal simplicity. Antipatr, who was now twenty, ached to enter the Naval Academy, but so far no officer of sufficient rank had been found who would sponsor his admission. Irina was fifteen, of marriageable age. She was a ravishing little beauty. dark-eyed, dark-haired, and fine-featured. She was also gay, good hearted, and well-mannered. She was still the pupil of the German governess who had been found for her and who had made something of a pianist of her.

Irina Baranova was loved throughout the colony and spoke many of the languages. And as for her father, he doted on her. She alone could handle him in his more cantankerous moods. When the castle had guests and she played piano for them, he was ready to burst with pride. He was also an ogre where she was concerned, fiercely shielding her from attentions unwelcome to him. But for whom he was keeping her, even he had to wonder. In this remote place few suitors could be expected to appear who would match her in attainments and station.

In July the Company frigate *Suvorov* arrived from Saint Petersburg in command of a Lieutenant Panafidin. She brought goods and letters, including one from headquarters disturbing to Baranov. He thought of that rumor from Okhotsk as he read that Captain Hagemeister was to be expected. He was on his way, in command of another frigate belonging to the Company, the *Kutuzov*. Pending his arrival, Baranov read, the *Suvorov* must be held in port. That was a strange sort of order. Frigate crews were large; keeping them idle was expensive.

Baranov questioned Panafidin, who knew what was afoot, had instructions to keep it a tight secret, and felt uncomfortable. When had Hagemeister rejoined the Company? Recently. When was he likely to arrive? In fall, perhaps November. November? That was four months hence. There were furs to be sent to Saint Petersburg. Why should the *Suvorov* remain idle all that while? Perhaps Captain Hagemeister wished all naval personnel on hand at his arrival. Baranov then bluntly asked what was going on, why they were saying at Okhotsk that Hagemeister was about to supplant him. To hear the secret was somehow known at a place as remote as Okhotsk so startled Panafidin that his expression was confirmation. His words were that he could give no explanation.

Baranov was grim. He had indeed been asleep. Yet, if it was true, why had he heard nothing official? Evidently Buldakov knew nothing about this. The Navy must be up to something monstrously underhanded. Well, he would have the truth when Hagemeister arrived. As was his custom, no matter his feelings, he banqueted his visitors. The *Suvorov*'s officers, especially the second-in-command, Lieutenant Yanovskii, were extremely appreciative of Irina's presence, giving her performance at the piano prolonged applause.

Before he left that evening Lieutenant Yanovskii asked if he might come again, call on Irina, who was delighted. Over the days that followed, Baranov got over his irritation at the prospect of having the *Suvorov* in port four months and presently was beaming. It looked as if his prayers had been answered. This young man seemed everything he had hoped for. Nor was he mistaken. Semyon Ivanovich Yanovskii was not only handsome and pleasant, liked by all classes, he had an excellent mind, he was widely read, he was exceptionally honest and straightforward. His future in the service looked bright. By October, when it was clear that his daughter and Yanovskii were madly in love, Baranov was ready to smile even at Hagemeister.

November was nearly over before the *Kutuzov* hove in. Panafidin hurried aboard to warn Hagemeister that his secret was out. It was known throughout the colony, Panafidin had ascertained, and there was widespread uneasiness, no one seemingly wishing naval rule. Hagemeister must have cursed at length. Part of his plan had been to have himself in control and Baranov shipped out before the colony in general knew. And now, with the old man on guard, it would be many times more difficult to ascertain where he kept his hidden loot, the clues to which were presumably in his books. Having those books audited was foremost on Hagemeister's agenda. He had even brought an accountant for the purpose.

How he thought out what he should now do, Hagemeister revealed when he had come ashore and was seeing Baranov. Panafidin, he said, had told him about the nonsense being talked. To tell the truth, he did have a special commission, but only to investigate conditions, the board wanting his independent report as an aid in obtaining a second charter. He hoped he would be able to say he had been freely allowed to glance over the books.

Baranov, who had listened with mounting certainty that the goings-on were as underhanded as he had guessed, snapped that he would turn over his books when his successor appeared, not before. Hagemeister had not the wit to reveal his orders then and there. For some reason, that did not seem clever enough to him.

He spent the next month, through Christmas, going about, questioning the employees, apparently in hope of hearing something to justify seizing the books. He learned only how extensive was the dread of naval rule and that he personally was cordially disliked. He did know when he was defeated. He recognized that for him to take over would cause such disaffection alike among natives and Russians as to dislocate the Company's operation. Then Panafidin came to him to say that Yanovskii requested permission to ask Baranov for his daughter's hand. As the superior officer, Hagemeister alone could approve the marriage of anyone on active duty.

Up to this point he could hardly have viewed Yanovskii's romance with much favor. A personal relationship on the part of one of his officers with Baranov was not desirable. But now, suddenly, he saw things differently. He had one of the few brilliant thoughts he seems ever to have had: Allow the marriage, then name Yanovskii governor. As Baranov's son-in-law, he would win the colony over to naval rule.

Yanovskii must have been well taken aback by the proposal. Even though he was Panafidin's executive officer, he seems not to have known the exact nature of Hagemeister's mission. Everything had to be explained to him, down to the fact that Baranov had been lied to. When the debate was over, Hagemeister had agreed to tell the truth as soon as Baranov gave his consent to the marriage.

Baranov was only too happy to give his consent, readily agreeing to an early date for the wedding: January 7—the year was now 1818. Now it was up to Hagemeister to do his part. He did it in a manner hardly envisioned by Yanovskii. Without apology or preamble, he laid his orders before the old man, brusquely informing him of the arrangement he had made for taking over the governorship and directing him to turn over his books within twelve hours.

It was more than Baranov could grasp at once. Was this truly Buldakov's signature? If so, why had he not been informed in regular fashion? Why had lies been told him? Above all, why was he ordered to give up his books in twelve hours? Only thieves were told things like that. When, finally, he understood, he had not the strength to master the supreme disillusionment of his life. He collapsed, crying like a child.

The castle servants put him to bed, and there he remained the next day and the next, staring at nothing, responsive to no one. Irina and Yanovskii could only hope that he would not emerge

with feelings so bitter he would withdraw his consent. Hagemeister behaved as if he had done nothing untoward. Functioning as governor for the time being, he ordered the *Suvorov*
readied for sailing to Saint Petersburg with his report and the
colony's furs. When, finally, Baranov arose, he sounded calm
and collected. He would, he said, see Kirill Khlebnikov with no
further delay.

Khlebnikov was the man to whom Baranov had been directed
by Hagemeister to turn over his books. He was the accountant
who had been brought to do the auditing, and he was to remain
as business manager under the new order. He was a friendly,
able man; he had long been with the Company and had been at
New Archangel before. Baranov received him cordially and
gave him the keys to the cupboards containing the books, with
an apology for the condition in which the older ones would be
found. Paper had been scarce with him in the early days. At
times he had had no more than scraps on which to keep the
accounts. But he would aid in deciphering the colony's twenty-
eight-year financial history. The work would begin as soon as he
had seen to the wedding of his daughter.

Unquestionably his desire not to complicate matters for Irina
influenced him to accept the situation. The little church in the
old ship was packed as Father Sokolov married the couple, who
then left on a wedding trip which, for Yanovskii, was also to be
an inspection tour of the colony. They planned to go as far as
the Pribilofs and, of course, to visit Kodiak so that Anna could
meet her son-in-law and old Father German give him his blessing. All the indications were that wherever they went they
would be met with great ceremony. Everyone was prepared to
accept the authority of the man who had married the daughter
of Aleksandr Andreevich.

When, near summer's end, the couple returned to New Archangel, Baranov and Khlebnikov were still at work on the books.
They were to be at it a total of seven months, into September.
Baranov's long lapses into reminiscences accounted for some of
the delay. Khlebnikov listened closely, drawing from him the

story of his beginnings and those of the colony. He was one day to write the only primary biography of Aleksandr Baranov.

With reason, Khlebnikov could admire his subject. The books, when the audit was over, were found to be in almost perfect balance. The figures were off in only one small supply account. Reported Khlebnikov, "In the cash accounts, involving millions, I found not one single discrepancy." Millions indeed. Baranov had produced wealth aggregating nearly 30,000,000 rubles. His net profit on the goods shipped him from Russia, showing his talent as a trader, was close to 90 per cent. Yet, far from having a fortune in foreign banks, as had been suggested, it now was clear that he was a poor man. He had given away so much of his cash and so many of his shares, it was even a question how he was going to live. Hagemeister was angered by the revelation. Baranov had to be guilty of something, he felt. He began sequestering records for examination in Saint Petersburg.

Baranov made no secret of his bitterness at having been voted no pension. The directors, he remarked, might at least have provided him with some small job. His problem concerned everyone. His means were too slender for him to live in any comfort in Russia; it looked as if he would have to remain in the colony. His own children were against that, foreseeing endless trouble. By interfering with Yanovskii, who had taken office, he was already showing he would never be able to keep his hands off affairs. He was testy with those who argued with him until, suddenly, he had what seemed to him the solution. He would go live in Hawaii. A man could live there on little, it was said. Kamehameha had forgiven him; they were of an age; they would have a wonderful time living out their lives together.

Everyone was aghast. The Schaeffer affair was fresh in mind; foreign governments were certain to ask Saint Petersburg what Baranov, of all people, was doing in Hawaii. But he would listen to no argument. Saint Petersburg had fired him; he could do as he pleased. At this juncture Captain Vasilii Golovnin arrived in command of a warship, having begun the inspection of the colony he had been commissioned to make by the government. Baranov, Hagemeister told him, must somehow be gotten out of the Pacific.

Golovnin, who had heretofore maintained that all connections with Baranov must be severed, went to him with the offer to see that the Company give him a position in Saint Petersburg. He was, Baranov replied, allowing no one to beg for him. It was his duty, Golovnin insisted; he had no right to deny his country the benefit of his knowledge and experience. The argument, which had always prevailed with Baranov in the past, might not have done so now had Golovnin not put him greatly in his debt by settling his last worry about his children. Antipatr would be sponsored at the Naval Academy by Golovnin, who went so far as to arrange to begin the boy's instruction himself by enlisting him with the personnel of his warship.

A month later, on November 27, the *Kutuzov* sailed for Saint Petersburg, and Baranov with her. All concerned had had a time helping him maintain his resolution. He had often been reduced to tears, so many had been the farewells he had had to say. Even the surviving Tlingit chiefs who had directed the Sitka massacre had come to see him, expressing the hope that the past would be forgiven.

Hagemeister commanded the *Kutuzov*. He saw to it that his principal passenger enjoyed little about the voyage. The usual stop at Hawaii was not made. Thus Baranov's hope of finally meeting Kamehameha was shattered. After ten stormy weeks, with a stop only at Manila, Java was reached, and Baranov at last saw Batavia, a name that had once filled him with such desire to see the world. He was now too old to enjoy it and too sick. His spirits were not lifted by the news that Kamehameha's death had occurred just after they might have met.

Five prolonged weeks Hagemeister stayed at Batavia, leisurely dickering with officials of the Dutch East India Company, either indifferent to the effect on Baranov or hopeful of hastening his death. Wrote Khlebnikov accusingly, "The climate of Batavia is known to be trying to any European, especially the advanced in years. It was worse for a man accustomed to the life Baranov had lived."

He was running a fever when the *Kutuzov* put to sea again. Four days later he was dead. The date was April 12, 1819, according to an official announcement later made by the Company. His body was committed to the Indian Ocean.

His son-in-law served a bare two years as his successor. Replaced in 1820, even before the Company was granted its new charter, Yanovskii returned to Russia with his exotic Irina. It was not that he had governed badly. He had done very well, earning everyone's liking, effecting a smooth transition to naval rule. But with that there were those who considered he had served his purpose. His marriage was seen as an undesirable link with the past.

XII

God Save the Tsar

The choice of man to replace Yanovskii as governor of Russian America was made with great care. It was evidently seen there could be no more Hagemeisters. Captain Matvei Muraviev, who came of a famous and brilliant family, was able, popular, scholarly, and strongly liberal of view. He was, in fact, one of the Navy's best men. He was chosen in the early months of 1820, before the new charter was ratified but in accordance with its provisions, by consultation between a naval committee and the company's board. The board retained the power to appoint, providing it chose from a submitted list of naval officers ranking no lower than captain.

The Company was going to have to spend a deal more money than of old on the colony, for churches, schools, and, at last, medical services. The cost of the colonial administration would, moreover, be much higher. The governor was to be paid 40,000 rubles a year, eight times Baranov's salary. He was to be given a number of aides, including an assistant governor, all from the Navy and likewise well paid. Not again would the staff at New Archangel be small. And no one worked on shares any more. All employees were paid salaries. That completed the break with the promyshlennik past.

Arriving at the colony in September of 1820, Muraviev began making changes at once, having orders to proceed without waiting for ratification of the charter. He inspected the posts, ordered much new construction, reorganized the administration.

One of his changes, his first, did not have quite the effect he expected. On the theory it would win the Tlingits' friendship, he abolished Baranov's rule forbidding them to live close to New Archangel. With alacrity they accepted the invitation, soon having some fifty of their communal dwellings close by, so close that Muraviev had ruefully to strengthen the walls of the settlement and order constant vigilance on the part of the guard. The Tlingits made themselves useful as suppliers of game and fish but, as their behavior indicated, it would be some time before they gave up the thought of seizing New Archangel at the first opportunity.

The barbaric air given the exterior of the settlement by the terrifying heraldic devices of the Tlingits was in queer contrast to the new order of social life within. Culture had come to New Archangel, putting it on the path of becoming what one writer was to call, not too wildly, "the Paris of the Pacific." Wives and children had been brought by the naval men, and all strove to live as well as they could according to the ways of upper-class Saint Petersburg, which was home to most of them and the place where they had all gone to school. The houses were furnished with a new elegance, as was Baranov's Castle, a name Muraviev kept. Evenings were given over to musicales, charades, whist, and balls attended in formal dress, with French commonly heard. But no foreigners were entertained during the five years Muraviev was governor.

When Muraviev came it was with orders to initiate an astonishing change of policy scheduled to be made official the following year, 1821. Foreigners were to be excluded. Russian American waters were to be closed, and by means of patrolling warships. He must, Muraviev had been told, halt the buying from Americans and all others, at the same time advising them not to return. He put as good a face on it as he could. For this part of his assignment he had no enthusiasm. It was a reflection of a situation at home about which he and many like him were unhappy in the extreme.

One expression of the bitterness was a small but true revolutionary movement taking shape among the younger nobles. The Decembrists, they would be called. Muraviev may have been one. As was to come out at their trials, the Decembrists numbered several naval officers and members of the Company staff. Intellectuals all, they were Russia's angry young men. Their anger centered on Tsar Alexander I, who had now been on the throne nineteen years.

The feelings of everyone where Alexander was concerned were the stronger for the recollection of the great joy there had been at his accession, following the assassination of his father, Paul, in March of 1801. Tyranny seemed a thing of the past that day. Russia was promised a place among the advanced nations of the world. He would, Alexander proclaimed, restore and finish the work of reform begun by his grandmother Catherine. The country was stirred to its depths. Over 20,000,000 serfs cried for freedom and land of their own. Taxation was heaviest on the poorest. The machinery of government was a jumble of unrelated parts. The law consisted of 30,000 decrees, many contradictory, which had not been codified in 250 years. So slow was justice that 100,000 men awaited trial. The changing of all these things was encompassed in the promises of Alexander, who spoke of abolishing the autocracy itself in favor of constitutional government.

Tall, twenty-four years young, handsome as an archangel, he had personified the hope he inspired. His every public appearance was greeted with the wildest acclaim. It was as if Christ had returned. People unhorsed his carriage and took the traces themselves; they kissed the dust his shoes had pressed. His admirers abroad included Thomas Jefferson, with whom he corresponded. It was seen as a mighty portent for the world that he and Jefferson came to power the same month of the same year.

For the first eleven years of his reign he was distracted and inhibited by Napoleon, who furnished a constant menace that forbade drastic alterations that might weaken the Russian state. Conceivably the story of Alexander might have been different had it not been for the wear and frustration of those years. His early acts indicated no instability of purpose. He put the conservatives out of power, surrounding himself with young advisers called by the reactionaries "the Jacobin gang." He freed the press, put down the secret police, welcomed foreigners, allowed travel abroad. He partly reformed the government and reconstituted education, spending vast sums for the creation of scores of lower schools and four new universities. There was more, and hope in him was sustained also by the work that was begun on a document granting civil rights with the intention of making it the nation's Magna Charta. Still another document was a charter based in part on the constitution of the United States.

It was a glorious period, those early years of the reign. Saint Petersburg advanced to second place among the cultured capitals of Europe. The liberated press blossomed, writers multiplied, discussion flourished. The exciting name was United States of America. Even the peasants seemed to know something about it. A shipmaster named John D'Wolf, who traversed Siberia in 1807, the first American to do so, told of encountering eager curiosity about him and his country in the remotest places. How he wished, he wrote, that he could have known the language and have answered all the questions. Wherever he went he was honored in a fashion unprecedented for a foreigner of any station. People opened their houses to him, officials tendered him banquets, he was even invited to be godfather at an Orthodox christening.

Pride was great over the fact that the empire was partly in the New World. Alexander underscored the feeling when he put the Russian-American Company under his "highest protection" and himself became a stockholder. And now the Company could claim to have an American on the board. He was Benedict Cramer, Jr., representative in Russia of the banking firm in which he was a partner, Cramer, Smith and Company. He was to serve on the board some twenty years, until 1825. His name, in practiced Russian script, was affixed even to orders sent the colony.

The official policy regarding the United States was friendly in the extreme. Alexander's government had taken the position that the infant republic on the other side of the globe was to be fostered and protected. One reason was unsentimental: the mutual antipathy to Britain, whose avowed aim it was to strangle American commerce. In 1809 John Quincy Adams became American minister to Russia, a post he was to hold nearly five years. "Our attachment to the United States is obstinate, more obstinate than you are aware of," the future United States president was told by Count Nikolai Rumiantsev, Minister of Commerce, Chancellor of the Empire, one of the nation's foremost liberals, and the chief architect of the policy. Rumiantsev explained the motivation in detail at his first private conversation with Adams, who noted it in his diary, as was his careful habit.

"He assured me," Adams wrote, "of his great attachment to the system of friendly intercourse with the United States and his conviction of long standing that the interests of Russia perfectly harmonized." Britain's "exclusive maritime pretensions and views of usurpation upon the rights of other nations" made it "essential to Russia that some great commercial state should be supported" as her rival. Fostering American trade was accordingly "to the highest interests of Russia," since they were certain never to be enemies, in Rumiantsev's opinion. Said he, Russia and the United States "could never in any manner be dangerous to each other."

The attachment was indeed "obstinate." It was not cooled by Washington's discourteous refusal to pass legislation forbidding traders going to Russian America from dealing in rum and firearms. By 1811 the trade with Russia was worth $6,000,000 to the United States, which went far to compensate for Britain's activities. That year at least a hundred American vessels visited the Baltic. Adams, whose years in Russia extended through the period of Napoleon's invasion in 1812, heard the note of friendship sounded personally and often by Alexander, who made him an occasional companion on his daily strolls. Preoccupied though he was with the invasion, and despite the fact he was then in alliance with Britain, Alexander offered himself as mediator in the War of 1812 between the United States and Britain. Nothing came of it because London felt that Alexander was too sympathetic with United States views on neutral rights.

Alexander gave all his attention to the international scene, following the final defeat of Napoleon. He had emerged the most powerful monarch in Europe, and he would, he stated, work for world peace, which he declared could be achieved through a true application of Christian principles. The league of nations that was formed to keep the peace was named the Holy Alliance. But it was now clear that Alexander was not the man he had been in 1801. Strange things had happened within him. Liberalism had fallen from him like a cloak he had always found uncomfortable. His Holy Alliance became a device for the preservation of absolutism in the world.

Russia was not left even half reformed. Much that had been done was undone. Liberals in the government, notably Rumiantsev, were thrust aside, conservatives brought forward. In order to devote himself wholly to Europe, Alexander appointed a virtual vice-tsar over domestic affairs, choosing the man who had been lackey to his father. He was Aleksei Arakcheev, a name that stood for tyranny, bigotry, and isolationism. The press was stifled, the secret police given new vigor. Again it was difficult for Russians to go abroad, for visitors to enter the country. Not even the universities were immune from Arakcheev; foreign teachers were dismissed, subjects such as Newtonian physics eliminated lest they corrupt the pious.

The great bulk of the people, having no way to organize, had despairingly to resign themselves. Not so the angry young men of the upper class, the Decembrists, a name given them by revolutionists of another generation. They formed various groups with various names, in and out of Saint Petersburg, among them princes and barons by ancient title. They were the first to plot on Russia's behalf in terms of the intellect and not simply to substitute one tsar for another. They talked of constitutions, of giving the people leadership, and of assassinating Alexander, who was informed of their doings by the police but would take no action. Said this curiously tortured man, he could not punish men for thinking as he once had done.

It was hardly surprising that members of the Company staff should interest themselves in the Decembrist movement. The merchant class had most to lose by the prevailing reaction. How the wind was now blowing was indicated by the fact that as well-known an enemy of merchants as Captain Vasilii Golovnin was chosen by the government to inspect Russian America as a preliminary step in deciding whether to grant the Company a second charter. To be sure, the directors saved the Company by taking the politically powerful Navy into partnership but, as they were now to discover, the price would be larger than they had thought. They were not to retain control over trade policy.

On his return to Saint Petersburg from the Pacific in 1819, his work of inspection over, Golovnin brought back the startling information that seizure of the colony by the United States was imminent. The Americans were everywhere; they had been allowed freely to ascertain the strength of all the installations; for years they had been committing the hostile act of selling the natives firearms—to prepare them to be allies, no doubt. There was the fact that Washington had refused to restrain the traffic, notwithstanding consequences such as the Sitka massacre.

Steps should forthwith be taken to exclude foreigners, Golovnin maintained. Warships should patrol the waters. Aside from other considerations, the Company was supposed to have a monopoly. No Russians other than its employees were entitled to hunt or trade. Why, then, should foreigners be privileged? It was nonsense that the foreign traders were essential. For its foodstuffs the colony could depend on Fort Ross, for commodities of other sorts on round-the-world shipments from Saint Petersburg.

The truth about United States intentions at this period is that she was willing, for reasons having to do with Britain, to see Russian America extended as far south as the present boundary of Canada. Golovnin could have had no shred of real evidence for his contentions, other than the sale of arms. But then he had never hesitated to manufacture whole cloth when it came to advancing his beloved Navy. Once before, in 1810, he had tried to make out a similar case. His motive would seem clear in the suggestion of the patrolling warships and the frequent round-the-world supply expeditions, all of which would help prevent peacetime deterioration of the service. Golovnin may have even hoped, not too unconsciously, to provoke war. Nothing keeps an armed service going like war.

The Company, which would be paying the bills, could expect its costs to soar like skyrockets. Whereas the foreigners brought goods at their own expense, every globe-circling expedition cost an average of 300,000 rubles. Nor could there be the profit of selling furs at Canton without the aid of Americans. Surely these objections were brought up within the Company, yet Golovnin prevailed. The pusillanimous among the directors and stockholders simply went along, and there were those who were even impressed by his arguments. Was it not the case that the foreigners made off with up to fifteen shiploads of furs each year? Was it not so that they callously dealt in rum and arms? Golovnin's plans were set forth in the Company's name by petition to the government.

There was certainty the government would approve, as is evident from the fact that Governor Muraviev was instructed to prepare the colony for the trade ban a full year before final action was taken. Golovnin, who became a member of the State Council, the body advising the board in political matters, made himself virtual dictator of affairs at Company headquarters. He did all or much of the rewriting of the charter in preparation for submitting it for ratification. One change in it was to contribute to the international uproar in the making: the colony's southern boundary along the American shore was advanced from 54 degrees, 40 minutes to latitude 51.

The charter was ratified by Senate decree in September of 1821, and so, with a difference of a few days, was the trade ban. Three war sloops were assigned to patrol Pacific waters north of latitude 51. Russian ambassadors and consuls were

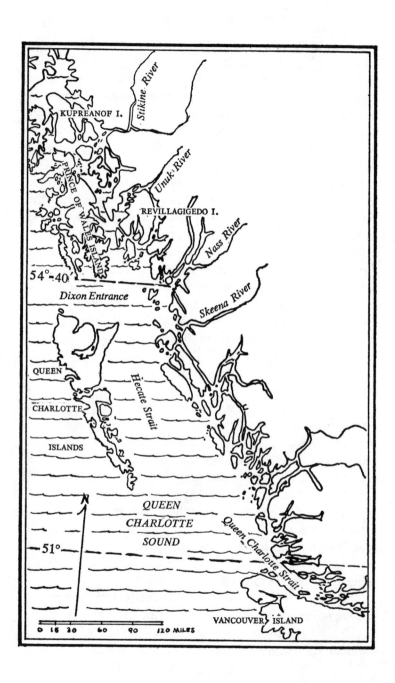

KUPREANOF I.

Stikine River

PRINCE OF WALES ISLAND

Unuk River

REVILLAGIGEDO I.

Nass River

54°-40'

Dixon Entrance

Skeena River

QUEEN

Hecate Strait

CHARLOTTE

ISLANDS

QUEEN

CHARLOTTE

SOUND

Queen Charlotte Strait

51°

0 15 30   60   90   120 MILES

VANCOUVER ISLAND

sent instructions to issue warnings. Foreigners were to set foot nowhere in Russian America. Indeed they were not to come within a hundred Italian miles of shore. Offending vessels would be confiscated.

How such a measure was ever passed, it would be interesting to know. Alexander professed to be working for world peace. And at the moment he had special reason for wishing cordiality with Britain, who was certain to be wrathful over the closing of an ocean. So was the United States, whose goodwill was still officially cultivated. Moreover, Britain and the United States were now given a cause in common against Russia, something highly undesirable from the standpoint of Russian foreign policy. Evidently the governmental right hand no longer quite knew what the left was doing. Alexander, who seems to have been given the impression that only smugglers were to be banned, was out of the country much of the time, attending to his Holy Alliance, and with him his able Foreign Minister, Count Karl Nesselrode. What suggests itself is that Golovnin worked through Arakcheev, whose power to act was wide and who would have seen merit in any proposal for the exclusion of foreigners. In any event, the consequences were all that could have been foreseen.

James Monroe was President of the United States. His Secretary of State was that old Saint Petersburg hand John Quincy Adams, who was no longer easy in his mind about Russia. For one thing, Alexander's Holy Alliance had developed the impractical but nevertheless disturbing aim of restoring to Spain the colonies she had lost in Latin America. In any such event, Adams felt, the United States could not stand idly by. And reports of a less clear kind had been coming that Russia planned a drive all down the Pacific, one portent of which appeared to be the Schaeffer affair at Hawaii. Then the shipmasters back from Russian America brought the news that they had been told not to return, and after that came the official notice of the ban. Adams, a pugnacious New Englander with strong views on free trade, replied in a fashion to leave no doubt of his country's position. "The President has seen with surprise . . ."

Saint Petersburg heard all it wished to hear on the subject. Protests came even from capitals having no interest in the trade, notably The Hague. In Naples the Russian representative decided not to announce the ban at all, "for fear of rousing discussion and objections." In Frankfort the papers had to be informed that war did not impend with the United States. Britain saw that its feelings were made known directly to the Tsar. The Duke of Wellington took the matter up with him at an Alliance conference in Europe. The embarrassed Alexander had lamely to say he would have to make inquiries. The ban had not long to live after that. But the consequences were not over. Far from it.

Adams had been given the chance to press for something he had long sought: a written understanding with Russia, defining rights on the Northwest coast. He addressed himself vigorously to the new boundary set forth in the Company's rewritten charter, calling it an infringement, though he had previously been willing to see Russian America extended much farther. He had the support of Britain, which had reasons of her own for wanting a treaty limiting Russia in America. Britain could be influential at this time because Alexander desired her aid in a matter having to do with Constantinople and therefore crucial to Russia's oldest ambitions in the foreign field. The result, following a complicated exchange of American, British, and Russian notes, was that Russia agreed to negotiate, the talks to to be held in Saint Petersburg, separately with Britain and the United States.

The Monroe Doctrine arose as a by-product of these events. During his correspondence with Saint Petersburg, Adams had sought to make clear his view of the Holy Alliance as it bore on Latin America: ". . . the American continents, by the free and independent conditions which they have assumed and maintained, are henceforth not to be considered as subjects for colonization by any European powers." It was decided to enlarge upon these sentiments, make them the basis of a clear statement of United States foreign policy to be given the world now, on the eve of negotiations in Saint Petersburg. Monroe enunciated his doctrine as part of his message to Congress late in 1823. The United States did no meddling in the Old World, which must similarly respect the New. The *de facto* governments of each were to be accepted by those of the other. Existing colonies would be respected, but there could be no further extensions of them, and the hemisphere was not a field for the implantation of oppressive political systems.

The treaty with the United States was signed in 1824, a year before Britain's, Foreign Minister Nesselrode in person having acted as a negotiator. The boundary was drawn back to 54 degrees, 40 minutes, Russia agreeing to establish no more posts outside the colony, which the United States would view as Russian soil. Freedom of navigation was assured both parties in their respective waters, with the proviso that settled places were to be visited only with consent of the local authorities. Both parties were also assured the privilege of fishing and of trading with the natives and of doing so in the interior seas, that is, the harbors and other shoreline indentations, Russia hedging that clause by making it reviewable after ten years. The United States at last agreed to prohibit liquor and arms, but it alone was to punish its offending citizens, Russia having no right to search or seize ships.

The British treaty, signed in 1825, comprised these things and much more. For the first time the colony was given an eastern boundary, substantially the line dividing Alaska and Canada to this day. In setting it, good use was made by the British of Alexander's hope for their aid in gaining Constantinople. The whole southern extremity of the colony, the section containing New Archangel, which had been won at the cost of so much blood, was hemmed in so closely that it was left a long strip of land no wider than thirty miles from tidewater. And the British obtained the right to navigate the rivers, enabling them to reach their territory in the interior by crossing that of the Russians. Reality had been given to Golovnin's warning that the colony was in danger of foreign aggression.

The Company was not silent during the negotiations. And a leading spokesman for the Navy, a former Minister of Marine, reminded the government of the national regret that the Amur had also once been thought so distant as to be dispensable. Alexander considered the objections only to reject them. Yet Russia was not to have Britain's help in gaining Constantinople.

The treaties were by no means all that had come of the trade ban. They were only the indirect result. The effect on the colony had been catastrophic. Its economy was in pieces. For the past four years the total catch of otter had been a mere 1500 pelts. How essential was foreign trade had been shown. The scheme to bring goods enough from the Baltic did not work. There was even want of food, Fort Ross proving an inadequate source without buying from the Spanish, which the ban forbade. In a sharp letter to the Company, Governor Muraviev made his feelings known, and he laid aside his orders, sending to Hawaii and California for food, even acquiring an extra vessel from the Yankees for the purpose. He had been removed from office, and now, in 1825, the governor was Ivan Chistiakov, who was to find that irreparable damage had been done.

As for the Company, its financial plight was such that the government censor had been asked to keep it out of the papers. Chairman Buldakov was close to a nervous breakdown. Not a kopek in dividends had been paid since 1821. Compounding the loss in revenue, the cost of the round-the-world expeditions, from which some of the directors were alleged to have profited, had been a monstrous 2,500,000 rubles. The stockholders' meeting of 1825 was a stormy one. As Rezanov looked lifelessly down from his portrait, the sumptuous board room rang with angry denunciations of the directors. But it came out all right for most of them. They were cleared by an investigative commission that included Vasilii Golovnin. All blame was put on the American member of the board, to wit, Benedict Cramer, who obligingly resigned.

The man who kept the minutes of that meeting was shortly to die on the gallows. He was the poet Kondratii Ryleev, who headed the Northern Society, the Saint Petersburg Decembrist organization. Recently he had been made office manager at Company headquarters. So numerous were now the Decembrists among the staff that, as the secret police were ascertaining, meetings were held on the premises. Involved also were at least one member of the board, a naval officer slated to head the colony, and another under consideration as commander of Fort Ross.

Alexander unexpectedly died late in 1825, a man worn out at forty-eight. The date by the Western calendar was December 1. Having no heir, he had named his brother Nicholas to the succession. Nicholas was twenty-nine, hale and uncomplicated. He was stiffly handsome; he looked imposing in the uniforms he loved to wear. Learning bored him; his talents were those of a conscientious general. He had a strong sense of duty; within the frame of his thinking he was kind and just. Absolutism was the simplest form of government; it was therefore best, and for all nations. The creed of Nicholas I came to be expressed by the three words Orthodoxy, Autocracy, Nationalism.

Before he took the throne in late December, he learned that the Decembrists were hastily moving in hope of setting off the revolution. Ryleev was among the leaders planning the action, which was to begin with a gathering of the military in a certain Saint Petersburg square. Though he seems to have known he was marked for assassination, Nicholas boldly went to the square, which at his appearance was jammed with some 3000 soldiers, sailors, and assorted civilians, with more arriving by the minute. Few knew exactly why they were there, the Decembrists having hesitated to make their aim widely clear, but all understood it was in defiance of Nicholas and they would not disperse. The result was that that night the snow was red with the blood of some 80 people. The December revolution died aborning. At Saint Petersburg and elsewhere the conspirators were all soon in jail.

Nicholas silenced even the Decembrist sympathizers. He ordered a widespread inquiry that lasted five months, himself taking a hand in questioning those brought before the tribunal. He gained the impression that the Company was virtually a subversive organization as all who were associated with it were thoroughly grilled, including Vasilii Golovnin. When it was over the remaining members of the Company staff paid studious attention to business—what business was left. Many a former colleague was on his way to Siberia, and among the five sentenced to hang was Ryleev. It was the first imposition of the death penalty since the reign of Elizabeth. Dead the following year, apparently from the strain, was Chairman Buldakov.

It was nearly three years before Nicholas brought himself to affirm the charter. The suspense was ended none too soon for the financially crippled Company, which was facing a new situation in the Pacific, where the British had become very, very active.

Britain's negotiators had worked from a well-laid plan when they achieved the 1825 treaty with Russia. Four years before, in 1821, a new expansionist instrument had been formed in Canada by the merger of two rival fur companies, ending a long feud that had impeded both. The combine, which kept the name of the older firm, the Hudson's Bay Company, was well financed, had a thoroughly seasoned organization, and was now headed by a man as resourceful and aggressive in his own way as Baranov, by name Sir George Simpson.

Hudson's Bay's immediate objective in the Far West was twofold: to secure Britain's hold on Oregon and to drive both the Americans and the Russians from the coast by supplanting their trade. The name Oregon then signified in its entirety the region west of the Rocky Mountains, from California north to Russian America. For the time being, Hudson's Bay could operate freely in Oregon, without fear of conflict with the United States, the territory having been opened by agreement to both Britons and Americans. The British expected to have the huge area in hand by the time the agreement expired.

They had been moving with great speed, yet with care, to establish themselves firmly. In the Columbia region, location of the main base, a large food-growing development was under way for the supply of the posts rapidly going up along the coast to the north. Each post was situated with an eye to the furs from the interior as well as those from the natives of the sea-board. Money had been lavished on ships and on trade goods of a quality above those dispensed by either the Americans or the Russians, whose prices were, moreover, undercut. When a post commander heard of an American trader in his vicinity, he sent the ship at his disposal, and his men, to compete. By 1828, only seven years after the amalgamation, Hudson's Bay controlled the trade almost as far north as the Russian border, most of the Americans having given up.

For the Russians, the British advance came at a calamitous time, what with the disorganization caused by the Decembrist troubles at home, the Company's lack of capital, the low state of the colonial economy, and the fact that Governor Chistiakov was a man of no great ability. Moreover, the Americans had been causing much trouble. Their treaty having given them the unrestrained privilege of dealing directly with the natives, a number of them were bringing in quantities of rum, notwithstanding the restriction. And now gloomy New Archangel saw source after traditional source of furs diverted to the British, who made their ultimate purpose clear when they began making use of the treaty privilege of ascending the rivers.

In 1830 a new governor took office, a small, testy man, red of beard and hair, an Estonian German by birth. He was Baron Ferdinand von Wrangell, a distinguished explorer and scientist. He was also the kind who gets things done with the means at hand. In the Company and the colony Wrangell found an interest that was to absorb him for twenty years. Gloom departed New Archangel at his advent. With vigor he pressed the search for new sources of furs, greatly stimulating exploration. He renewed the effort to better schools, missions, and medical services.

In 1834, the tenth year of the treaty with the United States, its traders having continued to deal in rum, Wrangell terminated the clause allowing them free access to shoreline waters. The problem of the traders had been compounded by a great influx of American whalers, three hundred of whose vessels were soon to be counted in one year. "Hell-ships," they were called, even in the United States, their captains often brutes and the crews no better. Having landed for the purpose of rendering oil, they stole the precious fuel of the Aleuts and the Eskimos; they also took their food and their women, in return giving rotgut and syphilis. Wrangell's action in canceling shoreline privileges was welcome to the colony, which had lost enthusiasm for Americans. As for the treaty with the British, Wrangell hoped to abrogate it completely.

The British had carefully refrained from creating incidents, making it difficult to come to open grips with them. A thought came to Wrangell when he learned that they had been navigating the Stikine River, which crossed Russian territory, with a view to establishing a post beyond the boundary, in their own territory. Since no Russian settlement stood on the Stikine, by the terms of the treaty the British had no need to ask permission to use the river. Wrangell decided that were they suddenly to find a settlement at the mouth of the Stikine, with a resident commander who forbade them to pass, they might be angry enough to try forcing their way, which would be reason to demand that the treaty be scrapped.

The settlement was named Fort Dionysius. The commander was instructed to be polite but firm when the British appeared, which they did in June of 1834, in a Hudson's Bay vessel, the *Dryad*. Unfortunately for the success of Wrangell's scheme, the local Tlingits interested themselves in the proceedings, lining up with the Russians. Faced with the likelihood of never getting up the river, the men of the *Dryad* withdrew, returning to base on the Columbia to report. At the time, that seemed the end of it to the disappointed Wrangell.

The tenures of the governors were brief, seldom over five years. In 1835 Wrangell returned to Saint Petersburg, where he was elected to the Company's board, eventually to become chairman. Along with his other qualities, he had an excellent business sense. His concern now turned to the Company's financial situation, which had remained wretched ever since the trade ban fourteen years before. The books were being manipulated to conceal the fact that dividends were coming out of capital, which had been ever harder to raise. Government aid had had to be sought.

Retrenchment on any scale was impossible without depriving the colonial institutions, which had been getting little enough. The losses due to Hudson's Bay had been compounded by the ever-rising cost of supplying the colony. For one thing, Fort Ross had become a liability. Circumscribed by the growing Spanish population around it, Ross was producing far less food than of old, at four times the cost. It could not, however, be simply abandoned, the grain and beef it did produce being too necessary. Wrangell had visited Ross; he had ascertained what was wrong and, for a time, had hoped that the Mexican authorities would allow more land, but he had been unable to persuade Tsar Nicholas to pay the price: recognition of Mexican independence.

Wrangell had been in Saint Petersburg two years, grappling with the many problems without finding a solution, when he received the dismaying news of the use to which the British had put his action on the Stikine. Russia was charged with violating the treaty, and the Company was served a bill for damages from Hudson's Bay amounting to 250,000 rubles. Nicholas disavowed responsibility on Russia's part, letting the Company down completely. Testily he ordered compliance when Hudson's Bay offered to drop its claim in return for a lease of the coveted southern portion of the colony, from 54 degrees, 40 minutes, all the way north to Cape Spencer.

There was no arguing with Nicholas, who, aside from his usual dislike of trouble caused by the Company, was these days striving for accord with Britain. Having to make the best of it, Wrangell met to work out the deal with his opposite number in the Hudson's Bay Company, canny Sir George Simpson. This was in 1838. The leased territory was made over for 10 years at an annual fee of 2000 land-otter pelts, a figure that surely made Baranov turn in his watery grave. The British would now be close neighbors indeed, all around New Archangel, the sole section retained. But Wrangell managed to turn the defeat into a most unexpected kind of victory.

He proved himself a master salesman, persuading Simpson, who had begun by disliking him intensely, to lay aside thoughts of further war and consider joining forces. Sealskins, the source of which the Company controlled, were much wanted in Britain. Payment in that commodity could be made by supplying the colony with food and merchandise. Another source of great profit to Hudson's Bay would be the processing of the furs of the Company, which had lost the eminence in that field, London's craftsmen having developed superior methods that were kept secret by law. When the bargaining was over, a contract had been made whereby the colony was guaranteed a regular supply of grain, beef, fruit, and other foodstuffs, largely from Hudson's Bay's Oregon farms. Its ships were also to bring, on demand, manufactured goods from England and elsewhere at the lowest rates per ton the Company had ever paid.

And so it came about that between the British and the Russians in Northwest America there was a virtual partnership, one destined to last for twenty-six years, although elsewhere in the world they were to be less and less at peace. The honored guests at what was still called Baranov's Castle would now be the Scots of Hudson's Bay; Simpson himself, eventually paid an extended visit. He could take satisfaction in the thought that he had supplanted American trade all the way down the coast to California. The defeat of the United States in the Far West seemed complete.

Wrangell had solved the Company's financial dilemma. Among the huge costs that could now be cut was that of Fort Ross, the food from which was no longer needed. That farthest of all posts established by Russians came to an end in 1841, following the sale of the property. Its people, numbering some four hundred, were transferred to Russian America, which was already undergoing a vast change. There was the money for the many things that had so long awaited doing.

XIII

The Flowering

Chief among the things that had awaited doing and for which there was now the money was the hastening of the process, which had been slowly going on since the colony began, of bringing the native world into the body of the Russian people. Entailed was a great increase in missionary effort, coupled with an equal advance in schooling. The beginning was witnessed by Sir George Simpson when he visited the colony in 1842, causing him to write musingly of Russia's ". . . long-tried policy, which has amalgamated so many uncongenial tribes into a compact people by means of one law, one language, one faith—a policy which England . . . has too much neglected. Through this policy, Russia, though apparently the most unwieldy state on earth, is yet more decidedly one and indivisible than any other dominion in existence."

The Company was motivated by a consideration having no parallel in Simpson's England, a situation without hope of change in the foreseeable future, owing to Tsar Alexander's failure to unfetter Russian society. Migration was not allowed the vast majority of the people, in particular those having knowledge of the soil and how to settle new lands. Most of that class was held immobile in the older parts of Russia by the paralyzing force of serfdom, the influence extending to all walks of common life, few having much more freedom to move from their birthplaces than had been permitted under Muscovy. Thus the phenomenal growth of the Russian empire had not been accompanied by a commensurate spread of its people. Much of Siberia remained sparsely colonized. Hence it was that so many of the native peoples had survived to be made compatriots upon adoption of the ancient tie of Orthodoxy.

The Company's employees were not settlers in any real sense. During the early years of Alexander's reign attempts were made to obtain true colonists, men and women free to farm, establish businesses and towns. One plan had had the backing of powerful Count Rumiantsev, Chancellor of the Empire, but even he could not prevail against the serf-owning nobles fearful of agreeing to the opening of the smallest gate to migration. No permission was on the books for even Company employees to settle for life. Only by tacit consent had some done so. Those below the official level were not supposed to remain longer than fourteen years.

The situation had always given the Company trouble, even in the matter of obtaining employees. It was worse now that the relatively footloose Siberian promyshlenniki were no longer wanted. Many of the so-called Russians now in the colony were Finns, the Company having found it easier to recruit men in the Baltic countries that had become Russian provinces. Even so, in all there were not a thousand, barely twice the number of men Baranov had had. With the European population both small and impermanent, in order to provide itself with a sizable stable personnel the colonial administration had had to go on doing as Baranov had done: educate natives. The ultimate future of Russia's overseas colony depended on extending civilization to the indigenes: the Aleuts, the Eskimos, the Tlingits, and the others, who, all told, numbered some 30,000. In the colony had long been a man of remarkable talent for the task, a very great man indeed.

In the tiny backwoods village of Anginskoe in Irkutsk province, on August 26, 1797, a big-boned, handsome, lustily healthy boy was born, the son of the sacristan of the local church. His earliest recollections were the scent of incense and the music of the Liturgy. He soon showed he was going to be a genius of some sort, so adept was he of hand and phenomenal of mind. He was reading with ease at six, although he had had no formal schooling. The family, which included a deacon, naturally hoped he would become a priest. At the age of nine he entered the theological seminary at Irkutsk. Thus was his course in life determined for the boy who was to become the great figure of the heyday of the Russian colony in America.

His name, which had been Ivan Popov, was changed to Ioann Veniaminov at the seminary, where he remained eleven years, making good use of every minute. The students slept in the classrooms, and the food was as poor as the accommodations, but the teachers were devoted and there were many books voraciously to be read; these were the years when Tsar Alexander was spending lavishly on education. The seminary library had new as well as old works on science and mechanics, young Veniaminov's favorite reading. The extent of his curiosity is indicated by his writings of later years, which show an all but professional grasp of fields ranging from anthropology to zoology. He also had a remarkable ear for languages. So retentive was his memory that, thirty years after his seminary days, finding himself among men with whom he had only Latin in common, he recalled enough of it to converse in that language.

He loved to work with his hands as well as his mind. He was forever inventing and making things. At fourteen, from a picture he had seen, and mostly with a simple knife, he constructed a clock that ran by dripping water, much to the fascination of Irkutsk, where timepieces of any sort were rare. Among his inventions was a sundial watch, duplicates of which he made for his classmates. No skill seemed too intricate for those remarkable hands to acquire, from carpentry and furniture-making to blacksmithing and the fashioning of musical instruments.

Nothing was puny about this man. When fully grown he was well over six feet in height and had a build to match. His personality seems to have been balanced to a degree extraordinary among geniuses. He was outgoing and gregarious, liked by everyone. And with it all went a rare sweetness, an uncommon gentleness, and a great capacity for sympathy. For that there is the word of Sir George Simpson, whom Veniaminov met when he was forty-five. The Scot wrote of his Russian friend that his appearance "impresses a stranger with something of awe," which wore off as "the gentleness which characterizes his every word and deed insensibly molds reverence into love." Added Sir George, who seems not to have liked most churchmen, ". . . he is sufficiently a man of the world to disdain anything like cant. His conversation, on the contrary, teems with amusement and instruction, and his company is much prized by all who have the honor of his acquaintance."

His seminary days over, he chose to work among the people, to do parish duty. He married, after which he was made a deacon and assigned to assist at a church in the Irkutsk diocese. Four years later, age twenty-four, in 1821, he was raised to the priesthood and given a congregation of his own. In choosing to belong to the married, or so-called White clergy, sharply distinct from the Black, who lived according to monastic rule, he closed the door on ambition for power. No man could be a bishop who had not first joined the Black clergy.

Young Veniaminov was soon immersed in the duties of his parish, in the teaching he undertook, and in the care of his family, which consisted of his aged mother as well as his wife and, presently, a son. His other interests were his well-equipped workshop, in which he made furniture and much else, and his books—as always, those on science in particular. He had no thought of becoming a missionary. In that he was no different from the great majority of the Russian clergy.

The Church had lost the pioneering spirit that once had made it so much a part of the frontier. No special training was given for missionary work, though much remained to be done within the empire itself, notably along whole stretches of Siberia. As for Russian America, which had just been brought under the Navy, little had come of the beginning made by Father Iosaf and his monks nearly thirty years before. In the whole vast region were only five priests, none young and one deranged. Nor had they taken much to heart the upbraiding given them by Rezanov for failing to learn the native speech and visit distant stations. Of the four or five churches and chapels that had been built, only two were in regular use, those at Kodiak and New Archangel. Elsewhere it was usually the Company agents who, reading from the book, conducted services on holy days and did the baptizing.

The Company, which paid salaries and expenses and now stood ready to be less parsimonious about this than in the past, wanted more and better priests, if only to improve the schooling. Professional lay teachers were all but impossible to get. As things were, the only priest teaching a school was old Father German at Kodiak. The school at New Archangel was taught by volunteers from among the Company's educated personnel. And that, together with the sending of a few youths to Russia for advanced work, constituted the educational effort. Small though it was, it had richly demonstrated the feasibility of looking to the natives for even bookkeepers and navigators. In the case of the creoles—as those of mixed blood had come officially to be called—the Company had no choice, the new charter requiring it to educate them.

Priests were not to be obtained simply by asking the Church. The situation of the colony in that respect was a peculiar one. It had long been part of the Diocese of Irkutsk but had never been declassified as a mission field, which meant that the bishop could order none of his clergy to go; he could only ask for volunteers. He sent out a general call in 1821, instructed to do so by the Holy Synod, in response to the appeal of the Company.

A volunteer was needed with special urgency at Unalaska, where no priest had been in such a long time the large Aleut population was in danger of forgetting what Christianity it had been taught. Even so, the bishop's call went unanswered for two years, Unalaska in particular seeming a post to be shunned, lonely and isolated, with few resident Russians now that colonial activity centered at New Archangel, a thousand miles away. When, in 1823, a volunteer finally stepped forward, and for Unalaska, the bishop was the more astonished that it should be the most scholarly of his young priests, namely, Ioann Veniaminov.

It seemed such a foolish thing for him to be doing that even the bishop argued with him. His mother was beside herself. He was doing so nicely. His two years as its pastor had made him immensely popular with his congregation. He was making a name as a teacher. But he was not to be dissuaded. He had been talking to a man who had spent forty years in the colony, loved it, thought highly of the Aleuts, and had movingly depicted their needs. In view of his character, it is to be surmised that Ioann Veniaminov was attracted also by the picture of a field where he would be largely on his own and could exercise to the full his ingenuity and resourcefulness.

He himself made it clear that the thought of getting rich played no part in his decision. So eager was the Company to have him, he was informed, he would enjoy the rarest of concessions: permission to deal privately in furs. He would be free to accept them as contributions from his parishioners, of whom he would have some 1200, located as far as the Pribilofs. He declined, saying that, aside from the unpleasant complications that might ensue, the natives should not have the impression they had to pay to hear the Word of God.

He was twenty-seven when, after a journey of almost a year, he arrived at Unalaska. He came prepared to stay for life. He brought his mother, his wife and son, a brother, the accouterments of his calling, his household effects, his books, his scientific instruments, and his large collection of tools. He found no house for a priest, no school, no church other than a tumbledown old chapel beyond repair. He seems to have been pleased. He would himself build what he needed and make the furnishings as well.

When he had his family temporarily housed, he visited the islands of his parish, making the acquaintance of the Aleuts and learning their language with thoroughness. They took to him, and he to them. They were all he had been led to expect, a gentle, generous, honorable people, their one great failing the improvidence that kept them beholden to the Company, for which they all worked in one way or another, mostly at gathering furs. It paid them, furnished their subsistence, guarded their health, shielded them, as much as lay in its power, from the traders and whalers with their rum and syphilis. The Aleuts were now to be classed as civilized, though they still lived by many of their old primitive ways. As was symbolized by the samovar that stood in each of their half-buried dwellings, they were Russian subjects, so defined in the second charter.

Their new priest had no trouble organizing a work force to help him build his house and his church. As he went along, he taught carpentry, metal-working, brick-making, and other skills, in turn learning how great was the Aleut aptitude for tools. The house was built first, as a school with residential quarters. When that was done, he had a well-trained crew for the building of the Church of the Holy Ascension, which was consecrated on July 29, 1826, the second anniversary of his arrival.

"When he preached the Word of God," an aged Aleut of Unalaska recalled more than fifty years later, "all the people listened, and listened without moving, until he stopped. Nobody thought of fishing or hunting while he spoke; nobody felt hungry or thirsty as long as he was speaking, not even little children."

His school had about a hundred pupils of both sexes, his wife aiding in teaching the girls, whose course included civilized housekeeping. Every boy learned some trade, such as carpentry, along with his three Rs—four, counting religion. The brighter were prepared for further work at New Archangel, where there was now a school of navigation, or in Russia, where a larger variety of courses had been opened to candidates from the colony. Gifted boys could now think of even becoming surgeons, and some were to do so. All males educated at Company expense bound themselves to serve the colonial administration for at least ten, and in some cases fifteen, years. Pay was according to type of work; subsistence was furnished; rank was conferrable after six years' honorable service. Those who chose to serve past the stipulated period could expect a pension. Creoles whose mandatory service was over and who were not in debt could choose to follow their trade or profession in Russia, the Company's responsibility for them ending with the payment of their travel expenses. The colonialism of the period offered few programs as enlightened.

Veniaminov did something at his school which was altogether unique in the annals of native education, something calculated to stiffen the pride of the Aleuts in themselves as a people. He instituted a course in their own speech—in fact in the local dialect, called Aleutian-Fox. And he invested the study of Fox with all the dignity of Russian, composing a dictionary, a grammar, and a primer. The alphabet he used was Church-Slavonic, which he declared better expressed the sounds of Fox than the secular Russian alphabet. For use as texts he translated three of the Gospels, the Catechism, a sermon he wrote, and a brief history of the Church. The value to the children was greater than the lift to their egos. Seeing their speech in writing gave them a concept of the uses of language they would otherwise have had trouble acquiring.

At the end of ten years, Veniaminov wrote, everyone in the district of an age to do so had some ability to read. He also claimed that all were Christians. Doubtless they were, and in more than name. He accepted no one who did not appear fully convinced. Later on he was to express himself forcibly on the subject of coercion. He was even against the custom of bestowing baptismal gifts. He once said proudly of his converts, "I do not mean that they know only how to make the sign of the cross, bow, and mutter some prayer. No! Some can pray from their souls, not only in church . . . but also in solitude."

Ten years he remained on the Aleutians, functioning as a scientist as well as a priest. He maintained a weather observatory, keeping records of winds and tides, thermometric and barometric readings. As, often, he made the rounds of his huge parish, visiting the various islands, he scrutinized each for knowledge of its plant life, wildlife, the rocks, and the soil. But his greatest interest was the people, the variances of physique, custom, and dialect. Unfailingly he noted every difference of dialect. In studying the Aleuts he anticipated the methods of present-day anthropologists. Disregarding the attitude toward pagan beliefs a cleric was supposed to take, he encouraged the oldsters to tell their myths and legends. He also gathered the sorry history of the promyshlennik period, glozing over none of it as he reconstructed in gruesome detail events such as the Soloviev massacre, which the very old could recall first-hand.

Never before had the Aleutians been examined by so knowing an eye or from so many standpoints. He wrote a series of articles that roused so much interest in Saint Petersburg scientific circles they were translated into French and German. Eventually he brought his observations together in a three-volume compendium which, modestly titled *Notes on the Islands of the Unalaska District*, has the admiration of scholars to this day and remains a basic text on the ethnology and other features of the region. His great interest in linguistics he expressed in another work, which also remains basic and is devoted to the varieties of speech. And, somehow, he also managed to find time to spend in his workshop. His special delight had come to be the making of watches. His wife was as busy. Along with her teaching she had the rearing of six children, two sons and four daughters.

In 1834, his tenth year in America, Veniaminov was persuaded by his friend and admirer Governor Wrangell to accept a larger field. He relinquished his work on the Aleutians to another priest and, with his family, was brought to New Archangel to serve as its priest, to improve the schooling, and to try his hand at converting the Tlingits, who, of all the natives, were the most resistant. Their liking for the white man's gadgets had not caused them to consider his religion or culture superior to theirs.

Veniaminov prepared carefully, learning the ways of the

Tlingits and their language. And he respected them, deciding they were the superiors of all the natives by virtue of "their activities, cleverness, and inclination for trade." Yet he won no large measure of their confidence until a disastrous smallpox epidemic swept up from the south, killing a quarter of the native population. The loss would have been far larger had the Company's medical service not been advanced to the point at which it could send serum even to stations far up the Bering. During the crisis, Veniaminov's preachment turned to acceptance of inoculation, and at the end the Tlingits had a certain respect for the white man's science. Whereas the incantations of their shamans had been futile, those who had listened to the priest of the Russians were nearly all alive. But no wholesale conversion followed. Not even Ioann Veniaminov, singlehanded, was enough for that.

The colony still had no more than a handful of priests and deacons, perhaps a score. The call for volunteers remained as largely ignored as ever. Among the posts that had never even seen a priest was Fort Ross, though it was now twenty-four years old and had a chapel. In 1836 Veniaminov was sent for a six-week stay, after which he met a set of men about whom he could not have been more curious: the Franciscan missionaries of California. The experience formed one of the great memories of his life. It was his first acquaintance with Roman Catholic priests.

Finding that his homeward journey from California would be delayed two weeks, he decided to do some sightseeing. He visited Mission San Rafael, and there, as he recorded in his travel diary, "I saw the Catholic service for the first time and met a monk of the Franciscan Order . . . padres, they are usually called." Now it was that, knowing no Spanish, he had to fall back on the Latin of his seminary days, finding he could converse well enough. Encouraged to do so by the padre, who was evidently most affable, he went on to the larger mission of San José, where the father superior received him with great cordiality and had him stay four days.

He was shown the entire mission, ". . . the workshops, the beautiful fruit orchard—in a word, there was virtually nothing that this padre through his good inclinations did not show me. . . . I saw the burial ceremony and the christening of children and was four times at Mass and saw all the sacred vessels and vestments." He and his host, whom he calls "most learned and virtuous," even talked shop.

He was accompanied by his host as, by horseback, he went on to visit Mission Santa Clara, the three or four resident padres of which also made him feel welcome. These Roman priests were evidently as curious about a Byzantine as he was about them. It was the same at the fourth mission he visited, San Francisco de Asis. It would appear the padres had indicated a need for more musical instruments. On his return home—as usual, with his own hands, in his workshop—Father Veniaminov made a number of barrel-organs, which he sent his friends in thanks for their hospitality.

As he returned to his task of attempting to convert the Tlingits, the sole hope of ever persuading them to lay aside their warlike ways, he surely reflected ruefully on the superior generosity of Spain when it came to providing her colonies with missionaries. His visit to California would seem to have contributed to the hard thinking given by the administration from this point on to the problem of obtaining more priests, thinking that expanded into the project of extending the missionary effort to all parts of the colony.

The thought was by no means new, Wrangell, for one, having entertained it. His term as governor having come to an end in 1835, he was now in Saint Petersburg, a member of the board and due to become chairman. The man who had been his assistant now served his successor in the same capacity and was slated to be the next governor, in 1840. The administration had no more insistent thinker on the subject of native education than Captain Adolf Etolin. He was utterly devoted to the colony, which he knew as well as any man, having explored some of its remotest parts. He could remember Baranov, having come as a youth twenty years before.

Etolin knew what it was to be an underdog. He was that rarest of ranking naval men, a man of illegitimate birth. He owed his rise entirely to the notice taken of his high moral character and keen intelligence. He was not a creole. The belief that he was has probably come of his preoccupation with the natives. He was born in Finland, the Russian governor general of which may have been his father. His interest in education was shared by his wife, a Finnish woman of great good breeding, whose contribution was the fostering of what amounted to a finishing school for girls, a boarding institution teaching the arts as well as the skills of civilized living.

New Archangel showed how responsive the natives had been through the years, small though the educational effort had remained. It had come to be a town of 1300 people, the largest civilized community within 2000 miles. Though over half the Russians in the colony lived there, two-thirds of the population was made up of Creoles and natives. At Kodiak, which was also growing, their proportion was 90 per cent. They were employed up to the administrative level. The trades were practically all in their their hands, even the tailoring. The men at the shipyard, including the foremen, were nearly all colony-born, Aleuts mostly, with some mainlanders from up around Cook Inlet, and here and there a Tlingit. It was the same at the water-powered sawmill and was only a little less the case aboard the ships.

Anyone doubting the reliability of the Russified natives had only to see what they were doing hundreds of miles north of New Archangel. They had even taken over the function of the oldtime promyshlenniki. By dog team and riverboat laboriously hauled upstream, they were opening the mainland, penetrating the vast region watered by the great rivers Yukon, Kuskokwim, and Nushagak, along which they were establishing posts. The work, which was of great importance, owing to the need for new sources of furs and the desire to forestall the British, had been under way for twenty years, but not one European Russian had yet appeared in the field. From the leaders on down, all the men were creoles and natives. They explored according to their judgment, they decided on the positions to be taken, they commanded and manned the posts they built. Some of Veniaminov's early pupils may have been among them. They kept records, calculated by instruments, made maps. And they had admirable relations with the Eskimos and Indians they were bringing under the flag which they represented fully as much as the Russians who had fathered some of them.

Many more such men were needed. And now a sharp new demand had risen for men who understood mechanics. The age of steam had arrived. The Pacific's first steamer, the Hudson's Bay Company's sidewheeler *Beaver,* already plied nearby waters. The marine and the shipyard had soon to adapt, if the Company was not to fall by the technological wayside. The colony's poor educational organization could not keep up. And there was Veniaminov's strong feeling of duty to extend Christianity to all the natives, a promise implicit since the foundation of the Company. The problem was, of course, the ways and the means—the indisposition of the clergy to volunteer, coupled with the Company's poor financial condition, due to the struggle with Hudson's Bay.

In 1838, even before New Archangel knew that the Company's financial difficulties would presently be over, Veniaminov was given leave to go to Saint Petersburg and present the colony's needs to the Holy Synod, which was to be asked in particular to make Russian America a separate diocese, able to develop its own clergy. He hoped also to obtain approval from the Synod for the use of translations into Aleutian and Tlingit which he had made of those parts of the Liturgy allowed in the vernacular by the Orthodox Church. He went by ship, planning to return overland for a visit at Irkutsk, which he had not seen in fourteen years. His wife and children were to meet him there. He was now forty-one, and a most impressive figure, according to world-traveler Sir Edward Belcher, who met him at this period: ". . . a very formidable, athletic man . . . standing in his boots about six feet three inches; quite herculean and very clever. . . ."

Arriving in Saint Petersburg in June of 1839, he was greeted by Wrangell with the glad news that the money troubles were a thing of the past, Hudson's Bay having agreed to peace and partnership. All that remained to secure the Company's immediate future was for Tsar Nicholas to grant a new charter in 1841.

It was soon clear that the bishops of the Synod intended to act only slowly, if at all, on the proposals of the visitor from overseas. He had to pin his hopes on Filaret, Metropolitan of Moscow, who seems to have been the one prelate greatly interested in him. Elsewhere he was a sensation. Scientific organizations raptly heard him speak. The rich organized benefits for his work. And of course he was made much of by Company officials, few of whom seemed to him to have knowledge equal to their rank. Then, suddenly, none of it mattered. His wife, he learned, had died at Irkutsk.

He went to Kiev to pray at the old shrines. Gone was all wish to return to America. But for his children, he would have entered a monastery. Returning to Saint Petersburg, he learned that the proposal to make the colony a separate diocese had passed the Synod and that his was one of the three names put up according to custom for election to the seat of bishop. He was in agony. This called for giving up his children, entailing as it did the first step of transferring to the celibate Black clergy. But he obeyed when the Synod gave a virtual command. He was tonsured and given the new name of Innokentii. Not that the act guaranteed his election by the prelates of the Synod, several of whom were known to favor the other two candidates. His sacrifice might well be idle.

Only one man could guarantee the election, and that was the Tsar. Presumably it was Wrangell who begged him to see his favored candidate. Nicholas may well have been irritated at having been asked to interfere in so small a matter, but he was enthralled on meeting his caller, showing what appears to have been the first real interest he had ever taken in hearing at length about the colony and its problems. Innokentii Veniaminov was consecrated bishop on December 15, 1840.

His work had been cut out for him. As if the colony would not have been diocese enough, he had also been assigned the Siberian coast. Nor had he been given a clergy of a size commensurate to the task. But he had obtained something he considered far more important: permission to relax certain rules, which would enable him quickly to develop a native clergy, in his view the surest foundation for the future. And he had the approval he had sought for the use of local languages in the conduct of the Liturgy.

He saw Irkutsk, on his way back, and his birthplace. He visited his wife's grave and said farewell to his children, who would now be brought up by the Church. On his way from Okhotsk by ship to New Archangel, which would be his see, he stopped at Unalaska. As his old parishioners knelt to receive his blessing, thanking God he had returned to look after them, perhaps he smiled again.

On schedule in 1841 Nicholas extended the Company's life for another twenty years, though work remained to be done on the new charter, the third. The clear intention behind this document, which was completed in 1844, was to retain the colony and, more, to draw it closer to the empire. Mention was at last made of settlers. Though the Company retained the form of a commercial corporation, the emphasis was now on its role as an administrative agency.

Several of the provisions sound as if they were written by Veniaminov. Force was not to be used on natives, save in keeping the peace. Posts among natives classed as "independent" were not to be established without their consent. Missionaries were explicitly instructed how to behave. "Clause 271: natives who do not profess the Christian faith shall be permitted to carry on their devotions according to their own rites; 272: the Russian clergy in making converts among the natives shall use conciliatory and persuasive measures, in no case resorting to coercion; 273: the colonial authorities shall see that the natives are not embarrassed under pretext of conversion to the Christian faith; 274: natives professing the Christian faith who, through ignorance, transgress ecclesiastical regulations shall not be subject to fines and punishment, instruction and persuasion being the only proper remedies in such cases."

By the time Veniaminov arrived at New Archangel in the fall of 1841, three years after his departure, he had seen at all the posts that the new era for the colony had already begun. Kodiak was getting a ten-bed hospital. Everywhere construction was under way. On becoming governor the previous year, Adolf Etolin had promptly begun to spend with a lavish hand the money released by the peace with Hudson's Bay, one benefit of which was larger pensions in which widows could now share.

Abuilding at New Archangel, or about to be built, were a forty-bed hospital, a playground for children, an addition to the castle, a new pier, new structures at the shipyard, a clubhouse with living accommodations for the unmarried employees. The Finns could now go to their own Lutheran church. That, too, had been built by the Company, which also supported the pastor.

The year 1841 was the centenary of Bering's voyage. It had been observed with a fitting indication of the way times had changed: the New Archangel shipyard had launched the first steam vessel built in the Pacific. The Hudson's Bay men had to concede the palm, their sternwheeler *Beaver* having been built in England. The *Nicholas I* was all colony-built, except for her sixty-horsepower engine, which had come from the United States. And the Aleuts at the shipyard's new machine shop were in process of constructing even the engine for the next steamer to be launched.

Etolin's touch with the natives was palpable in a new relationship with the Tlingits. He had instituted an annual fair for them at New Archangel, to which they came from as far away as Yakutat and Vancouver Island to feast, sing, dance, and show off their wares. Liquor was notably absent. Having forced Hudson's Bay to go along with him, Etolin had banned liquor at all the posts, even for the whites. Some of the Russians are said to have wept on receiving the order.

An even greater fury of building followed the return of Veniaminov, Etolin sparing no expense to provide the visible marks of a diocese. Plans went forward for a cathedral, a 30,000-ruble episcopal residence, and, first of all, that essential if a native clergy was to be developed, a seminary. Veniaminov saw to it that his seminarians were not to sleep in the classrooms as he had done. Foreigners who inspected the completed institution commented on the good dormitories and the other facilities, in particular the physics laboratory. By closing an ineffectual seminary on Kamchatka, Veniaminov obtained a faculty. The first group of students numbered twenty-three, all creoles or natives.

The art of teaching was designated a large subject for the seminarians, their bishop wanting each of his parishes to have at least one school, with texts in the local speech. His young clergy were set a formidable example for activity. He was forever on the go. By ship, baidarka, dog team, and foot he visited nearly all parts of his diocese, the world's vastest missionary field, making an organized entity of it within ten years. He was Paul Bunyan in a cassock. Even Italy-sized Kamchatka was given an inspection of a thoroughness for which few of its commanders had had the energy. Wherever he went he noted the dialect, with a view to providing school texts and vernacular parts for the Liturgy. He had posts marked out, some as far as the Yukon, for his new priests and deacons as soon as the seminary graduated them. All appear to have been imbued with some of his fire, and at least one reflected his genius.

Over a million rubles went to the work of the Church during the decade, clergy upkeep alone climbing to an annual 34,000 rubles. Up to 1850 the number of houses of worship was increased by seven times, as five new churches went up, one on the Asian side, and thirty chapels, the natives building some of them of their own accord. In 1848 the colonial clergy, who by then probably numbered some fifty, assembled at New Archangel for the dedication of the little Cathedral of Saint Michael, which is still very much in use, the modesty of its pioneer architecture belied by the treasures within. Adorning its façade is a six-foot clock, which was fashioned, piece by wrought-iron piece, by the hands of its first bishop. He still managed to find time to make things.

The era was as notable for work in science. The Imperial Academy and the Company jointly sponsored a mineralogical survey. Then there was the ten-year project personally conducted by famed Ilia Voznesenskii, later curator of the Academy, who made a comprehensive study covering such widely different subjects as geology and the handiwork of the natives, amassing a great collection in the process. The Academy published a text on the colony to which Veniaminov contributed part of the section on the ethnology. Magnetic and meteorological observatories were established at New Archangel, with substations elsewhere. Of vast importance to navigators was the compiling of the first set of standard charts and a hydrographical handbook. This was the work of Mikhail Tebenkov, who became governor in 1845, Etolin retiring to Saint Petersburg with the rank of rear-admiral and a seat on the board. Engraved and printed at New Archangel in a rarely artistic manner by two creoles named Terentiev and Kadin, the thirty-nine charts of the Tebenkov atlas are collectors' items today.

In 1859 a college was opened at New Archangel. It was small but indicative of the spread of schooling these eighteen years since 1841. The General College of the Russian Colony was under the Ministry of Education, its curriculum conforming to the standards of the Academy. The students, who were supported by the Company, were given five years of work in classical and modern languages, mathematics, various branches of science, including astronomy, with side courses in subjects such as navigation and accounting. Rezanov's dream had finally been given substance.

In 1860 a government inspector of the colony estimated the number of native Christians at 12,000, indicating that the task of conversion had been nearly half completed. And the population had increased, or, at any rate, that section of it, amounting to more than a third, which was directly under Russian rule and could be reliably counted, as was periodically done. The figures showed that from 1840, just after the great smallpox epidemic, to the 1860s, the increase had been 25 per cent, making up for even the losses from epidemics. The showing was a remarkable one for the Americas at this time.

On the debit side, two of the chief architects of the colony's great period were gone. Wrangell had left the Company. Veniaminov was in Siberia, head of the vast new Archdiocese of Yakutsk, created in 1850. The colony had been included, but serving it too had proven too much for him at his age. It saw him for the last time in 1854, when he had given it thirty years of his devotion. And New Archangel had lost the seminary to Yakutsk. Its former rector remained, having been named bishop. Bishop Petr well understood the methods of his predecessor and he was a conscientious man, but the momentum had been lost and, for other reasons beyond his control, he was not to complete the work in America begun by the fabulous Veniaminov.

In 1868, though seventy-one and losing his sight, Veniaminov was elected Metropolitan of Moscow. The boy from Anginskoe had become his country's foremost prelate. He bore the burden eleven years, and died at eighty-two in 1879. His Church, for which he had established a field even in Japan, had a changed view of missions. His influence was to go on making itself felt in the colony long after it passed to another power.

How that happened is a question the answer to which goes back to events in the Far East beginning the very year the colony entered its great period of development.

XIV

The Old Score with China

In 1839, 150 years had passed since Russia, forced to do so in 1689 by the Treaty of Nerchinsk, conceded to China in perpetuity all claim to the Amur River. Yet never in all those years had China put it to use. No ships of hers were on the mighty 3000-mile stream, the one route that would have given the Russians a simple connection between interior Siberia and the Pacific. Nor had China peopled the huge and fertile valley with any of her hungry millions. Indeed she had emptied it of what people there had been, evacuating all the natives save a very few thousand who had escaped notice by living in such remote areas as the one around the river's mouth.

Much the same thing had been done next door in Mongolia, which had been in China's exclusive control since the signing of the century-old Treaty of Kiakhta with Russia. The people had all been pulled back from the Siberian border to a distance of perhaps a hundred miles, leaving an empty space. It was China's policy to remove the tribes under her sway from contact with their neighbors. As in the case of the Amur Valley, she made use of Mongolia only as a buffer zone against the Russians. Russia had been done one service: the menace of the Mongols had long been a thing of the past. Years before they had resigned themselves to the yoke of China's Manchu rulers.

On her part Russia had scrupulously observed the treaties, herself aiding the Chinese guards in policing the border, harshly punishing her subjects caught in the forbidden territories. Russia's motive was the old one: the wish for no disturbance of the trade with China. In 1839 there had been no important disturbance in some fifty years; the two empires had reached a state at which they were altogether at peace. But the peace was a peculiar one, unmarked by cordiality. The quality of Russo-Chinese relations was summed up in the fact that never had permission been given for Russian ships to trade at Canton, though the favor would have cost Peking nothing and would have been of immeasurable benefit to Russian America. For a hundred years Kiakhta on the Mongolian frontier had remained the one place where the merchants of China and Russia could meet.

What most galled the Russians was, of course, Peking's refusal to allow them to navigate the Amur, the need for which had grown with every year since the foundation of Russian America. Peking had made it clear back in 1805 that the last thing to be expected was a concession with respect to the Amur. As for forcing Peking to do anything, that was impossible in the opinion of Saint Petersburg, which went on the premise, explicitly stated, that China was invincible.

Had it not been that the old breed of Siberian outlaws had died out, the Amur would probably have long since been reoccupied. But so few Russians had appeared on the river these 150 years that Peking had allowed the Chinese guard to dwindle to a few score men. And they were all quartered at the old post of Aigun, far upriver. Seldom did they patrol to any distance below that point. This fact was known at Irkutsk, which had imparted it to Saint Petersburg, where it was received with skepticism. Saint Petersburg could not bring itself to believe that the river was not thoroughly patrolled, one admiral who had been in the Pacific asserting it as fact that the Chinese even used war vessels.

Belief in China's invincibility was general in Europe and America. All the nations dealing with her did so on her terms at the dictation of the Manchus, who had grown arrogant in the extreme after two hundred years in power. Huge though China's trade had come to be, Hong Kong, Shanghai, and all other ports remained closed, with the sole exception of overcrowded Canton, where those who wanted to do business, save for a favored few, were forced to put up with insults, capricious rules, and graft on a grand scale. China had little sympathy in the world, even on the issue of the opium from India to which she had been introduced and which she had lately been endeavoring to exclude.

In 1840 the British opened their famous Opium War on China, soon smashing the myth of her invincibility. Within two years, having, for one thing, taken Canton, they forced the Manchus to beg for peace. The terms included the payment of a huge indemnity, the admission of opium and Christian missionaries, the opening of ports other than Canton, and the cession of Hong Kong for use by Britain as a base.

Russia was conspicuously not among the nations allowed the use of the ports, Britain having no intention of seeing the scope of Russian maritime activity enlarged. She had been waging a cold containment war against Tsar Nicholas, who had been advancing on various fronts, notably Persia—too many fronts, in the opinion of his cautious Foreign Ministry, whose advice Nicholas took when it suited him. He was riding high these days, confident he had the support of the crowned heads whose thrones he was doing so much to protect. He had made himself the supreme enemy of revolution, "the gendarme of Europe," a phrase for him in which he gloried, sensing none of the mockery it conveyed.

The victory of the British had sent a great shock-wave shuddering through China, disorganizing the government and rousing long-smoldering disaffection with the Manchus, disaffection that was presently to flare into open rebellion. The confusion was such that within months the trade with Kiakhta began going rapidly downhill, causing great concern in Russia but at the same time removing the usual reason for leaving the Amur alone. To Nicholas this was an opportunity to make a countermove against Britain in the Far East.

A question had first to be settled: the actual value of the

Amur as a waterway. Of late years the armchair geographers had, for various reasons, developed the view that the river was unnavigable at its mouth. When the matter had been debated by a committee which developed plans for an exploration so public that the British would have known of it at once, the Foreign Ministry called in Company Chairman Wrangell. His reply to the query put to him was that the Company would consider it its "sacred duty" to oblige the government by making a thoroughly secret exploration, one that would also carefully ascertain just how well the Chinese patrolled the Amur.

Governor Tebenkov at New Archangel received Wrangell's instruction in early 1846. He entrusted the mission to a Lieutenant Gavrilov, assigning him the brig *Constantine,* with instructions to remove all indications that she was a Russian vessel. Gavrilov and the crew were to disguise their nationality, even to using only American tobacco.

When, in fall, Gavrilov returned from the Asian coast, it was with an encouraging report. Despite the lack of charts, the poor visibility through fog and rain, and other hazards, he had penetrated a region never before seen by a European from the deck of a ship. He had located the estuary of the Amur, he had traced channels. The local natives, a simple and friendly people who had proved very helpful, had reported seeing no Chinese in living memory. A second exploration made later confirmed the navigability of the Amur and cleared up old misconceptions concerning the complicated topography of the region.

The Company was empowered to begin the occupation of the lower river, taking care not to let the fact be known to the Chinese at Aigun, 2500 miles upstream. Men were moved in from New Archangel; trade was established with the local natives, who had sable skins to sell, a commodity now rare. Command of the project was given to an energetic young naval lieutenant named Vasilii Zavoiko, who had already established a new port on the Okhotsk Sea. He soon had a lively operation under way, with explorations extending in several directions, but he was not to remain in sole charge.

It was by the wish of the cautious Foreign Ministry that the task had been assigned the Company, which could be trusted to proceed by peaceful means. Nicholas, urged to do so by individuals impatient for results and inimical to the Company, gave divided authority over the project to a military man, at the same time naming him governor general at Irkutsk. He was Nikolai Nikolaievich Muraviev, and, with his appointment, though the fact was not to be evident for some time, the destiny of Russian America was determined.

Nikolai Muraviev was exactly the kind of man to appeal to those who wanted spectacular action. Already a lieutenant-general at thirty-eight, with wounds to show for having fought Turks, rebellious Poles, and the warlike peoples of the Caucasus, he was a bold, flamboyant man with singular energy and drive. He was also a ruthless man, hesitating at nothing when he had an end in view. He was vastly unpopular at the Saint Petersburg ministries, with which he frequently had head-on collisions when his requests were denied.

For six years following his appointment to command at Irkutsk, Muraviev was in constant battle with the Foreign Ministry, which managed to keep Nicholas on its side. Muraviev's desire was to take the Amur in one grand move, if necessary fighting the Chinese at Aigun, though neither he nor any other living Russian able to estimate its strength had ever seen Aigun. The Ministry, anxious as always not to expose Russia on another front, in this case a very distant front indeed, wanted no explosions that could reach the ears of the British, who would be delighted in this instance to come to the aid of Peking. Meanwhile, during the six years, the Chinese at Aigun learned absolutely nothing about the activity on the lower river.

Muraviev was finally given his chance by the Crimean War— a name that has obscured the memory of the fact it was partly fought in the Pacific. In that brief but violent conflict, which took place from 1854 to 1856, Russia faced an alliance headed by England and France. It was Europe's first upheaval of the sort in the forty years since Napoleon, and the first war between white men in the Pacific, to which it was carried jointly by the English and the French. Before that happened, the Company and its colleague, the Hudson's Bay Company, obtained an exemption from direct attack for their American holdings. They were to be subject only to blockade and seizure of their vessels on the open sea. The exemption meant that the Siberian coast must take all the fire of the allies.

Muraviev hastened to Saint Petersburg prior to the outbreak of the war with a plan for the strengthening of the coastal installations, which were very weak. As he pointed out, the only way to get men and matériel quickly to the seaboard was by the Amur. He argued that the Chinese at Aigun could have no logical objection inasmuch as the British were their enemies as well. Nicholas agreed, on the condition that no violence be done the Chinese even if they resisted. "I want no smell of powder about this."

On returning to Irkutsk in the early weeks of 1854, Muraviev sent Peking a statement of his case with the request that the answer be sent to Aigun. He then turned with furious energy to the mobilization of the war resources of the Irkutsk region and to the building of a small shipyard on the Shilka, the Amur headwater lying in Russian territory. He had no time to waste if he was to be on the coast by summer, in time for the expected onslaught. It was May when he set out down the Shilka. He was in a newly built steam launch at the head of a line of some ninety boats and barges laden with men, supplies, and artillery.

Four days of sailing down the Shilka, and they were on the Amur. Two days more, and they sighted Albazin, scene of the last Russian stand against the Chinese, 165 years before. Presently they neared a small walled town guarded by ancient cannon. Here Muraviev beached his armada, drew a long breath, and sent his interpreter to ask the governor what had been heard from Peking. This was Aigun.

Nothing had been heard from Peking. It was all a surprise to the governor, who "was quite embarrassed by this situation," according to historian Aitchen K. Wu. ". . . He let the unwelcome guests pass through in order to get rid of them." And that was all there was to it the day Russia faced up to China after all the years.

Muraviev now knew who was afraid of whom. As he chugged on down the Amur, the Orient was elsewhere undergoing momentous penetration. Japan, responding to the implied threat presented by Commodore Perry's American warships, opened certain of her ports to the United States.

Muraviev would have arrived on the coast too late had the enemy squadron not been behind schedule. Consisting of three British and three French battleships, it was under the command of Britain's Admiral Price, who knew nothing about the installations on the Amur. He was headed for Petropavlovsk in the expectation of easily destroying the little town together with all ships that might be in the harbor. Its defenders, who had had word of his approach, awaited him nervously, having only a few old cannon. Numbering perhaps fifty, they were mostly Company officers and men hastily assembled by Lieutenant Vasilii Zavoiko, who had yet to see a battle. Then came 350 of the men brought by Muraviev, and the bulk of the field guns, with orders to Zavoiko to take command with the rank of admiral. No sooner did he have the new guns in place to guard the harbor and the ships within than the enemy appeared.

The first casualty was Admiral Price, who shot himself, much to the disgust of the French. Those hastily placed new guns, the source of which was a puzzle, had shown him what use the Russians had made of his lateness in arriving. The French admiral to whom command fell was made of sterner stuff; he ordered that the original plan be carried out. Zavoiko and his men fought fiercely, but one by one their guns were silenced by the fire of the allies, who then tried a landing. That proved a mistake great enough for a French account afterward to deny the outcome was "a shameful rout." In any case, the Battle of Petropavlovsk was over, the victory Zavoiko's. The enemy departed in search of easier prey, leaving town and ships unharmed.

Even though exempt from direct attack, the colony suffered. Ships were lost; the blockade caused want; local activity was at a standstill, most of the naval men having left for the front. Everything about the Battle of Petropavlovsk and all the other engagements along the Asian shore was soon known and passed along the native grapevine. The conflict was brought close also by the frequent sight of allied warships—monsters, the newer ones seemed, steam-driven and capable of firing the new missiles that exploded when they struck.

The knowledge that white men were killing each other affected the natives like a contagion. There seems no other explanation for the sudden and widespread unrest, even in places that had known only peace, in British as well as Russian territory and farther down the coast. At New Archangel, the Tlingits, angered by a trifle, uprose with a fury they had not shown in years. The astonished townspeople found themselves fighting for their lives. Two of them died and nineteen were wounded before the attackers were driven off with a loss of sixty dead and wounded. The church built for them was a wreck. Plainly the war was a setback for civilization among the natives.

The allies again struck the Siberian coast in the summer of 1855, this time succeeding in destroying Petropavlovsk. But that, together with the shooting up of a little Company station on the Kurils, the burning of ships, and the doing of other damage of the sort, constituted their triumph. The allied commanders still did not even suspect the existence of the posts on the Amur, which Muraviev had been at tireless pains to add to and strengthen.

Only in the Far East had Russia gained, as could be seen when peace was made in 1856. The world now knew that the Russians were on the Amur, and great had been the surprise in Europe when the news of it came out of China, the opinion having been general that the river was unnavigable. To their chagrin, the allied commanders in the Pacific now understood how it was that pursued Russian ships in the vicinity of the

Amur had managed to disappear in a manner altogether puzzling at the time.

The war had cost Russia heavily, in lives, prestige, and money. The treasury was empty, the government deeply in debt. And the huge army of which Nicholas had been so proud had proved, despite the great bravery shown by many, corrupt beyond measure.

Nicholas was now dead. He had died when the war was a year old, in February of 1855, in a sense by his own hand, for he had deliberately exposed himself in a fashion to bring on pneumonia. The truth had been borne in on him by then, about his army, about the hatred for him in Europe, about the degree of respect for him from his own subjects. His son and heir, Alexander II, was now Tsar.

Muraviev had been made supreme commander in the Far East by Alexander, with authority to proceed at his discretion. One of the first uses of his new power had been to oust the Company from the Amur and substitute an organization of his own creation. At war's end he prepared to take the river permanently from the Chinese, who were even less able to resist than they had been. China was in chaos, the rebellion against the Manchus being at its height.

In the summer of 1856 Muraviev set out down the river with a contingent of settlers drawn from the convicts in Siberia. Stopping at Aigun, he bluntly informed the governor of his intention, adding that he would be by again in two years, at which time he would debate the matter, should Peking care to have an emissary meet him. With that he went on, Aigun putting up no resistance. This reached the ears of the British, who went to the aid of the Manchus, restoring them to power and quelling the rebellion, but not in time to forestall Muraviev.

When, in 1858, he reappeared at Aigun, it was with more settlers. Awaiting him was Manchu Prince Yi-Shan, who was told that Russia wanted the left bank of the river down to its mouth and the coast of Manchuria south to Korea. Yi-Shan "at first had no intention of accepting the humiliating demands," states Wu, "but, owing to the furious attitude of Muraviev during the conference, he finally acceded. . . ." He acceded to the extent of putting his name to a new treaty with Russia.

Another and different treaty was negotiated at much the same time by Russia's envoy to China, but that did not trouble Muraviev. He made good his Treaty of Aigun by simply occupying the Manchurian coast, founding Vladivostok among other towns of the future. He then called it a day and retired to Paris in 1861 with the title of Count Muraviev-Amurskii. It is another story that Russians were again in Mongolia and presently were to attain all their old objectives in the East.

To all outward appearances, the future of Russian America was never brighter. The Amur was open; the old problem of communicating with Siberia had been further simplified by the seizure of the Manchurian coast. Nor was that all that had been done. Company ships were buying 30 per cent of Russia's tea at Shanghai. By diplomacy, China's ports had at last been opened to Russian trade, and likewise those of Japan. Yet there were those who for some time had been urging that the colony be disposed of.

XV

The Sale

". . . The United States are bound to spread over the whole of North America. . . . Sooner or later we shall have to surrender our North American possessions." Nikolai Muraviev wrote those words. He set them down in 1853, fourteen years before the sale of Alaska—to begin using the name it then acquired.

He saw the surrender as no sacrifice. In his view, Alaska was not worth retaining. Russia belonged in the Far East. There she should concentrate her energies. Avoid trouble, "gracefully yield" Alaska, and the United States would be won to alliance, serve as guardian of the Siberian back door.

This thesis set in motion the forces that led to the sale. And it remained the core of the argument to the end, although by then its premise had long been imaginary. Far from wanting to take Alaska by force, the United States proved uneager even to buy. She bought in the belief she was obliging Russia. Since Russia believed she would oblige the United States, the transaction was a thoroughly bizarre affair, not at all the reasoned, logical thing time has made it appear. It was a case of the fallibility of international intelligence.

In 1841 an elegant bachelor of thirty-three who liked his name spelled Edouard de Stoeckl came to the United States fresh from Europe, never dreaming he would stay for twenty-seven years. A career man with the Russian Foreign Service, he had been assigned to the secretariat of the legation in Washington. Though he styled himself Baron, his antecedents are difficult to trace. He was educated in Russia but not born there, and he was of Austrian and Italian parentage, according to the hazy information on him. Russian biographical works are curt on the subject of the man who climaxed his diplomatic career by engineering the sale of Alaska.

Washington, with its mud-filled streets, gun-toting politicians, and omnipresent cuspidors, was regarded as a place of exile by most European diplomats, and Edouard de Stoeckl shared the view, but Washington loved him. His manners were as polished as his appearance; his air was friendly, his English fluent. Capital society quickly took him to its bosom. Not that his charm was the only reason. Discounting the occasional diatribes against Tsar Nicholas from press and platform, which could be taken with salt, Russia's representatives were generally treated with cordiality bordering on affection. The current Russian minister, who had been emboldened to marry an American after four years in the United States, was called "Papa." The warmth came of the fact that for forty years the most consistent friend of the United States in Europe had been Russia.

For all his detestation of republics, Nicholas had taken care to sustain his predecessor's policy of amiability toward Britain's growing maritime rival. There was a constant exchange of goodwill messages. American representatives in Saint Petersburg were accorded flattering attention, Nicholas himself occasionally joining in the effort to impress them. He did so with such success in the case of James Buchanan, who became American minister in 1832, that this future United States President was charmed into thinking of the champion of reaction as "a man without a moral blemish." Nor was it all gestures. Russia was the diplomatic ally of the United States on the great question of neutral rights. And the volume of business between them had grown large. American vessels did much of Russia's shipping for her, to and from many ports, enjoying by treaty a rare set of privileges in the matter of tariffs and the like.

From the American point of view the relationship had one

flaw. It had to do with the 1824 treaty dealing with Alaska. Russia refused to reinstate the canceled clause under which American ships had freely frequented bays, harbors, and other inshore waters. Direct trade with the natives was practically at an end. The fact that the Company was in league with the hated British of Hudson's Bay made this all the more irritating. Washington had been moved to protest in 1836, following the forcible expulsion of a trespassing ship by Company officials, but Saint Petersburg had upheld the action, contending that peace was best served by excluding the traders. They had, it was charged, continued to deal in rum, contrary to the treaty. This was denied, but Washington could not truthfully say that much had been done to restrict cargoes, and there the matter had rested ever since.

The issue by no means outweighed the general good feeling for Russia, but it did create enough trouble for the legation at Washington to make Stoeckl uneasy. Despite the friendliness he was shown on all sides, he was unsure how far to trust these Americans. There was much about the United States he was never to understand, and once he got an idea into his well-barbered head it stayed there. In his view he understood the United States very well indeed. His writings, which are voluminous, set forth many confident predictions, only a fraction of which stood the test of time. The quality of his insight into the American make-up is indicated by his written remark that the authorities ought to restrict the frequency of voting, "since elections cause disorders and anarchy."

His uneasiness over Alaska came of his view of Americans as a violent people, not to be trusted no matter how friendly they seemed. For that opinion he had a certain reason. The country was ringing with oratory on Manifest Destiny, the preachment that the United States was bound to possess the entire continent, despite treaties and the promise contained in the Monroe Doctrine to respect existing colonies. How ready was the United States to take advantage of her opportunities was indicated by the events occurring in the Southwest. Manifest Destiny was a holy cause in the eyes of some of its exponents. It was the duty of the United States to extend to all her neighbors her law, her institutions, and her culture.

European logicians generally disbelieved that the thinly populated United States could reach the Pacific inside of a hundred years. In the Pacific indeed destiny seemed to be with Britain, what with her successful war in China, her position in Oregon, and the headway she was making in California. Then came 1844 and James Polk's campaign for the presidency with the slogan "Fifty-four-forty or Fight," threatening Britain with war unless she released the coast all the way to the boundary of Alaska at 54 degrees, 40 minutes.

Stoeckl was ever after a complete believer in Manifest Destiny. Within five years, the discovery of gold in California contributing, the coast was American from Mexico to the present boundary of Canada, which Polk established by compromise with Britain. Hudson's Bay was forced to withdraw north of the line, into British Columbia, a name that had yet to be bestowed. In the United States there were those who viewed the compromise as no sacred pledge, declaring that Britain would yet be completely defeated, some going so far as to speak of taking Alaska as well.

Threats of the sort aside, the westward surge of the United States seemed to bode only good for the Russian colony, for which a wholly new avenue of trade was opened. Petr Kostromitinov, who was stationed at San Francisco as consul and Company agent, wrote New Archangel in 1849, describing the gold rush. Anything and everything from shoes to shovels could be sold, he wrote, so great were the needs of the thousands of men flooding in. The shipload of stuff he was sent, some of which had lain in the colony's warehouses for years, all went quickly at fabulous prices.

With that as a starter, Kostromitinov built up a regular trade over the next three years, giving the colony its first market for commodities other than its furs. Burgeoning San Francisco was in need of lumber, coal, fish, and much else that Alaska could supply, including ice. The ice was a brilliant thought on Kostromitinov's part, the first shipment fetching seventy-five dollars a ton. It led to the formation of a distributing corporation in San Francisco called the American-Russian Commercial Company. Paid in gold, the New Archangel shipmasters bought food in Hawaii for California as well as for the colony. The Company invested heavily in the new trade, ordering seven new steamers, small and large, built at eastern United States yards.

The wish of the Company was to have no callers at its ports, to do all the shipping itself. That presently ran counter to the wishes of San Francisco's new and aggressive businessmen, who had soon developed a keen desire to investigate Alaska's resources, precisely what the Company did not want. Gold, something for which the San Franciscans had a keen eye, had been found—not much, but it took little these days to rouse Americans. What could happen had been shown by California's recent history. Pointing to its right under the 1824 treaty, the Company forbade free entry beyond New Archangel. In vain the irritated San Franciscans pointed to the lack of restrictions on Russian ships in American waters.

The complaints were brought to Washington by a man to worry the Russian legation. He was William Gwin, the senior of California's first pair of senators. Gwin had been in Congress once before, as a representative from Mississippi, and was known to get what he wanted. Alaska had greatly roused his interest. Stoeckl, who was evidently assigned to deal with him, wrote Saint Petersburg that the Company must be made to act reciprocally, else the United States might close her own harbors to Russian ships, which she could do under the 1824 treaty. Saint Petersburg stayed calm. The Company, Stoeckl was informed in effect, was to handle its own affairs. Washington also stayed calm; in fact Russia was offered the consular services of the United States in China and Hawaii. And, to Stoeckl's delight, Gwin indicated the wish to be friends. A good politician,

Gwin knew how to bide his time. Eventually he obtained approval for an exploring expedition in Alaska, the findings of which did not include gold.

Russia's long-time policy of amity paid a handsome dividend from 1854 to 1856, the years of the Crimean War, creating one of the more curious episodes in American history. The nation appears to have concluded that the world was picking on its overseas friend. With scarcely a dissenting voice, press and public uprose in wrath against Russia's enemies, as the government of President Pierce all but went to open war in Russia's behalf. American crews rescued Russian ships. Arms were furnished, a whole shipload of powder going to the defenders of the Siberian coast. Among the popular demonstrations was the offer of three hundred Kentucky riflemen to go to the Crimea, where volunteer American surgeons served with the Russian forces. James Buchanan, who was minister in London, was practically a Russian spy, passing on what he learned to Secretary of State William Marcy, who relayed it to Saint Petersburg through the Russian legation.

Feeling ran especially high in California. Senator Gwin won re-election after calling for all-out support of Russia. San Francisco's American-Russian Company, by operating New Archangel's ships under the American flag, ran the blockade of Alaska. The flag was used also to bring the Company's new, United-States-built ships from the east coast to the Pacific. "By the time it was over," wrote Frank Golder, no Russophile, "the United States was the only nation in the world that was neither ashamed nor afraid to acknowledge boldly her friendship for Russia."

And all the time Edouard de Stoeckl had been at the center. Just before the outbreak, owing to the emergency created by the death of the minister, he was made chargé d'affaires for the duration. His first endeavors had been to be clever. He sought to involve the United States directly until reminded by Saint Petersburg that his first duty was to guard relations. It was a command he was always to remember. Having also had the uninhibited advice and guidance of Secretary of State Marcy, he emerged with such distinction that he was named minister by the new Tsar, Alexander II. All Washington was glad to see The Baron get the promotion. He had done nothing to diminish his popularity by marrying an American, Eliza Howard of Springfield, Massachusetts, who was to help him maintain the capital's foremost salon. After the inauguration of Buchanan in 1857, Stoeckl had only to walk into the White House.

". . . We shall deeply regret the downfall of a great nation with which our relations have always been friendly and intimate and which, on one memorable occasion, was virtually the only power sincerely sympathetic to our cause." Those words were to be written by Stoeckl at the outbreak of the Civil War. The behavior of the United States during the Crimean War had unquestionably impressed him deeply, but he had not lost all his old mistrust. The friendliness, the intimacy had not caused him to lay aside his conviction that in pursuit of her Manifest Destiny the United States would not hesitate to take even Russia's colony. In his view, the solution was to sell the territory.

He had been told that the United States would buy and "pay handsomely." This assurance was given him when, one day in the course of the Crimean War, Marcy and Senator Gwin called on him to ask, much to his surprise, whether Russia might sell, rumor having it that she was in great need of money. Earlier, at the outset of the war, before it was known that Alaska would not be attacked, Kostromitinov in San Francisco had conceived a notion of protecting the colony by pretending it had been sold to his friends the owners of the American-Russian Company. In this roundabout way the idea of actually buying had come to Gwin, who had learned something of the value of the Alaskan fur resources. Stoeckl was at the time greatly shaken by the interview with its confirmation of all his fears that Alaska was coveted. Reporting the conversation to Saint Petersburg, he referred to Americans as "dangerous neighbors." He begged his visitors please to forget their question. But he himself had not forgotten it. On the contrary. Now he was minister, his intention was to persuade the government of the new Tsar to oblige the Americans.

Judged by his achievements, Alexander II, who was thirty-seven at his accession, was a man of singular will and energy. He it was who freed the serfs at historic last, a task that took him five years. He reformed the courts, decentralized the government, effected many another change overdue by centuries. Yet, until he came to the throne, he had shown no promise of going against the ways of his father, Nicholas. He had, however, the intelligence to understand that change was imperative if the dynasty was to survive, so many were the evils exposed by the war. As he informed the representatives of the nobility at the outset of his reign, they must either work out a plan for the liberation of the serfs or expect revolution.

At some other time in the empire's history his reign would have been easy-going, uneventful. He had never wanted much to be Tsar, it would seem. Once he confessed that as a boy he had dreamed of running away to America. He leaned heavily on certain of his advisers, men he had chosen for the will he lacked. He had a brother nine years younger who was his direct opposite. Energetic Grand Duke Constantine lacked neither inner drive nor love of power. He was an annoyance to his brother in that he sought often to spur him to this action or that, showing he would gladly have reigned in his stead. He played as large a part in the government as he was allowed. Though not yet thirty, he was Admiral-General of the Fleet and a power in the Navy. In the years ahead he was to be chairman of various committees, Viceroy of Poland, and President of the Imperial Council.

Constantine was a revolutionist, or so he considered himself. His father had left him a fiery advocate of the radicalism of the period. The passion with which he expounded it at times mounted to fury, foreshadowing his loss of reason late in life.

"Fools" was the least of the expletives he hurled at those who disagreed with him. Nor was he disposed to forgive and forget. He was a dangerous man to cross.

In Constantine the Company had a mortal enemy. In his view it was no more than a monopolistic colonial corporation, an offense to advanced economic thought. He saw it as a contradiction in terms that it could have done anything praiseworthy for natives. The claim that it had given the colony a model government of its kind he rejected as absurd. It served only to enrich the stockholders, no matter what the charters said. He was unswayed by the knowledge that not a single merchant was any longer on the board, which was now made up of such highly respected figures as Admirals Etolin and Tebenkov. No one associated with the Company was respected by Constantine, whose belief was, in short, that it should be destroyed.

One man whom Constantine idolized was Nikolai Muraviev, whose complexities of character included a view of himself as a radical of the most advanced kind. He was well acquainted with such figures as Bakunin, who had debated the future of the world with him. Muraviev loved debates of the sort, throwing out as he talked great showers of startling ideas like so many sparks. If he believed in all the thoughts he is known to have expressed, he held to a strange mixture of anarchism, socialism, and inventions of his own, all without seeing any inconsistency among them, or with his behavior as a ruthless imperialistic conqueror. Herzen seems to have summed him up well when he called him ". . . a democrat and a Tatar, a liberal and a despot." Constantine could understand perfectly.

Muraviev professed a great admiration for the United States. An idea he once flung out called for a United States of Siberia, affiliated with the overseas model. For all his admiration, he was evidently not aware of the well-known American policy regarding "foreign entanglements." He did know about the success of the United States in California and Oregon, and he had heard of Manifest Destiny, a concept that enchanted him. His complete faith in it he indicated when he wrote that ". . .

sooner or later we shall have to surrender our North American possessions," a proposal he was first to make. His exuberant imagination had no trouble conjuring up a vision of the United States, made grateful by the surrender, collaborating with Russia in the Far East. Indeed that was the immediate reason for giving up the colony. "Unfortunately we allowed the English to invade this part of Asia, but the mistake can be rectified by a close alliance between us and the United States."

A frequent explanation for the sale of Alaska has come to be that the Crimean War showed Russia how easily it could fall to Britain. Aside from the question whether the war could have revealed anything new along that line, the sources are completely clear on the point that talk of aggression centered on the United States. And Muraviev made his proposal *before* the Crimean War, as is clear from the date: 1853. Nor had the idea of sale then risen. Stoeckl had yet to discover that the United States might buy. Muraviev was, in short, willing to donate Alaska, which he never saw. Having the faculty of believing what he wanted to believe, he had arrived easily at the conclusion that the colony was worthless alongside the benefit of satisfying the United States.

The behavior of the United States during the Crimean War did give him some reason for believing the alliance possible. He was sent munitions, American shipmasters kept him informed of enemy movements. Great interest in the Amur development was shown by American traders. When he had won the Amur and had gained coastal Manchuria as well, Muraviev was even more convinced that Alaska was unnecessary to the empire and that it should be ceded to the United States, whose role would be that of protector of the Siberian back door.

Few in Saint Petersburg regarded him as a great thinker, and he removed himself from the argument when he retired to Paris. His thesis might have died had it not been taken up by Constantine, who believed that all his ideas should be carried out. Constantine first put himself on record as champion of the thesis in 1857, the year following the Crimean War, and the second of his brother's reign. He initiated a ten-year battle having one aspect of classic drama in that it came down to a struggle between two men for control over the Tsar's actions in the matter. Constantine's antagonist was the man his brother had chosen to be his Foreign Minister, Prince Aleksandr Gorchakov.

A calm, dispassionate sort of man, a scholar of history, and a linguist, graying Prince Gorchakov was one of Europe's leading statesmen, having behind him forty years' experience in the foreign-service field, much of it gained at difficult posts abroad. His respect for the United States was great. "For the more than eighty years it has existed, the American union has owed its independence, its towering rise, and its progress to the concord of its members, consecrated, under the auspices of its illustrious founders, by institutions which have been able to reconcile union with liberty. This union . . . has exhibited to the world the spectacle of a prosperity without example in the annals of history."

As he put it, he saw no "political necessity" for selling Alaska, which was contrary to the view Stoeckl was already expressing in his correspondence. Evidently Gorchakov wanted his representatives abroad to say what they thought, without regard to his opinion. Stoeckl was calling Alaska "a breeder of trouble" and was presently to urge sale in as many words, some of which would be in key with Muraviev's utterances. And with every new threat of trouble, however nebulous, Stoeckl was to hasten to sound the alarm. Yet Gorchakov was never to be moved. Nor was the Company to be made substantially to change its mode of operation.[1]

---

[1] How Gorchakov reasoned may perhaps be deduced from an argument against the sale written in 1866 by a Baron Fedor Osten-Saken, an official of the Asian Department who had served in the United States: ". . . the position of our American colonies from a purely political sense can be called particularly favorable. . . . Whoever acquaints himself with the history of the continual rivalry between England and America . . . will begin to understand how it was that the insignificant power of our Company could survive alongside such powerful neighbors. . . . As

On occasion Gorchakov showed Stoeckl's letters to Alexander and seems not to have kept them secret even from Constantine, who of course had heard, like many others in Saint Petersburg, that back in 1854 highly placed persons in the United States had asked to buy Alaska. In March of 1857 Gorchakov opened a note from Constantine which said in part that ". . . we must not deceive ourselves. We must foresee that the United States, aiming constantly to round out their possessions and desiring to dominate undividedly the whole of North America, will take the aforementioned colonies from us and we shall not be able to retain them." It was Constantine's opening shot. Evidently he had been told by his brother to go argue with the proper authorities. He also wrote the Minister of Finance, whose jurisdiction included the Company. Other things he said were that Alaska was valueless, that the treasury needed the money, that the Company was a detriment to international relations.

Gorchakov indicated that he would be swayed by only one consideration: the amount the United States might pay. And she must open the negotiation. Russia would do no peddling. In any event, the debate was premature. Nothing should be done until the expiration of the Company's charter in 1861, four years thence. Meanwhile, lest harm be done, they should all be careful how they talked about this thing. Constantine agreed to secrecy but was otherwise undampened, seizing on every opportunity to reopen the subject.

The next year brought word that 30,000 men from the United States were swarming into British Columbia in response to a gold strike, giving Hudson's Bay great trouble and causing London to take hasty legal steps to hold the domain. Though that was indication of what could happen in Alaska any time,

---

long as the present state of affairs exists in North America there is hardly any ground to fear seizure. . . . The more or less unaccountable fear of losing our colonies . . . could be set off against other fears with respect to the misunderstandings, disadvantages, further seizures, et cetera, to which we should be subject if we were to receive a new next-door neighbor in the person of the United States. . . ."

Gorchakov stayed calm, as he also did on learning from Stoeckl that the Mormons were thought to be planning to leave Utah, possibly to go to Alaska. Why that would be a bad thing Stoeckl did not explain. That dispatch was too much for Alexander. He said they had better decide now what to do about the colony. But no action followed. Gorchakov's calm supervened. The Mormon threat proved a myth; Britain did not lose British Columbia.

The Company, which had become aware that something was afoot, was assured that all was well. It was permitted to renew its contract with Hudson's Bay for the third time and told to proceed with its plans to seek another charter. The government arranged to have the usual preliminary inspection made of the colony. But Gorchakov lost control of the situation when, in 1859, Stoeckl came to Saint Petersburg. He had much to discuss, notably the disquieting prospect for Russia that the United States might presently cease to be a strong, single nation. Undoubtedly questioned by Constantine, Stoeckl had truthfully to say that if Alaska was to be sold it had to be now or possibly never. He returned to Washington empowered to seek an offer.

The Secretary of State was not in favor of new territory, but Stoeckl knew how to bypass him. He went to Senator Gwin, who went to Buchanan. In early 1860 Stoeckl happily wrote Gorchakov that they had an offer of $5,000,000. Far from enough, replied Gorchakov, evidently back in control of the situation. Crushed, Stoeckl went back to Gwin, whose comment on the feasibility of raising the price revealed the actual extent of desire for Alaska at the time. He thought the Western senators might go for more money, but not the others. Stoeckl went on trying, but it was hopeless. And that fall of 1860, Lincoln was elected; war ensued. The question after that was whether the United States would remain whole and ever again be able to buy new lands.

In Saint Petersburg the government proceeded to consider the Company's petition for another charter. As usual a committee was appointed to hear the evidence and make a recommendation. On the surface the outlook was for a cut-and-dried affair. The Company's record had never been better, and its financial condition was excellent, its capital standing at the all-time high of 13,000,000 rubles. The committee, which numbered four-teen, mostly officials and scientists, included Company stock-holders. And a favorable decision was wanted by the Finance Minister, who had charge of the proceedings. The cost of pro-viding the colony with a substitute administration would be a heavy one for the government, the financial burden of which had not lightened markedly since the Crimean War. A fight nevertheless loomed. Constantine was determined to sway the hearings to his way of thinking, which was that the Company's existence had forthwith to be ended.

The hearings were lengthy and stormy. Constantine himself took the stand, charged that the Alaskan natives were serfs. That brought Etolin out in hot denial, and so it went. The committee, in an evident effort to please both sides, rendered a decision shot through with contradictions. Charter-renewal was recommended, but for only twelve years instead of the usual twenty, and on conditions which the Company refused to accept, calling them unworkable. It could continue to operate on the old charter for the time being, and there the matter hung, but to no one's benefit. The uncertainty as to the Company's future, together with the knowledge, now widespread, that a try had been made at selling the colony, destroyed its credit, and its capital was soon gone. To keep it afloat the government found itself contributing an annual 200,000 rubles. Meanwhile the American war raged on.

In that war Russia was the only major European power ac-tively sympathetic to the Lincoln government, which came to be beset by fears of open intervention on the part of nations hope-ful of disunion. In 1861 Gorchakov instructed Stoeckl to say that "in any event the American nation may count on the most cordial sympathy . . . during the serious crisis through which it is passing." In 1862 Gorchakov told the American chargé d'affaires that "we desire above all things the maintenance of the American union. . . . I cannot express to you how profound an anxiety we feel, how serious are our fears."

Russia herself, owing to a situation in Poland, presently faced the threat of intervention from England and France, with the probability that hostilities would spread to the Pacific. The fleet was ordered to proceed in secrecy to American waters, a better position for offensive movements in the event of outbreak of actual war. And so it was that in September of 1863 the people of New York were astonished to see, entering their harbor, a number of wicked-looking battleships flying the Russian flag. Days later San Francisco had the same experience, as the Russian Pacific fleet put in, also to cast anchor for an apparently indefinite stay. No public explanation was ever made by the very few in Russia and the United States who knew the facts. The deliberate silence on the part of the two governments heightened the impression that Russia had sent her fleet as a warning to the world to keep its hands off American affairs, most notably the Union blockade of Confederate ports.

This was the belief in the United States for years after the Civil War, until an American unearthed the pertinent documents from the Russian archives. The episode is now considered debunked, a judgment that ignores the effect at the time, which hung on the very fact the world was left to draw its own conclusions. Morale in the North was low when the ships appeared; Washington was most in fear of intervention. The visitors were received with the wildest acclaim. Wrote War Secretary Gideon Welles in his diary, "Thank God for the Russians." They remained seven months, their ships visited by shoals of people, including Mrs. Lincoln. The chancelleries of Europe were greatly taken aback on learning where the Russian fleet had gone. The maneuver ended fear of intervention alike in the United States and in Russia.

In October of 1863 Gorchakov considered making a formal alliance, the United States showing signs of willingness to lay aside her old feelings on the point. His eventual decision was that the entente needed no written attestation. The freeing of the serfs and Alexander's other reforms, his several acts on behalf of the Union, the fact that Russia had given support for over sixty years, these things had of late been widely stressed by the American press. Relations were in a state that could only be called ideal.

The end of the war left Washington defeated on one front. Great economic pressure had been exerted on the provinces of Canada in the belief that if reduced to want they would forego their shreds of allegiance to Britain and join the United States. Their reaction had been to tighten their belts along with their ties to Britain, and now they were fast moving toward a union of their own, eventually to be known as the Dominion of Canada. The fact had decisive bearing on the situation of Alaska, which was now unlikely ever to be contiguous to the United States.

The Canadian movement was a personal defeat for William Seward, who had been Lincoln's Secretary of State and was now Andrew Johnson's. A onetime governor of New York, a former senator, and, until lately, head of his party, he had been within sight of the presidential nomination in 1860 and was determined to succeed Johnson. An old exponent of Manifest Destiny, with a specific eye to Alaska, Seward hoped to emerge as the great national figure through the realization of large plans he had conceived for the extension of the United States, even to distant islands in the two oceans. Though his vision of the future was hardly unjustified, at the time only a man of his ebullience could have believed he had a chance.

These were Reconstruction days. The atmosphere of Washington was never so highly charged. Seward had forfeited the support of his party by choosing to stay with Johnson, who had enemies in Congress so virulent they were not to hesitate to try impeaching him. No administration measure could expect easy passage, least of all one for the purchase of new territory. The country was in no mood to think of enlargement. Manifest Destiny had become a phrase to make Americans wince; they saw for one thing where it had led in the case of Canada, much of the blame for which could be laid to the over-eager Seward. Alaska was to be his only acquisition, and that was to come of peculiar circumstances.

Alaska had not, as has been supposed, been waiting to be sold at the close of the Civil War. Grand Duke Constantine had had the thought but he had been forced to put it out of his mind. Gorchakov had been given large new authority in 1863. He was now the Tsar's right hand, Chancellor of the empire as well as Foreign Minister. The plan now was to keep the colony and, as the quickest way to make it self-supporting again, to revitalize the Company, which had been authorized to raise new capital and promised another twenty-year charter. This pledge was affirmed by Constantine as President of the Imperial Council on April 2, 1866. The decision not to sell was made well before that, as is indicated by orders given a new colonial governor appointed shortly after Gorchakov's authority was extended.

Events in Canada and the United States had obviously made retention of the colony the only wise course for Russia. With the United States weakened by a long war, bound to remain torn by dissensions for some time to come, and clearly unable to control the Canadians, it was folly to think of her as any sort of guardian of the Siberian back door. As for the old thought that she might seize Alaska, the Canadian confederation was making that even more absurd than it had been. In any event, there was the great debt of friendship now owed Russia by the United States.

As a further indication that Alaska was off the market, in 1866 Stoeckl was informed that he was finally to leave Washington, that he was to be transferred to The Hague. That fall he was in Saint Petersburg, discussing his new assignment. He was happy about it. It was a promotion, and he would again be living in his beloved Europe. He had been well rewarded for his work in the United States. He had been decorated, given two elevations in rank and a raise in pay so high the amount was kept secret from others in the Foreign Service. His son had the

Tsar himself as godfather. Carried away perhaps by the respect accorded his views, he allowed himself to talk loosely. One of his views was that the United States would yet triumph in Canada, that Britain would voluntarily withdraw from North America. He believed he should have been allowed to proceed with the sale of Alaska in 1860. He said as much to Constantine and to Finance Minister Mikhail Reutern, who was glum about the large subsidy he would have to go on furnishing the Company for some time to come. Asked what he thought the chances of selling now were, Stoeckl airily replied they were good, well though he knew the political situation in Washington.

Taking Reutern with him, Constantine went to his brother, who was sufficiently upset to ask Gorchakov to reopen the question. Gorchakov methodically asked Constantine, Reutern, and Stoeckl to state their views in writing. The United States was destined to possess the continent, he read, the colony was an encumbrance, the Far East was Russia's sphere—not a word was new. It was as if these ten years had not passed. And, clearly, Constantine was never going to give up, pledge or no pledge given the Company. Something seems to have snapped in Prince Gorchakov, who bore a heavy burden for a man close to seventy. He went to Alexander, gave him the statements, suggested a meeting at which he would preside, and asked him to make up his own mind this time.

The meeting was held in secrecy at the Winter Palace on December 16, 1866, Alexander presiding as requested. Present were Gorchakov, Reutern, Stoeckl, and Minister of Marine Krabbe, a notable opponent of the Company whose presence Constantine had requested. Krabbe brought a map on which a line had been drawn to indicate the proposed division of the waters. Gorchakov let the others do the talking. Alexander, who was perhaps also tired of hearing about the matter all these years, at the end asked Stoeckl whether he minded returning to Washington to close the deal. There must have been a pause. Until this moment Stoeckl had not realized he had been risking his appointment to The Hague. But he managed to say the right thing. Krabbe gave him his map, Reutern told him not to take less than $5,000,000, and, with that, Stoeckl irritably wrote later, he was sent on his way.

By the time he was back in Washington, in March of 1867, the outlook for administration measures in Congress was even poorer than before and growing worse. He had, nevertheless, to pin his hopes on the ambitions of Seward, whose influence was practically gone. No longer was there a Senator Gwin, his Southern sympathies having long since removed him from the political scene. Seward's eagerness was boundless when he understood that Alaska was for sale. For him the proposal was in time's nick. The Canadians might be given second thoughts about proceeding with their confederation. And what a territory to be able to claim to have added to the United States—bigger even than Texas. Congress surely would not refuse to accept this one, not if the proposal was put as a favor to Russia.

Enjoining great secrecy on everyone, Seward obtained the approval of Johnson and the cabinet, lukewarm in both cases, then got back to Stoeckl with an offer of $5,000,000. Stoeckl got him up to $7,200,000, which was still little enough; in Russia the Navy alone cost twice as much each year. Seward was to offer $300,000 more for two small Danish islands in the Atlantic. The price made Alaska practically a gift.

Seward was in a great hurry, wanting the treaty passed before the Canadians took the final step toward confederation. That called for asking the Senate, which was about to adjourn, for an extended session. And that in turn called for writing and signing the document in a single night; Seward, Stoeckl and their aides worked until four in the morning of March 30. The senators reared back on learning they had been held over to consider a treaty negotiated in secrecy and haste. They were unimpressed by the argument about Canada, and few among them knew anything, or cared, about Alaska, which was the less appealing for the fact it was non-contiguous territory.

Atop everything was the feeling against the administration. Senators went to Stoeckl to say they were sorry but they could support nothing proposed by Seward. The measure might simply have died in the Foreign Relations Committee had it not been for the chairman of that body, Massachusetts' brilliant Charles Sumner, whose view was that, despite the circumstances, Russia had to be obliged. Having gathered all available information on the worth of Alaska—he it was who proposed the name [2]—Sumner gave a three-hour oration with all the force at his command, concluding with the one argument that had real weight: "Even if you doubt the value of these possessions, the treaty is a sign of amity. It is a new expression of that entente cordiale . . . which is a phenomenon of history."

Alaska was, nevertheless, bought by only one vote above the two-thirds required for passage of a treaty; of the thirty-nine senators present, twelve dissented. Another vote was taken, following a plea for unanimity, but two held out. The vote of record is thirty-seven to two. The news of the purchase left the Canadians unmoved.

Stoeckl could not yet call it a day. The House had still to appropriate the money, but he was assured that would be done at the next session, in July. So went the pledge on the honor of the United States given by Thaddeus Stevens, majority leader of the House, chairman of its Appropriations Committee, and mortal enemy of Johnson. So sure was Seward that all would go well, he prepared to take possession of Alaska that fall.

By letter from Gorchakov, Stoeckl learned that the Tsar had awarded him 25,000 rubles, which was not quite $17,000—a pittance, all things considered, Stoeckl thought. Added Gorchakov, "On my part I now take my share of the responsibility for this," meaning by that the blame. The government, which had maintained secrecy, had now to inform the nation and the Company that the pledge not to sell had been broken. And the money, which came to less than 11,000,000 rubles, would be small solace to the Company, the Finance Ministry planning to keep most of it. When its debts were paid, the Company would

---

[2] The name Alaska had, with variant spellings, long denoted the land east of the Aleutians. It derives from the Aleut word for "continent."

be left with only enough to pay off its stockholders at the rate of 200 rubles per share, less by seventeen times what the shares had once cost. The Company was then simply to go out of business.

No meekness marked the reactions of Company officials. The furious outcry was led by Vasilii Zavoiko, hero of the Battle of Petropavlovsk and initiator of developments on the Amur. Now a Board member, Admiral Zavoiko declared that he would sign no papers indicating acceptance of the government's action. Nor would he fall silent when threatened with loss of his rank and banishment from Saint Petersburg. "He was," his grandson succinctly told this author, "cashiered."

Protests were heard within the government itself. The press was widely critical, some journals not hesitating at sarcasm, causing the government censor to rule out as "seditious" remarks on the price and the treatment accorded the Company. That brought public discussion to a practical end, but not the national feeling, which seems to have been one of shame. Never before had the nation voluntarily relinquished any part of itself. And the religious considered that a great sin had been committed in selling peoples converted to Orthodoxy. The sense of guilt remains to this day.

The sale earned Russia no credit abroad. From that standpoint the sacrifice was worse than useless. Britain was angry, and the United States, far from showing gratitude, made trouble about paying. The relationship, so carefully cultivated by Saint Petersburg for so many years, would never be the same again. How poor a prophet was Muraviev, to say nothing of Stoeckl, was seen before the year of the purchase was over.

Nothing in all his twenty-six years in Washington had prepared Stoeckl for the ordeal of getting the United States to pay. As his lawyer and lobbyist he had to retain no less a personage than a former Secretary of the Treasury. The honor of the United States went by the board as Thaddeus Stevens weaseled on his promise to see the appropriation through the House. There was even an attempt, in which Stevens took part, to besmirch both Russia and Stoeckl by resurrecting a disreputable old claim against the legation, which the American courts themselves had disallowed.

The bill was fifteen months reaching the House floor, the delay due in part to the attempt to impeach Johnson, which failed by one vote. During the long wait, the press built up a body of highly adverse criticism in key with the minority report of the House Foreign Affairs Committee, which categorically damned as worthless the timber, the fish, the minerals, and all the other resources of Alaska down to the furs, adding that it was "unfit for civilized men." There had been vigorous support from some of the press, but not enough to drown out the catchy catcalls invented by the opposition, notably "Seward's Icebox" and "Seward's Folly," which did damage from which the territory was to suffer for many a year.

It made no difference to the opposition that Alaska had been in American hands for eight months when the bill finally came up in late June of 1868. The debate lasted two weeks, the sessions extending far into gaslit nights, despite the humid heat of the Washington summer and the fact the House was behind with all its business. Nothing about the measure was left undenounced, speaker after speaker dwelling in particular on the doubt as to the value. A suspicion had risen that the territory had been bought to compensate Russia for sending her fleet during the war. One representative proposed that she be simply given the money and told to keep her colony.

Then, all of a sudden, in mid-July, the debate ended, the vote was taken. It showed 113 in favor of payment, 43 against, and 44 not voting. Had Stoeckl finally resorted to bribery? So great was the suspicion that a committee investigated but, to its "regret and disappointment," without success at persuading Stoeckl to let himself be questioned. Nor would he allow anyone to explain in his behalf what had become of over $125,000 missing from his bank account. Johnson was told by Seward that bribery was used, or so the bitter ex-President wrote in a note he left to be discovered after his death.

Stoeckl returned to Saint Petersburg unacclaimed. He asked for but was not given another post. Pensioned off, he lived out his years in Paris with his family. The wish to forget him is evident in the failure of Russian reference works even to mention his name.

A nation having small desire to sell did so to a nation that was not eager to buy, their motives the belief they would please each other. History does not invariably make sense.

XVI

The Uprooting

It was 1861, six years before the sale. The stamp of Russia on Alaska seemed as permanent as that of Spain on California. The bulbed domes of Orthodoxy showed above 43 communities. The 12,000 adherents were served by 35 chapels and 9 churches, 2 of the latter at New Archangel, counting the cathedral, seat of Veniaminov's successor, Bishop Petr. Seventy-seven years had passed since the founding of the first permanent settlement by Shelikhov. The Russian names borne by some of the families of mixed blood went back much farther than that. Nor were the wholly Russian families by any means all new. One dated prior to 1800. Feeling for the country ran deep. Ex-governors such as Wrangell, Etolin, and Tebenkov had always remembered it with affection. After spending eight years in it, one family transmitted through three generations a nostalgic memory of the mountains, the islands, the seas, and even the rain.

The colony cherished its history. Baranov had emerged the great figure. He was seen as the father of the country. His name had been given to a mountain range and to the island in Sitka Sound on which New Archangel had stood for the fifty-seven years since he retook the site from the Tlingits in 1804. His name was also borne by a ship. The governor's residence was, after three remodelings, still called Baranov's Castle. The song he had written to inspire his men had all but officially become the colony's patriotic hymn.

The will of our hunters, the spirit of trade,
On these far shores a new Muscovy made,
In bleakness and hardship finding new wealth
For fatherland and tsardom. . . .

New Archangel had some 2500 people in 1861, many of them children, the families tending to be large. The settled air was emphasized by the leisurely public gardens adorned with pretty teahouses. It was a music-loving town. According to one American observer, the home of no upper-grade official was without a piano. The Lutheran Church boasted the only pipe organ in Northwest America. The upper story of the castle had been converted into a theater. The plays were in French as well as Russian. There were four lower schools as well as the college. A public library dispensed books and periodicals of many sorts sent four times yearly from Saint Petersburg. There were two scientific institutes, both under the Imperial Academy and supported by the Company. One was zoological. The other, in which the British had a joint interest, was for the study of terrestrial magnetic phenomena.

The colonial schools seem to have numbered some fifty. Orphans as well as illegitimate children sired by Company employees were supported and schooled at least to the age of seventeen. Nine boys and three girls were doing graduate work in Russia, one in medical school. There were four hospitals. Danger from smallpox epidemics had been wiped out by widespread and periodic inoculations. Other infectious diseases, including syphilis, were fought by all the means then known. The pension system had been enlarged. And those employees entitled to settle and who wished to do so when they had served out their contracts were given land and equipment.

Economically the colony's future looked secure. The current governor, Finnish-born Ivan Furuhelm, had been appointed because he was a mining engineer. The plan was to enlarge the exploitation of minerals and other resources heretofore secondary to furs. Nor were the furs gone. The conservation policy instituted by Wrangell was restoring the otter and had brought

the Pribilof seal herd to the large figure of three million. The old
relationship was maintained with Hudson's Bay, although that
organization had never fully recovered from its defeat in Oregon
and was ceasing to be a colonial force. Communication was
frequent and cordial between New Archangel and Victoria, capital of British Columbia, a name now three years old.

The port of New Archangel was, after forty-three years under
naval officers, a model of efficiency. The harbor had been laid at
great cost with a system of cables that made for safe anchorage
in all weather. Marvelously for its day, a searchlight atop
Baranov's Castle threw a beam that penetrated the night for
miles, a large concave mirror concentrating the illumination
from a number of seal-oil lamps. What with the direct trade by
ship it was now carrying on with the Orient, notably for the
purchase of 30 per cent of Russia's tea at Shanghai, the Company had the largest fleet in its history. Great pride was taken in
the fine, screw-driven 1200-ton *Alexander II*. New York and San
Francisco were among her American ports of call. The
Company's flag was also to be seen these days at Bremen, at
Hamburg, and on the Thames.

The colony was economically self-contained, having even its
own currency. The administration was well organized by dis-
tricts; the vast domain was thoroughly in hand. Communication
was maintained by a system of boats delivering mail and supplies in season as far west as the Kurils and northward to Fort
Saint Michael at the Yukon. But for the Tlingits, there would
have been small need for the military force, which consisted of
only 270 men. And the Tlingits had been growing ever more
peaceable. Some had even taken up gardening in order to add
vegetables to the fish and game they brought to the market set
aside for them at New Archangel.

The life was disciplined. Employees were expected to attend
church and otherwise live strict moral lives. No longer could
they freely take native women. Among the many small regulations was one limiting workingmen to two rations of liquor a
week. The most regimented of all were the educated creoles

and natives. Although they were the most beholden to the Company, it is not surprising that they were also its severest critics. Its rule was not without a seamy side. The administration was all-powerful, judge and jury over all but the most serious crimes. Everything bought was at Company prices. Yet on the whole the colony was better governed than Russia, that "sublime, universal, ordered chaos," in the words of Dostoievskii. Forgetful of that fact, or ignorant of it, a number of the educated colony-born and others hoped to see the Company done away with and the colony brought directly under the crown as, perhaps, a province.

It was known throughout the colony that this was a year when the Company must seek another charter. It was also known, probably less generally, that this time the Company faced an opponent of unimaginable power in the Tsar's own brother, Grand Duke Constantine. Speculation as to the future was great, the agents at the distant stations no doubt impatiently awaiting the mail boats for news, and grasping at what came over the grapevine. But the speculation could have encompassed no thought of sale to another power. That was a totally foreign idea. In the Russian view, land was never to be voluntarily relinquished. Land had ever been to the glory of the Tsar, the more distant the more glorious. The news that came this summer of 1861 was therefore of a shatteringly unexpected kind, causing all feeling against the Company to be forgotten.

The indications are that the news was brought by the officers and crew of a Company ship that had docked at San Francisco. There it had recently been learned that in Washington the previous year, with the aid of California's Senator Gwin, the Russian minister had attempted to sell the colony. San Francisco was greatly excited. The view was that but for the outbreak of the Civil War the sale would have taken place, and that it would take place with victory for the Union, which everyone expected soon. Governor Furuhelm, who seems to have been as disconcerted as anyone, no doubt hastily queried Saint Petersburg. However he afterwards tried to explain to the colony, he could not deny the essential fact: sale had indeed been discussed.

Before the summer was out, the story was all over the Pacific. Company crews were hearing it at Shanghai, Honolulu, Portland, Seattle, Victoria, where the British were very disturbed. At Kodiak, where ships from San Francisco regularly put in, the conviction was soon firm that sale was inevitable. Everyone was filled with anxiety. Thinking as to the future was in utter confusion. What would the Americans do when and if they became the masters? Would they require those who were called Russians to go to Russia? For that matter, would the Tsar, to whom they had all taken the oath of allegiance, so require? Going to Russia would be no great hardship for those born there, but for the colony-born, the great majority, it was an unfathomable prospect. How would they make new homes, find new ways to make a living?

Those who, like Bishop Petr, could look beyond their personal situations asked graver and larger questions. What would become of the orphans and illegitimate children being cared for? How would the Church fare? All support still came from the Company, not the parishioners. And what about the schools? The general American view of race was well known in the colony. Would the United States take over the work of educating the natives? The Aleuts posed a problem all their own. How would they fare in the event the fur resources of their islands were reopened to unrestricted pillage by shipmasters of all sorts? In the long run that would mean extinction for them. But perhaps some of them shrugged and said that at least they would no longer have the Company telling them how much sugar and tea was good for them.

Among the Tlingits there was probably a certain licking of the lips. For the past twenty years, ever since the Company and Hudson's Bay made their pact, liquor had been scarce. The Americans might have larger hearts. They had been the best source of rum in the old days. That this aspect of the old days might return was another source of worry for New Archangel.

Few could have gone on doubting that Saint Petersburg intended to sell when it was learned that the Company had failed to obtain the charter it wanted, that it was operating on a temporary basis destructive to its credit and capital. The effect was soon felt in the colony. Activity ground to a halt. What profit was made came mostly from the trade in tea at Shanghai. By the time two years had passed, some of the people may well have begun to wish the Unionists would win the American war, buy the country, and get it over with.

The assistant governor of the colony was a noteworthy man by the name of Dimitrii Petrovich Maksutov. Though he was by no means wealthy, he belonged to the oldest nobility. He was Prince Maksutov, the title stemming from a fourteenth-century Tatar forebear. In him aristocracy had not gone to seed. A captain in rank, he was one of the Navy's best men, a very capable administrator, fair and just. He was a man of great honor and truthfulness. And he was fearless. He had conspicuously proved this fact about himself when he fought under his friend Admiral Zavoiko at the Battle of Petropavlovsk during the Crimean War. He was nearly killed trying singlehandedly to reload a deserted cannon in the face of the withering fire from the enemy warships. The act, intended to rally the men he commanded, was one of the high points in the bitter engagement.

His wife, the former Adelaide Bushman, daughter of his English instructor at the Naval Academy, had recently died, leaving him with three children, the youngest only a few months old. He had been, as he was now to learn, the subject of much discussion at Company headquarters. Furuhelm's term as governor was nearly over, the plan to use his talents as a mining engineer a forgotten thing among the many discontinued activities. The sort of governor needed now was primarily an administrator, one who, if it came down to that, could be trusted to preside over the liquidation of the colony in all decency and honor. Called to Saint Petersburg to discuss the matter, Maksutov took his two oldest children with him, evidently thinking of putting them in some school or with relatives.

As is made clear in a family memoir written by his son and namesake,[1] Maksutov was strongly opposed to sale. Shortly after his arrival in Saint Petersburg in the fall of 1863, he made his feelings known directly to Grand Duke Constantine, which took some daring inasmuch as the Company's implacable foe was the Navy's foremost officer. But things were already happening within the government to change the outlook for the colony, Gorchakov having been made Chancellor this year. As President of the Imperial Council, Constantine was presently to have to put his name to the pledge to give the Company another twenty-year charter, a clear promise not to sell.

The Company believed that all was well as early as February 3, 1864. That is the date on the orders given Maksutov for his guidance as the new governor. The document, which was preserved by his family, enabled him to give the colony entire reassurance. The numerous, lengthy, and detailed orders all dealt with the future, some with long-range plans. Not a word of instruction was given in the event of sale.

New Archangel was no doubt beside itself with joy over Maksutov's news on his return in the fall of 1864. So sure was he his term would be untroubled, he brought back his two children and a bride. The new Princess Maksutova came of an old Cossack family. She was Mariia, daughter of Vladimir Aleksandrovich, Governor-General of Irkutsk. She was nineteen, fun-loving, and beautiful, just the one to lead New Archangel out of the gloom that had possessed it for the past three years. Never had there been so much music, dancing and laughter. The renewed tie with the empire seemed the more secure for the fact that the line of governors, which had begun with the lowly Baranov, had achieved such standing it was now graced by a prince whose house went back to Mongol times. The colony seems to have loved its near-royal family, which was to grow by two more children over the next three years.

Those three years brought Maksutov no hint of the end to come. On the contrary, he was empowered to form a new for-

---

[1] See listing under MAKSUTOV, at the end of this volume.

eign alliance when, in 1865, the old one with Hudson's Bay came to a close, the latter's business having changed character. A similar arrangement had long been sought by businessmen of San Francisco. Talks having been opened with them, in 1866 they organized a California corporation for the purpose of engaging in the fur trade with the Company. New Archangel was surely regretful at having to part with Hudson's Bay, whose men had been the best of neighbors, often helping, as they had been helped, in time of crisis, notably with the Tlingits. The twenty-six-year-long association had been a great one, no less so for the business reasons that had determined it, reasons that had surmounted even the bitterness of the Crimean War. But now it was over. The American connection meant $5,000,000 of new capital. But that was soon over too. In less than a year, in May or June of 1867, apparently through San Francisco, Maksutov learned that in April the United States Senate had bought Alaska.

He was coldly, furiously angry. The secrecy told the story. Honor had meant nothing. Much as he probably wished he could express his feelings by resigning, his sense of duty to the colony was too great. His determination was to remain until his usefulness was over. His first task was to inform the colony. He did so when he had the details from Saint Petersburg and Washington.

The word went out to all the stations, carried by the mail boats to the old forts on Cook Inlet and Prince William Sound, to the posts on Bristol Bay, to Saint Michael, Kodiak, and Unalaska. From those places it was relayed to the many islands, to the crews working afield, to the posts up the inland rivers. At New Archangel the people had the news directly from Maksutov, a thousand of them listening as he spoke to them from the steps of Baranov's Castle.

They had not long to wait, the people learned. The United States planned to take possession in October. It was hoped the San Franciscans interested in the furs would obtain a franchise from their government like that of the Company. That would mean employment for those whose trade was peltry. With the exception of the naval personnel, all who wished to do so could choose to stay in the country. They could choose to stay and become American citizens. The treaty of cession provided that the inhabitants of the ceded territory ". . . with the exception of uncivilized native tribes shall be admitted to the enjoyment of all the rights, privileges and immunities of citizens of the United States and shall be maintained and protected in the free enjoyment of their liberty, property and religion."

A vast sigh of relief surely went up all over the colony at having the greatest of the questions answered in this unequivocal fashion. And not a word about race. The only distinction was between the civilized and the uncivilized. Moreover, there would be opportunity to see what American rule would be like before a decision had to be made whether to stay. Three whole years were provided. Within that time anyone choosing to do so could go to Russia with transportation furnished. Nor was that all to make the news of the sale palatable when the initial shock wore off. Everything possible would be done to enable those wishing to stay to do so. Individuals would be given title to dwellings and lands they occupied. The Company would likewise make over shops, mills, equipment, in short the facilities for carrying on trades and professions. It sounded like heaven. No one could lose by waiting and seeing. Impatience began to mount as October neared.

What was in store for Alaska was a military occupation. Seward, in his haste to take possesssion of the territory before it was even paid for, secured an executive order placing it under the War Department. He believed the arrangement would be of short duration, that surely Congress would do the usual in these circumstances, which was to provide the appurtenances of territorial government: a civilian governor, a legislature, courts, and appropriate laws. President Johnson so requested when, in July of 1867, three months before the occupation began, he formally notified the House of the need to pay Russia. But the belief that Alaska was worthless had taken extremely stubborn root in Congress.

Alaska was made a customs district, and that, aside from granting certain corporate privileges, was to be all that Congress was to do about it for seventeen incredible years. No historian was ever to have a good word to say about this "era of no government," during which no one was to be legally entitled to settle, buy or sell, be married or buried, the legislation remaining unprovided. The lawlessness was to be abetted by the military, which was to remain for ten years. That was the shape of the future as Seward prepared to take possession.

There was to be a formal ceremony of transfer at New Archangel, the purchase treaty stipulating the appointment of commissioners to represent Russia and the United States, the one to declare the territory made over, the other to accept. These two commissioners were also to certify to the division of property, agreement having been reached as to what was to pass to private individuals, what the Company could sell, and what was to go to the United States. This last consisted in general of the vacant lands, the town sites, the public buildings. Seward named the commissioner for the United States, and Stoeckl named Russia's, choosing a man from his diplomatic staff. The two appointees took ship for Alaska from New York in late August.

As he planned the ceremony at New Archangel, Seward seems to have envisioned a happy event marked by banquets, toasts, and speeches. He had personally given his commissioner the flag that was to be raised when that of Russia had come down for the last time, the central act of the ceremony. Present would be the troops who would initiate the new occupation. The choice of these troops together with their commander was made by the general commanding the Pacific area, who seems to have been under the impression that Indians were to be fought.

The commander chosen for Alaska had begun his career as a teen-age private fighting Mexicans in the 1840s. He was a tough one even then; the Battle of Buena Vista made him a second lieutenant. His name, not to be confused with that of the

Confederacy's great leader, was Jefferson C. Davis. This Jeff Davis fought the Civil War with the Union Army, first as a lieutenant at Fort Sumter during the bombardment. He saw further action at Pea Ridge, Corinth, and Stone River. He was also with Sherman on the march through Georgia. Quick on the trigger, he killed Union General Nelson during a quarrel, but that was somehow forgotten by the end of the war. Brevetted a major-general, he went out West to fight Indians. That was his occupation when, at thirty-nine, he was ordered to Alaska with a force of 250 men. They sailed from San Francisco in mid-September on the transport *John L. Stevens*. On ahead had gone two gunboats with baggage and supplies.

The harbor of New Archangel, a name soon to be dropped in favor of Sitka, was crowded with shipping, most of the Company's fleet having been called in. The two American gunboats had to moor some distance out. So did the *John L. Stevens* when she arrived on October 8. She had had a rough three-week passage but Davis and his boys were not to go ashore just yet, he learned. They had to wait for the arrival of the two commissioners, and when that would be, nobody could say. The Russian governor was being sticky about it. So there was nothing to do but swear at all the rain and speculate about the Russian women in that funny town over there with the onions on the churches.

Sitka was already jammed with people, men, women, and children having come in from all parts of the colony with tons of baggage. They were the officials and their families, who, together with a number in Sitka, were scheduled to leave directly Russian rule was over. The exodus would begin with the departure of the ship being readied for sailing to the Baltic. The town was filled with the sound of hammering and sawing as crates and boxes were made for the shipping of pianos, books, clothing, and other personal belongings. No joy went with the activity. According to an American witness, the townspeople ". . . seemed as though they were preparing for the funeral of the Tsar, going about the town in a most dejected manner."

Maksutov, who would not be leaving until the last day of the year, was busy with a number of businessmen up from the United States, most of them representing the California interests hopeful of persuading Washington to give them a franchise like the Company's. They had come to Sitka to bid on the Company's salable property: the ships, the machinery, the equipment, the suppplies, ranging from sheepskin coats to sugar in the colony's far-flung warehouses. Maksutov sold it all cheaply, hoping it would stay in the country and help the people, hardly foreseeing that to get their money's worth most of the buyers would have to resell elsewhere. One ship bought for $4000 resold for nine times as much.

Although the Company had paid for everything in the colony short of personal belongings, Maksutov sold nothing that was necessary for the new administration to use in carrying on. The donation included the basic furnishings of the governor's residence. The hospitals, the schools, all the public institutions were left their equipment, the churches their treasures. Church property, which by the treaty had passed to the ownership of the congregations, was in the custody of Bishop Petr, who with most if not all his clergy planned to stay, hoping they would be enabled to carry on their work.

At length, on the morning of October 18, when Davis and his 250 soldiers had waited out in the harbor 10 days, the U.S.S. *Ossipee* arrived, bringing the commissioners. The one representing Russia was Captain Aleksei Peshchurov. His American counterpart was Brigadier-General Lovell Rousseau. Things began happening immediately. Davis, who lost no time seeing Rousseau, no doubt complained of the length of time his men had been cooped up on that ship. When he had seen Maksutov, Peshchurov announced that the transfer ceremony would be held that very afternoon.

The hour was set for three. To the beat of their drums, under the command of Peshchurov, the 90 sailors and 180 soldiers from a Siberian regiment who made up the garrison of the town marched up to the knoll, crossed the parade ground fronting

Baranov's Castle, and were brought to attention before the 90-foot flagstaff flying the imperial emblem. Now more drums were heard. The Americans had come ashore. Presently onto the parade ground came Generals Rousseau and Davis, the commanders of the Amercan warships, and a company of Davis's troops. They too were brought to attention. A nice ceremony had been worked out. As one flag came down and the other went up, the salutes were to be given alternately by the guns of the *Ossipee* and of Sitka. Happily for a day in October, the rain had ceased; the sun shone. There was, nevertheless, a heavy emotional overcast.

Maksutov was there as an onlooker, his face impassive. With him was his wife, her emotions plainly near the breaking point. Few other Russians had brought themselves to attend. The spectators were mostly the San Francisco businessmen. The very first act of the ceremony brought things to a nerve-racking halt. The wind-whipped Russian flag seemed not to want to come down at the will of the man operating the flagstaff ropes. It curled itself around them, the more tightly the harder the ropes were pulled. Finally a bosun's chair had to be rigged in order to get a man up there to cut it loose. It fluttered down on the bayonets of the soldiers below. The overwrought Princess Maksutova crumpled in a faint.

The rest must have seemed anticlimactic. The guns belatedly saluted. The American flag went up without incident. Peshchurov declared the territory made over, Rousseau accepted. "And," wrote a witness, "we stood upon American soil." Out of deference to the feelings of the Russians, Rousseau tried to stop the giving of three cheers, but he could not.

Years numbering 126 had passed since the discovery of the region by Bering, 122 since the arrival of the first Russians in search of furs, 68 since the founding of the Company. The sale was the greatest event of its kind in peacetime history. But no one adverted to these facts. The ceremony was followed by no banquet at which speeches were made and toasts given. What did follow the ceremony, the moment it was over, was an announcement from Davis that he was in command now. The Maksutovs were immediately to make room for him and his wife at the castle. Nor would he wait until the Russian garrison could be shipped home before his troops took over their barracks. By the time October 18, 1867, had passed into history, the new occupation had begun.

The commissioners remained a week, listing the divided properties, making out the deeds to the lands, homes, and shops going to private individuals. Rousseau was impressed by the people of Sitka. He tried to sound a warning when he wrote his report, remarking that the majority would stay "if treated kindly." The pity was that he, a man far above Davis in character and training, had not been put in command of the occupation. That he would be had been Seward's understanding.

The American period seemed at first to promise only prosperity. Would-be settlers began arriving by the boatload soon after the transfer. The papers all over California, Oregon, and Washington had been full of the news. In San Francisco the bookstores displayed Russian dictionaries. Sitka had several hundred new people by mid-November. They were real-estate dealers, cooks, miners, lawyers, homestead seekers, owners of ships and barges, whores, gamblers. They had one thing in common: they knew how to organize a prosperous, self-governing country.

They liked Sitka and its old inhabitants. The idea was that they would all get rich together. They extended the townsite for miles, staking out lots and building shanties, charging newcomers high prices for them. Among the buildings they put up were a restaurant, two saloons, two tenpin alleys. A newspaper was started. A city charter was framed, ordinances drawn up, the plans calling for even a school board. The first mayor was William S. Dodge, who had come to Sitka as Collector of Customs, the only government official aside from Davis. Everybody knew that Alaska did not as yet have the laws that would make these acts valid, but it was inconceivable that Congress would not soon provide proper territorial government. And when that happened the soldiers would go.

Instead, more soldiers arrived, until there were five hundred stationed in various parts of the country, all under Davis, with the largest detachment at Sitka. They caroused, raped and looted. They looted even the cathedral. That exploit was one of the few for which Davis meted out punishment. It was useless to inform Washington. That was discovered by Collector Dodge, who wrote that ". . . many has been the night when soldiers have taken possession of a Russian house and frightened and browbeaten the women into compliance. . . ." Dodge could do nothing, lacking the means of enforcing even customs regulations, but the people could turn to no one else. "Many is the night I have been called upon, by men and women, Russian and Aleutian, in their night-clothes, to protect them. . . . Officers have carried on with the same high hand among the Russian people. . . ."

Among the Tlingits syphilis and drunkenness spread quickly. Contrary to federal law, the military connived at the importation of hundreds of gallons of rotgut and the molasses with which to make it locally. Davis himself got one chief drunk after dressing him up in a cast-off uniform. The chief thought he had been honored until a guard set him straight with a kick. The cost of that incident was four lives. Quiet was not restored until Davis had a Tlingit village shot up.

Even the Americans could not take Davis's rule for long. Sitka's boom began to peter out a year after it started. As for the Russians, they began to leave within months after the transfer. With no amusement could they have recalled that the purchase treaty had assured them the "rights, privileges and immunities" of American citizenship. Some went to British Columbia, some to California, most went to Russia. With the Maksutovs when they departed on December 31, 1867, went 150 men, women, and children. The last ship furnishing free transportation carried 300, twice her supposed capacity. How they fared, the colony-born who had never seen Russia, seems not to be known. In the observation of old Father German, the colony-born tended not to survive in cities for long.

Northern Alaska was spared miltary rule. That part of the

country was given something quite different in 1870, three years after the purchase, something ironic: another monopolistic fur corporation. Washington had recognized that, short of detailing the Navy to patrol the waters against the irresponsible pillagers, there was no other way to protect the fur resources. The Alaska Commercial Company was given a twenty-year franchise over the Pribilof Islands for an annual fee plus a royalty on the products. It was the heir of its Russian predecessor in that, through Maksutov, its organizers had acquired the buildings and other facilities on the islands.

The organization soon extended itself beyond the Pribilofs, building stations all along the Aleutians and trading with the mainland. The Aleuts were saved from want and demoralization. They were paid, housed, schooled, and doctored. The Alaska Commercial Company has been bitterly denounced, but most historians seem to think it ran its house well. It maintained the only mail and passenger service in the territory. Its part of the country was given a prosperity and an order utterly lacking elsewhere. The enterprise, which reaped the harvest of the conservation measures instituted by Wrangell, was enormously profitable, giving the lie to Stoeckl, whose arguments for selling had included the allegation that the fur resources had been hopelessly depleted.

The peace and prosperity in the north emphasized the anarchy elsewhere. Davis made no use of the governmental facilities so carefully bequeathed him by Maksutov. But then Washington had provided him with no ships and no money. The hospitals were staffless. So were the schools. Sanitation had gone unserved. When, in 1877, after ten years, the soldiers were finally pulled out—because of an Indian uprising in Idaho, not because Alaska had as yet been given civilian government—they left the places they had occupied virtually empty of Europeans. Sitka was a ghost town, the old searchlight atop the castle turning crazily with every wind. The families numbered twenty, only five of them Russian. The cost to the United States had been a culture.

The one remnant of the culture is the adherence of many of the natives to Orthodoxy. The Church in Russia sent funds for nearly fifty years through the missionary organization established by Veniaminov after he was made Metropolitan of Moscow the year following the purchase. The fathers in Alaska were enabled to maintain most of their churches, three or four orphanages, and seventeen schools. In 1887, twenty years after the purchase, according to the bitter comment of the territorial governor, the Russian Church was annually spending more on schooling than the $40,000 the United States was spending for the education of both whites and natives in the entire territory.

No more money could be sent from Russia after the revolution of 1917. Still the fathers stayed at their posts, some supporting themselves by laboring with their hands. It was some time before help came from the North American Orthodox Church, which now has jurisdiction. The Liturgy is still celebrated on the Pribilofs, at Unalaska, Kenai, and elsewhere. Sitka still has a bishop. The cathedral retains its old treasures. It is now one of the oldest houses of worship in continuous use on American soil. Three histories meet in this little Byzantine fane. Names such as Benson and Mather are borne by the members of the congregation, who are mostly Tlingits. With characteristic tenacity they have clung to the faith they first adopted. English or Tlingit or both may be heard in the parts of the Slavonic Liturgy given in the vernacular. In that part of the ritual where once the Tsar was prayed for, the petition is now for the President of the United States.

October 18, the anniversary of the transfer, is now called Alaska Day. The ceremony is re-enacted annually at Sitka. Again the old Russian tsarist flag flies from the tall staff that still centers the knoll overlooking the town. Again it is hauled down and replaced by the Stars and Stripes, the thunder of the saluting guns reverberating down the mountains and causing grave consternation among the millions of seabirds. Otherwise the re-enactment bears little resemblance to the original event. The townspeople are all there. No one is sad. The Orthodox bishop gives an invocation. He is followed by notables with speeches. Bands play, the Tlingits sing to the beat of their old drums. It is a holiday throughout the state. Alaskans are like their Russian predecessors in that they have a great passion for the country. It is thanks to that passion, which drove them to work for statehood long, hard, and consistently, that, in 1959, ninety-two years after the purchase, the President proclaimed that Congress had at last agreed to bestow full membership in the Union. For the first time in the two hundred years and more since the coming of the Russians, the land was no longer a colony.

On the Sources

Unsurprisingly, in view of the fact that the Russians did little printing until the time of Peter the Great, the first published literature of any size on Russia was in English. Britons were so fascinated by the subject that even poet John Milton felt the urge to contribute, which he did by writing a history of Muscovy. The privileges bestowed on the merchants of England by Ivan the Terrible in the sixteenth century gave them the observational advantage over all other foreigners. Happily their curiosity centered on the doings of the Russians in the East. Among the items of information they somehow obtained for publication in London was the account of the first Russian mission to China in 1618.

When, in the 1760s, it was learned in England that the Russians were in the Pacific, a special literature sprang into being, fed by reports of shipmasters, by the observations of the explorers quickly sent to investigate, and by what could be gleaned in Russia. One book, a review of the whole subject titled *Account of the Russian Discoveries between Asia and America,* the work of a young clergyman named William Coxe who had toured Russia, went into four editions, the first appearing in 1780. Coxe was more sensational than accurate, but he told the story down to the doing of Russo-Chinese business at Kiakhta, a full description of which he had obtained. The writings of Vancouver and other explorers, which came out in handsome volumes, generally show a disposition to judge Russians fairly, with particular reference to their treatment of the natives. Much the same can be said of the highly valuable reminiscences of Sir George Simpson, who was given an unmatched opportunity to study the colony in its heyday.

The literature in Russian started relatively late, in 1787, with the publication, by order of Catherine the Great, of a geography of the empire that comprised the Pacific possessions, a work that sets forth historical facts of value to this day. The next eighty years saw the production of a substantial number of works ranging from well-printed narratives of voyages to personal reminiscences of life in the colony. But the writing stopped abruptly with the sale of the country. So completely did the Russians then turn their backs on that phase of their history, they even allowed the colonial records at Sitka to go to the United States. As for the records in Russia, many disappeared, among them a large section of the Company's papers. Further losses of documents were caused by fire and war.

The sale caused the British also to lose interest, but the growth of the literature in English did not end. A new section had for some time been forming in the United States, an observational literature, for the most part, and very important, the work of shipmasters and other travelers. An example is the little book by Rhode Islander John D'Wolf, which deals with the year he spent in the colony (1805–1806), as well as with his journey across Siberia, the first by an American. This work, along with certain others mentioned in my text, is fully cited at the close of these remarks.

The literature still continues to grow, indeed faster than ever. It is now of a size requiring whole bibliographical volumes to list merely the main titles in the various languages, the histories, the works on the explorations, the essays, all of which number perhaps half a thousand. A representative portion of the titles, published up to the 1940s, together with a listing of the bibliographical volumes that have been compiled, is to be found in Stuart Tompkins' excellent *Alaska, Promyshlennik and Sourdough* (University of Oklahoma Press, 1945), which also contains a discourse on the losses of materials in Russia.

For all the richness of the literature, the researcher in the field remains a species of detective, constrained often to seek his information from many sources as he strives to reconstruct the happenings. And some of the sources on which we relied in past years have been found wanting. The generally accepted, harrowing picture of early New Archangel created by G. H. von Langsdorff is seen as personally venomous in the light of the relatively neglected book by his friend John D'Wolf.

The entire truth about some things may never be known, owing to the losses of materials in Russia and the gaps in the colonial records bequeathed to us. A complete history of the colony was never written by the Russians. What they did write is, for the most part, so good as to make the lacks that much more regrettable. The chief historical text is a two-volume work on the Russian-American Company, written to its order from its archives by historian Petr Tikhmenev and published in 1863, four years before the sale. This work is the more valuable in view of the losses of Company records. We are given, along with facts from the Company's history and details concerning its mode of operation, a number of documents in full, including several lengthy letters from personalities such as Baranov and Rezanov. Without those letters we would have little real understanding of, among other things, Rezanov's voyage to California.

Explorations were well covered, and of late years the Soviets have been building up the literature in this area. Biography was also a strong point with the Russians. Their reference works in the field give the main facts on most of the personalities at the forefront of the colony's history. Khlebnikov's biography of Baranov covers a wide area. Veniaminov's life was detailed in an anonymous biography published on his centenary. This work came to our attention late and is still rather neglected, although the Church has issued an English translation. Then there are works that indirectly shed light on events in the colony, also recent discoveries in some cases, notably a history of Transbaikalia which gives details on that highly determinative element, Russo-Chinese relations.

Reasons are good for believing that the history of Russian America may grow and develop further. In 1951 the Harvard University Press published a translation by Carl Ginsburg of *The Russian-American Company* by Soviet author S. B. Okun, the first work of its kind to come out of Russia in eighty years. It is an impressive job of research. By patient work in the archives, Okun found materials which made up for some of the losses. He added a whole new dimension to understanding of the workings of the Company, its relations at home and abroad, and the careers of the men involved. But rousing admiration for those men formed no part of Okun's purpose, which was, on the contrary, to show the nefariousness of private enterprise in terms of the Stalinist period. Lies are told to that end—e.g., "To the very end of the Company's existence, the governing board opposed any increase in the number of missionaries." Merchants are excoriated after, curiously, the fashion of the old nobility. Okun nevertheless showed how much new material may yet be discovered.

American scholarship in the field of Russian studies was slow to develop. The United States historian who knew much about either the history or the language of Russia was for a long time a rare bird. Not until the second decade of this century did a scholar of ours, Dr. Frank Golder of Washington State College, investigate the archives in Russia in order to ascertain what they contained of interest to American history. This was nearly fifty years after the purchase of Alaska, about which a number of histories had already been written.

The first of these texts, H. H. Bancroft's *History of Alaska,* a work still in wide use, appeared in 1886, nearly thirty years before Golder began his epoch-making research, which gave United States writers on Alaska's Russian period their first inkling that they had much to learn despite the size of the printed literature. But some of the errors made by the old writers remain rooted to this day. The prime one has to do with Russia's motive for selling Alaska, which was not fear of Britain.

Golder made himself the father of Russian studies in this country. He gave United States scholars a published guide to items bearing on American history in the Russian archives. He wrote a number of books and articles, each of which was a landmark. Yet this man who corrected so much has himself been corrected. It is now seen that Frank Golder was Russophobic, that on subjects such as Russian expansionism he was not above coloring what he wrote.

The United States now has no lack of specialists in Russian studies. Their books, theses, and articles account in large measure for the recent growth of the literature we are discussing. New light has been shed on the character of Russian Amercia by, in particular, searching studies on the practices of Russian colonialism down through the years. Mysteries have been solved, notably the one that long surrounded the attempt of the Russians on Hawaii in the early 1800s. Neglected Russian sources contained the answer, as was shown only this past year by Richard Pierce, who translated the documents and wrote a text that awaits publication as I write this.

It has been a great experience for me these thirty years, watching a supposedly dead history round out.

The following brief listing is for the purpose of (a) completing the citations of certain writings mentioned in my text and (b) crediting works of recent date to which I am specially beholden.

Dallin, David J. *The Rise of Russia in Asia.* New Haven: 1949.

D'Wolf, John. *A voyage to the North Pacific and a journey through Siberia* . . . Cambridge, Mass.: 1861.

Fisher, Raymond, H. *The Russian Fur Trade 1500–1700.* University of California Publications in History, vol. 31. Berkeley and Los Angeles: 1943.

Gruening, Ernest H. *The State of Alaska.* New York: 1954.

Jane, Sister M., S.H.F. *Concepción Argüello* . . . Unpublished M.A. Thesis, University of San Francisco: 1962.

Khlebnikov, K. T. *Zhizneopisanie Aleksandra Andreevicha Baranova* . . . (Biography of A. A. Baranov . . .). Saint Petersburg: 1835.

Langsdorff, G. H. von. *Voyages and Travels* . . . London: 1813–1814. 2 vols.

Lantzeff, George V. *Siberia in the Seventeenth Century* . . . University of California Publications in History, vol. 30. Berkeley and Los Angeles: 1943.

Maksutov, Dimitrii (Jr.). This is the memorial on his family. "Iz proshlago Rossiisko-Amerikanskikh kolonii" ("Out of the past of the Russian American colonies"). From *S beregov Ameriki; iubileinvi istoricheskii sbornik* (*The Shores of America; Jubilee Historical Collection*). Association of Former Russian Naval Officers in America. New York: 1939.

Pavlovsky, Michel N. *Chinese-Russian Relations.* New York: 1949.

Pierce, Richard A. "Georg Anton Schäffer, Russia's man in Hawaii, 1815–1817." *Pacific Historical Review,* November 1963.

———. *Russia's Hawaiian Adventure, 1815–1817.* Berkeley, Calif.: 1965.

Shenitz, Helen A. "Father Veniaminov, the Enlightener of Alaska." *American Slavic and East European Review,* February 1959.

Sherwood, Morgan. *Exploration of Alaska, 1865–1900.* New Haven: 1965.

Simpson, Sir George. *Narrative of a journey round the world, during the years 1841 and 1842*. London: 1847. 2 vols.

Tarakanov, Vasilii. This is the narrative of his captivity in 1808–1810. "Krushenie Rossiiskago-Amerikanskoi Kompanii sudna 'Sviatoi Nikolai' . . ." ("Wreck of the R-A Co. ship *Saint Nicholas* . . ."). In V. M. Golovnin's *Opisaniia primechatel'nykh korablekrushenii* (*Descriptions of remarkable shipwrecks*), vol. 4. Saint Petersburg: 1853.

Tarsaïdzé, Alexandre. *Czars and Presidents*. New York: 1958.

Tikhmenev, P. A. *Istorischeskoe obozrenie obrazovaniia Rossiisko-Amerikanskoi Kompanii . . .* (*Historical survey of the establishment of the Russian-American Company . . .*). Saint Petersburg: 1863. 2 vols.

Veniaminov, Ioann. Diary of visit to California, 1836. Extract in Bancroft Collection, manuscript translated by Richard Pierce.
———. His biography. "The Life and Works of the Most Reverend Metropolitan Innocent." Anonymous English translation in *Russian Orthodox Journal*, July, August, September, and October 1940.

Vernadsky, George. *The Mongols and Russia*. New Haven: 1953.

Wu, Aitchen K. *China and the Soviet Union, a Study of Sino-Soviet Relations*. New York: 1950.

Index